No More Teachers, No More Books

No More Teachers, No More Books

The Commercialization of Canada's Schools

Heather-jane Robertson

M&S

Canadian Cataloguing in Publication Data

Robertson, Heather-jane

No more teachers, no more books : the commercialization of Canada's schools

Includes bibliographic references and index.

ISBN 0-7710-7575-8

1. Education – Canada. 2. Education and state – Canada.
3. High technology and education – Canada. I. Title.

LA412.R62 1998   370'.971   c98-930378-0

We acknowledge the financial support of the Government of Canada through the Book Publishing Industry Development Program for our publishing activities. We further acknowledge the support of the Canada Council for the Arts and the Ontario Arts Council for our publishing program.

Typeset in Goudy by M&S, Toronto
Printed and bound in Canada

McClelland & Stewart Inc.
The Canadian Publishers
481 University Avenue
Toronto, Ontario
M5G 2E9

1 2 3 4 5 6   03 02 01 00 99 98

Contents

For Caitlin and Mark,
the best of the responsible rebels,
with my loving admiration

– Mom

PREFACE

Education is in the news, and the news isn't good.

Thousands of teachers and parents march on the Alberta legislature, urging the government to reinvest in public education. They claim that Alberta is funding its budget surplus by squeezing more kids into the most crowded classrooms in the country, while a government task force travels the province to discuss giving more public funding to private schools. In Nova Scotia, the minister of education is embarrassed when the details of a smelly private-public partnership deal on school construction surface. Violence in a Cape Breton school rips a racially segregated community apart. In British Columbia, a fourteen-year-old girl is beaten and murdered by other youths. The media blame schools, although the kids involved are streetmates, not classmates, and students interviewed say school is the only place they actually feel safe.

Apropos of little except ratings, both national television networks cover a story about a Kentucky teacher convicted of sexually assaulting her twelve-year-old student, and a tragedy in Tennessee, where a fourteen-year-old murdered three classmates. The message is clear: teachers and kids are out of control, and so are their schools.

In Mexico, protesters shut down the stock exchange, demanding that the government back down on national tests that will stream students into vocational schools. In Ontario, resistance to legislation intended to restructure every aspect of public education

– from who can teach to who can levy taxes – results in constitutional challenges and the largest teachers' strike ever witnessed in North America. New Brunswick begins a new era of education governance without school boards but with total electronic connectivity. Prince Edward Island schools discover that among all sixty-three Canadian and American jurisdictions, they rank dead last in per-student spending.[1] The American per-student average is now $6,469 (U.S.); the Canadian per-student average is $5,228 (U.S.); P.E.I. spends $3,782 (U.S.).

Manitoba considers merit pay, basing each teacher's salary on standardized test results. It is rumoured that gangs run Winnipeg's inner-city schools. Newfoundland finds its education system enmeshed in federal-provincial politics and old religious jealousies. Saskatchewan cuts its suit to fit the cloth, closing rural schools and hoping distance education will make up for the resulting loss of community. Quebec turns away from school boards based on religion, and decides to put its faith in parent councils and language-based systems. Television footage shows parents weeping over the schools that are about to be closed to accommodate the new system. A McGill student from British Columbia launches a suit against the Quebec government, claiming that the tuition-bounty placed on out-of-province students constitutes discrimination.

The backdrop to these disparate events – most of which are covered only by provincial media – is nonetheless familiar everywhere. Wisdom has it that schools are failing. Despite the enormous amounts spent on them, schools are delivering a poor, or perhaps even a terrible, product and wasting public dollars in the bargain. According to politicians, business leaders, and the media, it isn't education restructuring that poses a threat to public education, but resistance from greedy or sentimental special interest groups that refuse to accept the fact that education must change to meet the new realities of globalization.

Predictably, it wasn't until "the education crisis" hit Ontario that school reform became a fit topic for national debate. Throughout this period, governments were constructing an official framework to contain the so-called problem of public education, and the framework was taking hold. The problem would be called a power struggle. Guests and callers on CBC radio's Cross-Country Checkup wanted to debate education standards, teachers' working conditions, education spending, the role of teachers' unions, the responsibilities of parents, and the achievement of students. In no particular order, callers were disgusted, sympathetic, frustrated, fearful, angry, and, above all, alarmed that somehow they would have no say in what would happen next. Host Rex Murphy kept trying to shoehorn their opinions and emotions into the question of the day: "Who should control education?"

Picking up the same spin, the *Globe and Mail's* extensive report on the power struggle over education reform across Canada exposed the issue as a political headache that threatened to become a migraine.[2] However, a second education story that contained no reference to power struggles only made it to the inside pages of the same edition. It reported that a UBC survey of senior high school students had detected an "alarming" decline in students' inclination to vote and to volunteer in their communities.[3] Students also reported less confidence that they could make a difference in the world. The British Columbia Ministry of Education blamed these results on "the large number of immigrant and special needs children integrated into regular classrooms." Ministry officials didn't elaborate on how these children caused a decline in other students' citizenship skills.

One of the prerogatives of power is the right to decide when power is an issue, and when it is not. Students' deteriorating citizenship skills don't make the cut. Whoever controls which information and points of view will be considered pertinent, and which will be marginalized, controls public thought and private action. In the debate over public education, the terms of the discourse (as the academics like to say) have been set. We may talk about who has power, but not about who profits. We may talk about measuring outcomes, but not about assessing effects. We may talk about what is illegal, but not about what is unjust.

Gradually, we ease into the framework and lose sight of the picture it frames. On talk shows, there is little reflection on whether public education has a role beyond training the work force (or out-of-work force) for the short-term future. There is almost no debate over whether the word *partnership* could accurately describe the relationship between a fast-food giant and a school full of pre-teens, or whether a provincial ministry ought to sign an agreement with a brewing company to supply curriculum promoting safe drinking for underaged students. Only the opponents of the privatization of education ever mention these concerns, so their fears are dismissed as delusional.

Along with the right to define the problem goes the right to identify the solution. Below the headlines and behind the bad news about our schools, many believe in one beacon of hope. Like the students' loss of interest in their communities, this one bright light is also exempt from any analysis of power, for it is about possibilities. Indeed, in weeks of unprecedented public and media attention to education reform, the topic of technology did not even surface as one of the forces leveraging education reform.

With one exception. In October 1997, the *Ottawa Citizen* ran a short item under the lead "Study ponders teacherless society."[4] It reported that a leaked Ontario government document, stamped confidential, contained the minutes of a meeting billed as the "Minister's Round Table on Technology in Learning." Along with the minister, those in attendance included senior ministry officials responsible for curriculum, the chair of the Ontario Arts Council, the president of TVOntario, and a college president-turned-privatizer. One of their recommendations would merge the ministries of education and economic development, the better to emphasize "learn-to-earn" right from the start. Their other ideas were somewhat more radical.

The round table recommended the elimination of schools in "the new Ontario."[5] By the year 2000, students would be learning with the help of "virtual communities, smart agents and mentor networks" – and personal computers, of course. Students would soon learn, they said, "anytime, anywhere" (a copyrighted Microsoft slogan) on their own time, whenever they chose. Without schools to staff, teachers would no longer be required. Since students would be able to "access the curriculum using their personal electronic notebook," teachers and books would be as vestigial as tails and extra toes. Although schools as we know them would be out, business would be in. Parents would guide their children's education (or, in the document's words, "their children's future") with the help of "business advisors."

When the sleuthful reporter who had obtained these minutes asked John Snobelen, then minister of education, about his group's recommendations, the minister said the ideas were only "blue sky thinking," that personally he had never believed all that stuff about technology replacing schools and teachers. Technology, he said, is only a tool.

With other education developments posing a more imminent threat than the blue sky falling, it was not surprising that this news report received little attention. After all, the minister was clear he hadn't really meant what he had said. Since he was about to be shuffled to the allegedly techno-proof portfolio of the environment, his peculiar views on how technology could eliminate schools were surely irrelevant and, at any rate, inconsequential to the rest of the country.

Many Canadians may not see the connection, but the link between education restructuring and computer technology tantalizes people in some sectors. An item in the *Ottawa Citizen* reads: "Minister wants $4 billion to give each student a computer."[6] A report distributed to Canadian investors claims that the education industry is about to replace health care as the next hot sector. "If health care is a good indicator, private companies will benefit strongly from a climate that emphasizes change."[7]

Welcome to ed.com, where global money and globalizing technology will determine the future of Canada's schools, where no exaggeration is too extreme, no promise is too expensive, and no downside is too steep. Thoughtful reflection on technology and school reform has become unfashionable. Debate is now limited to what brand of technology should be purchased and how fast it can be adopted. In the midst of a power struggle about everything else touching schools, both the Left and the Right, both experts and amateurs, seem to have found common ground in welcoming information technology.

Ontario's Royal Commission on Learning (1995) hailed technology as "a lever," a "driving force," and "an engine," creating "excellent learning institutions." It concluded that "the true promise of technology lies in the classroom"[8] – although, traditionally, the classroom is where students, not machines, show promise. Speaking from the other end of the political spectrum, Ontario's Tory deputy minister of education has said that information technology can tell us what "our students need to know and what kinds of skills and attitudes they should have . . . to enable them to live productive and personally satisfying lives."[9] If computers can indeed provide the definitive answer to the source of happiness, which has eluded philosophers for centuries, surely hesitation is futile as well as irresponsible.

With this level of buoyant consensus, the technology sector does not have to be discreet about its own enthusiasm for the windfall implications of ed.com. As the high-tech lobby known as ITAC, the Information Technology Association of Canada, led by AT&T, Bell, IBM, and Northern Telecom, bluntly tells its members, "Investing in education is investing in the future of business."[10] The shared future of business and education will be realized through "a restructuring of the classroom curriculum to permit the full integration of information technology in the delivery of education."

Misplaced enthusiasm for techniques and technologies that promise to transform education dates back at least to the invention of the radio. At various times we have been assured, for example, that continuous progress would eliminate grades, and that open area classrooms would dissolve curriculum boundaries. Revisited ten years later, education reforms such as these tend to be revealed as duds. Traditionally, when innovations have not led to results, schools have reverted to what worked in the past. But the technologies of the digital classroom will not have to prove themselves on their merits, because the rules have changed.

Subjecting ed.com, with its leveraged investment in technology, privatization, and profit, to the ordinary rules that govern innovation (does it work? is it worth the cost?) would be too risky. Too much ideological, political, and financial capital is involved. Overhyping ed.com is only part of the business plan; the other part relies on eliminating the competition.

I

ME,INC.@ED.COM

THE POLITICS OF EDUCATION

People who are determined to change the world are drawn inevitably towards schools. Some of them want schools to foster the growth of human potential, and others are looking for greater work force productivity. All of them, however, recognize the power flowing towards the ideas and institutions that can capture and drive school reform.

Enthusiasm for their own ambitious ideas can delude reformers into underestimating the complexity of education systems. In reality, nothing is simple about schools, especially about changing them. Education policy makers may believe that a regulation here and a strategic plan there will bring about the changes they seek or the results they promise, but schools and education systems prove hard to redirect. They are entangled not just by regulation and history, but by the values and attributes of their students and communities.

Thoughtful observers of public education in Canada talk about how schools are shaped by the context in which they operate. No provincial task force or commission has concluded that a school is a closed system. Its context is dominated by the strengths and limitations of students, and moulded by social and economic forces that the classroom cannot control and can barely mitigate. As social institutions, schools reflect the society they serve, and sometimes our reflection frightens us. Nor can schools do much about other powerful influences: fear of the future, loss of community, growing anxiety about our continued national and personal prosperity.

Social, economic, and personal anxiety seeks outlets: reasons, excuses, magic bullets. When U.S. president George Bush said that "there is no problem in America that our schools can't solve,"[1] people may have inferred that he was praising schools. If schools are supposed to hold the solution to society's problems and these problems escalate, however, it follows that schools have failed. The weaker the economic indicators, the higher the rate of teen pregnancy, the lower the voter turnout – whatever the problem – the greater the failure of public education.

From a political standpoint, making schools responsible for every societal problem is clearly expedient. Better that schools take the blame than politicians and their friends. And it is so much easier to scapegoat education than to examine economic and political realities. Several American presidents have campaigned on becoming "the education president." According to polls conducted during the 1996 American presidential election, 60 per cent of respondents said Bill Clinton's position on technology-driven education reform was a decisive factor in their voting decision. Fewer than 10 per cent mentioned the economy. More than two-thirds of Clinton's inaugural address was devoted to school reform via technology and charter schools; the economy received only a passing mention.[2]

In different times, this attention and optimism might be good news for public education. In other times, such faith in schools might lead to increased spending, greater innovation, more respect for teachers, thoughtful public debate about how to achieve the ambitious list of goals we have set.

But these are not other times. For many, these have been hard times, when the determination of governments to reduce deficits and hold the line on inflation has hit close to home. We are told that these policies, combined with taxpayer resistance, have forced governments to target any institution that consumes tax dollars, including schools. Schools, certainly, have experienced hard times.

For some people, of course, recent years have been easy: witness the unprecedented transfer of wealth from governments and citizens to the private sector. As both wealth and poverty increase, cutting public spending to fifty-year lows entrenches private profit and power at the expense of public services. There are few public schools on Easy Street. The rich send their kids to private schools.

We can explain the pressures bearing down on education in other ways as well. Perhaps they have less to do with the economy than with the capacity of public education – only partly realized – to create the public, not just to serve it. "To safeguard a revolution," wrote linguist and social critic Noam Chomsky, "first you have to get to the teachers and the priests."[3] Schools transmit ways of seeing the world.

The historian and philosopher John Ralston Saul defines public education as "the single most important element in the maintenance of a democratic system."[4] However, decisions about which children learn, what they learn, and why they learn it are equally important to totalitarian states. Chinese youngsters chanting from their Little Red Books in the 1960s and Hitler's Young Pioneers thirty years earlier were the shock troops of their respective revolutions. Surely, if we are experiencing a fundamental restructuring of our societies and economies, then capturing the public mind by capturing its schools becomes a plausible explanation for the nature and pace of education reform. This argument is rarely advanced, however. Prevailing wisdom concludes that education reform is an economic imperative, driven by the best interests of young people, who will be subject to the uncontrollable appetites of the global economy.

Appeasing these appetites has already required, in the words of Finance Minister Paul Martin, "enormous sacrifices" on the part of Canadians. Our leaders continue to claim that the long-term gains will be worth the short-term pain. Neither the pain nor the gains have been evenly distributed, however. The young, the elderly, the poorly educated, the unemployed, welfare recipients, people with disabilities, and every other group of limited power have paid and paid again as the public services they depend on, and the jobs they might hold, disappear. While the "recovery" our governments boast about has paid off handsomely for some, the rest wait for the benefits of globalization to trickle down.

The Global City

Is this just a transitory phase of the modern economy, one that will likely be corrected by the invisible hand of ever-freer markets or by governments reasserting their right to distribute wealth? While some people still think so – and others deny that any fundamental shift is taking place – a growing number read a different message between the lines of the business press.

Rather than witnessing self-centred nation-states gradually transform into a verdant global village – a metaphor that suggests trust, community, and neighbourliness – they believe we are being force-marched into the global city. The global city has none of the reassuring warmth of the global village. Its music is not the new rhythms of world beat but the ringing bells of the stock exchange. There are no wide, curving streets or flower gardens in the global city, except perhaps within its gated communities. Mansions and luxury condos are less common than the tight quarters of the low-rent districts or the tin huts of the no-rent districts. The UN reports that the richest one-fifth of humanity now pockets sixty times as much income annually as the poorest fifth, a multiplier that has more than doubled since 1965.[5] The rich live well in the global city, and they intend to keep it that way.

Who runs city hall in the global city? Who oversees the management of worsening inequality? Some say the powers-that-be resemble an occupying force more than a government of the people. The private sector has moved from standing behind the throne of power to sitting on the throne itself. Once in charge, these unelected business leaders represent the interests of the system that has allowed them to maximize profits by externalizing social, environmental, and economic costs – costs that are the unavoidable effluent of the unlimited pursuit of quick profits. This is the system of deregulation, less government, liberalized trade, and investment mobility. No corporation can deviate much or for long from the pursuit of maximizing returns, for the unsentimental marketplace will punish it by favouring a more ruthless competitor. Such are the rules of the unrestrained market.

THE INSTITUTE FOR Policy Studies in Washington, D.C., lists fifty-one corporations among the top one hundred world economies, which means that Wal-Mart, at number twelve, is larger than 161 countries, and General Motors is bigger than Denmark.

Source: Canadian Centre for Policy Alternatives, *CCPA Monitor*, February 1997

These may not be new rules, but our umpires are no longer neutral. The game is changing. Governments that might be expected to regulate the market's waste emissions have sided with global corporate interests against citizens. While certain governments of particular political stripes are enthusiastic about their new compact with business, others beg for public understanding – after all, they say, they had no alternative. Just as the market will punish corporations that break the rules, so it will punish governments that refuse to furnish the key conditions for enhancing competitiveness.

To maximize profits, corporations look for a well-trained but anxious work force, along with low labour costs, low corporate taxes, and low rates of inflation – the better to protect the value of capital. Lax environmental standards, minimal government regulation, and unfettered access to markets grease the skids. The fewer strings attaching a corporation to a particular country, the better. Governments comply and even boast. As Federal Industry Minister Sergio Marchi says, "The role of government is to reduce the impediments that reduce competitiveness, and thus add value."[6]

Value to whom?

Are Canadians – or the citizens of any other country – enjoying more value from their governments as politicians cut and destabilize the public sector? Most Canadians want their governments to be business-friendly, but not at any cost. Indeed, even as we elected governments that would devise and implement tools of corporate control such as the Free Trade Agreement and NAFTA, we were assured that these agreements posed no threat to the public institutions Canadians value most. Culture would remain a sacred trust, the environment would never be put at risk, public services would thrive, and the social safety net would always be there to catch us. We now know that every public principle, service, and institution is in peril. However, the source of the threat is neither corporatism nor markets, we're told, but the deficit, the debt, or – as an all-purpose excuse – globalization.

THE COMBINED SALES of the largest two hundred corporations exceed 25 per cent of the world's economic activity, and their wealth is double that of 8 per cent of the world's population. Despite their size, or perhaps because of it, these corporations employ less than 1 per cent of the estimated global work force of 2.6 billion.

Source: CCPA Monitor, February 1997

In the name of trade – the vehicle of globalization – we are reneging on environmental standards, decimating social services, increasing child poverty, and restructuring the relationship between people and their governments. At the same time, we are assured that if we will just march more briskly and willingly towards the global city, we will be able to replace what we discarded to lighten our load.

Don't count on it, says Tony Clarke, who has written a richly detailed chronicle of what he calls "the big-business takeover of

Canada."[7] Clarke accuses the Business Council on National Issues (BCNI), the lobby group representing Canada's business elite, of successfully orchestrating the "coup d'état" that has transformed Canada's political relationships. The BCNI doesn't refer to the new order as corporate rule, of course, but as the return of minimal government. Minimal governments fulfil their role by doing as little as possible. While every government has internalized this doctrine at least reluctantly, some have embraced state minimalism enthusiastically. In the words of Lloyd Axworthy, still considered to be on the left of the Liberal government: "Like a good waiter in a high-class restaurant, government increasingly should be as effective but as inconspicuous as possible."[8] In the global city, of course, only preferred customers dine in Mr. Axworthy's restaurant. The kitchen help don't share in the tips, either.

The flip side of downsizing government is upsizing the private sector, turning over to it anything in which it has an interest – namely, activities that turn a profit. Health care, pensions, welfare, corrections, transportation – and, perhaps the most vulnerable public service, education – all show the promise of profit. Governments sometimes find it difficult to persuade citizens that privatizing these services and institutions is in their interest, and that they should walk away from a vision of the public sector that Canadians have invested in for generations.

And so, paradoxically, minimalist government sometimes requires forceful intervention. In the name of less government, Ontario premier Mike Harris (whose province's new official slogan, "open for business," graces the government's Web site) has led an activist government that has forged ahead on all fronts simultaneously, creating unprecedented public resistance. This in-your-face leadership style has less subtlety than Axworthy's smooth maître d' tack, but both approaches have produced the results intended to please the people who really count.

The rest of us are isolated, relatively easy to manipulate, and increasingly disconnected from somewhat esoteric debates about the appropriate role of government in an advanced democracy. Taxes get our attention. We wake up when our health care system is threatened; we get angry when mail service is interrupted. We worry about our jobs and our pensions. But as successive governments demonstrate that protest will not alter their agenda, disillusioned Canadians conclude that "they're all the same," and decide to shut down as citizens and reboot as consumers. No one was surprised when only 67 per cent, fewer of us than ever before, bothered to vote in the 1997 federal election.

Swimming in Darwin's Pool

Canadians seem to have chosen acceptance over outrage. Sixty-four per cent expect that, within ten years, governments will provide little or no assistance to people who lose their jobs. The figure rises to 72 per cent among youth aged eighteen to twenty-four, who were also reported as the most likely to find this scenario acceptable. Meanwhile, 86 per cent of their parents aged forty-five to fifty-four believe that, by 2005, "many people will never find full-time work." Pollster Allan Gregg says Canadians have become "borderline nihilists" about the relevance of government to the quality of their lives,[9] and for younger Canadians in particular, the private sector has displaced the state's role. Eighty-seven per cent of respondents said that, in the future, "they expect private enterprise to play a much bigger role in society." More to the point, almost as many – 83 per cent – say they find this acceptable.[10]

THE 1996 MACLEAN'S/CBC News year-end poll found that 80 per cent of Canadians, and 89 per cent of those eighteen to twenty-four years old, think it likely that government pensions will disappear within ten years.

Source: Maclean's, December 30, 1996

In some quarters, this poll brings welcome news. To maintain harmony in the global city, residents must accept the inevitability of the new order. A substantial number must come to believe that they can thrive, not just survive, under the new rules; the rest must believe that they have no choice. Many Canadians think we can and must make it on our own, despite our shaken personal circumstances. Unemployment touched one in three families in 1997. While the official unemployment rate remained at about 10 per cent, the real rate exceeded 18 or 19 per cent.[11] Hardest hit is the best-educated generation Canada has ever produced: the official unemployment rate for youth is 16 per cent.[12] Many within this group are also parents, whose children are at extreme risk. Child poverty in Canada increased by 58 per cent between 1989 and 1995, and the fastest-growing family type living in poverty is young parents, whose children now have a 44 per cent chance of growing up poor.[13]

Bankruptcies have hit record highs and savings have hit record lows. RRSPs have been pillaged by those with urgent financial needs that overshadow dreams of Freedom 55. Even Freedom 75 looks increasingly unlikely as consumer debt piles up. Despite international admiration for our proclaimed economic recovery, Canada remains the only country among the G-7 to have seen real incomes fall during the last decade. Some families have maintained something close to their previous standard of living by balancing several part-time jobs or by becoming two-paycheque families. This is a one-shot strategy, however – few families have a second wife to send out to work.

Traditionally, public spending has mitigated income disparities and their consequences. But in 1996, public spending in Canada as a percentage of GDP hit record lows, just as the stock market hit record highs.[14] A Toronto food bank ran out of food on the same day a car dealership ran out of Jaguars.

The widening gap between rich and poor – the largest gap ever recorded in Canada, and the second-highest among industrialized countries – is showing up around the world. In the United States during the 1980s, the richest 1 per cent of the population captured 62 per cent of the total gain of net wealth; the richest 20 per cent took 99 per cent.[15] In Canada, the real wages of the best-paid 20 per cent rose 7 per cent during the 1980s for full-time male workers and 11 per cent for comparable women. The wages of the worst-paid 20 per cent fell by 9 per cent for men and 8 per cent for women, and all but the top 10 per cent saw declines in their average weekly earnings.[16]

The underclass of the global city is more visible every day. Its members were once confined to the developing countries of the southern hemisphere and to the American inner cities that Canadians boastfully condemned. But as the number of Canadian victims of economic and social restructuring grows, tension mounts. Societies with deep class divisions are unstable. Jealousy and resentment among the have-nots endangers governments and civic order. As long as the South remained a geographical entity, northern hemisphere countries could exert control by propping up political dictatorships, using both pliant governments and the World Bank as economic disciplinarians. But when the South appears in your community as homeless people and the hopelessly unemployed, it poses a more immediate threat. Establishing a measure of physical distance provides some comfort and security – gated communities, charter schools, anti-begging legislation – but, in the end, the poor still out-number the rich.

Damage control becomes an important political objective. Controlling the message by refusing to control the media serves important political goals. Gutting public broadcasting while refusing to acknowledge the danger of print media monopolies ensures that certain views are expressed with authority ad nauseam, while others are relegated to the margins of opinion essays. Profits in the banking community, as it is bizarrely known, will still be reported, of course. But they will be followed by commentary explaining that record-breaking profits within a sector that has laid off thousands of employees are good for ordinary Canadians, since many of us indirectly own bank shares through our employee pension plans. But which mainstream news source will speculate on the Canada Pension Plan reforms that move citizens' security into bank-controlled investments? Which business pages will tell us that the federal government has chosen to borrow 80 billion dollars each year from chartered banks – a loan that costs Canadians (and nets the banks) $7 billion annually – although it could borrow from the Bank of Canada at nominal interest?[17] If

NESBITT BURNS, MIDLAND Walwyn, KPMG Peat Marwick
Thorne, Scotia McLeod, Richardson Greenshields, RBC Dominion Securities, and Toronto Dominion Securities were the
biggest contributors to the federal Liberal party in 1995,
donating more than half a million dollars in that year alone.
Source: The CCPA Monitor, February 1997

they knew these truths and others, would Canadians still accept
the orthodoxy of program spending cuts as the unavoidable cost
of appeasing the deficit?

While governments manage the mechanics of minimalist government and benefit from an agreeable harmony among corporate
opinion and editorial writers, Canadians are encouraged to blame
each other and themselves for their worsened circumstances.
Long-term stability requires that the marginalized be held responsible for their own marginalization, to dissuade those who are teetering on the brink and those who aspire to moving up from
sympathizing with "special interest groups." Thus the solution to
poverty is to blame and shame the poor into giving up their
dependency on the state. Variations on this theme abound. Racism
is not a problem; the real blight is the anti-racism industry (funded
by government). Unemployment is not the problem; it is the laziness of the unemployed. (If unemployment insurance causes
unemployment, perhaps the Canada Pension Plan causes us to
grow old.) Child hunger is not a matter of too little money, said
Ontario's Premier Harris. It is caused by mothers too preoccupied
with their own careers to cook hot breakfasts. In the current political environment, the mean-spirited refrain of "not in my backyard" finds an echo in "not my problem" and, most certainly, in
"not with my tax dollars."

Occasionally, we see signs of a vestigial Canadian conscience.
For a few weeks in early 1997, it looked as if the federal government might experiment with the traditional Liberal pre-election
strategy of espousing popular social causes. Child poverty was once

again in the news, and it was widely rumoured that substantial federal money would be invested in children. Paul Martin cursed his way through an interview with the *Ottawa Citizen*: "What kind of a society do we have when we see these gigantic salaries up here and this huge amount of poverty down there? . . . I mean, Christ, you should say 'What in God's name?' . . . We support the deficit targets, but Jesus Murphy, there's more to it than this."[18]

Expectations grew among child-poverty activists and poor parents, only to be dashed when it became clear that Martin's "down payment on child poverty" would look more like a Leon's ad: "Do not pay until 1999!" The finance minister was reigned in; his political advisors "wondered whether Mr. Martin had lost his mind. . . . [He was] fuelled more by a sense of guilt than an appreciation of realpolitik." A party insider said, "It was the welfare message. He'll never do that again."[19]

"I THINK YOU CAN live below the poverty line but still have a good standard of living if you have loving parents."

Source: Comment by a participant in a focus group convened by the federal government to test its campaign platform on child poverty, *Globe and Mail*, June 17, 1997

An access-to-information request revealed that the government had commissioned two surveys and convened twelve focus groups to taste-test different campaign slogans about child poverty, and to gauge how little money it could promise to spend without losing too many votes. Surely this is one of the most cynical political strategies ever launched. However, assuming party strategists heeded the feedback, Canadians should share some of the shame. According to reports from the focus groups, the well-to-do were less sympathetic than what were called "the economically insecure." The secure classes focused on the perceived "emotional, moral and intellectual deficiencies of parents," and were the least likely to consider the "child poverty problem" related to government action.[20]

"THE GOVERNMENT IS almost as dedicated to the fight against child poverty as it is to having a good public relations strategy. This is very encouraging."
Source: Charles Gordon, commenting on the Liberal government's focus groups on child poverty, *Ottawa Citizen*, June 19, 1997

While we are busy playing "blame the victim," the real game is moving well beyond the control of citizens and their focus groups.

New Game, New Rules

The problem with democracy, some say, is that it allows citizens to make changes. Since elected governments can be replaced, new governments at least in theory can insist on new rules that make greater demands of corporations, such as job creation. To get around this problem, multinational corporations are seeking to write the rules at a new level, to establish through international negotiation and consensus certain corporate entitlements that could never survive scrutiny by alert voters. Trade agreements that take precedence over national laws make public opinion irrelevant and public resistance futile. Michael Walker, free trade advocate and president of the influential right-wing think-tank the Fraser Institute, explains that the role of trade deals is to make democracy less powerful: "A trade deal simply limits the extent to which signatory governments can respond to pressure from their citizens."[21]

Behind the photo-ops of G-7 meetings, amid gatherings of the Organization for Economic Co-operation and Development (OECD), and, most blatantly, through APEC (Asian Pacific Economic Co-operation) dialogues, world economies dare each other not to blink as they enhance corporate freedom. In another forum, the world's political and corporate leaders seek agreements – rules of the game – to enshrine corporate power and entitlements that can never be superseded by national governments.

Leaked drafts of the Multinational Agreement on Investment (the MAI), now under negotiation through the OECD, foreshadow a frightening world of unrestrained corporate power. The goal of the MAI is to protect foreign investment capital. Under the rules of the MAI, it would be considered protectionist and thus illegal for states to make demands of transnational corporations. The corporate rights spelled out in the MAI include the right of any corporation, whatever its country of origin, to own the natural resources of another country without undertaking any obligation to sustain them; the right "to bid for and own any privatized public infrastructure, social good or cultural transmission without any limit on foreign control"; and the right "to reject as illegal any national standards or human rights, labour rights or environmental protection on goods produced . . . in other nations."[22]

Under the MAI, goods and services that governments provide to the public would be deemed monopolies that by definition "interfere with business freedom." Thus monopolies such as health care and education would be required to compensate by acting "solely in accordance with commercial considerations in the purchase or sale of goods and services" – meaning that business principles could be the only policy consideration applied to these areas. Governments that refuse to privatize services such as education would be liable for the payment of compensation to corporations that had lost the "opportunity to profit." John McMurtry, a Canadian philosophy professor who writes about the ethics of global markets, calls this appropriation of public power "an act of aggression against democracy."[23]

Some MAI-watchers accuse critics such as McMurtry, and the nationalist lobby group the Council of Canadians, of overreacting. Forced into a limited round of hearings on the MAI, the federal government assured Canadians that it would never sign the agreement – the same agreement it once claimed didn't exist – unless the deal contained exemptions that met the "high standards" of NAFTA. According to the government, these exemptions have protected our national sovereignty and unique culture, if not the actual jobs of Canadians.

Are Canadians up in arms about the MAI, or denouncing their government's role in its negotiation? Few have heard of it. But even if the intent and content of the MAI had been detailed in the media, and even if Liberal candidates had not been coached to avoid any reference to the MAI during the federal election campaign,[24] would Canadians have taken notice? International organizations, their meetings and their agreements, hardly preoccupy most of us. When free trade advocates mention APEC, they describe it in dulcet tones as apolitical, as a forum that only promotes trade. When two thousand protesters at the University of British Columbia tried to draw attention to their view of APEC's real agenda, forty-eight were arrested, and news cameras caught dozens of others being pepper-sprayed by the RCMP. The scenes of police dogs and physical confrontation between police and protesters should have shocked Canadians, many of whom are old enough to remember Kent State. Quick to dismiss the incident, Jean Chrétien responded to a question about the RCMP's use of force by joking, "Pepper? Me, I put pepper on my plate." Laughter could be heard from the press. The next morning, the *Globe and Mail* headlined its story "Human-rights protest noisy but non-violent," and dismissed the protesters as merely "young and enthusiastic."[25]

"WORDS ARE, OF COURSE, the most powerful drug used by mankind."

Source: Rudyard Kipling

Since Canadians have been repeatedly assured that pursuing trade is always in our best interests, we go about our business. Even the language of APEC is intended to soothe and reassure us. Jane Kelsey, a New Zealand economist, says the dialect of APEC is as unique as Esperanto: "These economies aren't inhabited by people, but by 'human resources.' They don't have elected representatives but 'economic leaders.' It is cold and grey and mechanical and scary as hell."[26]

This is not the way APEC is promoted to high school students, of course. Through convoluted laundering processes, a corporation known as TGMagazine, together with a group called the Students'

Commission, used Human Resources Development Canada (HRDC) and private technology money to consult Canadian youth about APEC and its agenda. They sponsored face-to-face and virtual conferencing under the theme Global Vision, also the name of a "non-profit educational organization committed to invoking enthusiasm in Canada's youth towards business in a global market." Particularly enthusiastic youth are invited to take part in Team Canada's trade adventures.[27] At the APEC forum, a wired-to-the-max booth trumpeted the consensus of today's youth. A quote in foot-high font read, "I want to be a leader in the world of the future. In my world, there won't be any borders."

APEC Means Business

The leaders of the eighteen economies of the Asia-Pacific region regularly report progress on trade liberalization and globalization, and discuss how participating economies can further nurture global capital – money that knows no borders. Since the conditions most favourable to corporate opportunity require a work force with certain characteristics, human resource development is an APEC priority. Thus APEC seeks region-wide consensus on restructuring education along business-friendly lines.

Canada plays a lead role in APEC's aggressive human resource/ education strategy. APEC's working group on education is led by Stewart Goodings, an experienced Canadian civil servant with impressive credentials. Goodings speaks of globalization as an opportunity, not a threat: after all, "Wasn't it a Canadian, Marshall McLuhan, who came up with the phrase, 'Global Village'?" he asked a small but sceptical crowd of educators gathered to protest the APEC summit in Vancouver.[28] No doubt Goodings thought invoking the blessing of a Canadian cultural hero such as McLuhan would bolster his credibility. Perhaps he was unaware of McLuhan's rather testy retort to a question that probed his views: "I don't *approve* of the global village – I say we live in it."[29]

Goodings explained modestly that although he chairs the education working group, his role is not all that important. APEC calls all its chairpersons "head shepherds," Goodings pointed out,

"MORE THAN ANY other institution, corporations dominate our conceptions of how life should be lived. If you switch on your radio, flip on the television, or open your newspaper, corporations speak to you. They do it through advertising. . . . The average viewer now watches 22,000 commercials every year. That's how many times corporations place images in our brains to suggest that human life is most satisfying when inundated with their commodities. . . . And between commercials there are programs, also created by and for corporations, that espouse values consistent with the ads."

Source: CCPA *Education Monitor*

although he confessed that he had no idea why this term was chosen. His audience groaned.

Some sheep lead; others follow. Because of APEC's transnational structure, it does not arrive at policies per se, and there is no legislation that sets out an APEC agenda, of course. Instead, APEC's positions are determined by consensus. Economies that assume the lead responsibility for a particular topic shape this consensus by producing a concept paper outlining basic principles. This is how South Korea came to write APEC's concept of education.

South Korea's paper is admirably straightforward. In subsequent rewrites, its blunt statements will no doubt be massaged into the innocent-sounding jargon of edbiz-speak. But in its original form, this document asserts clearly that since globalization is inevitable as well as desirable, human resource development must be forced to supply its requirements. The implications for schools are obvious. Canada's Web site promoting the APEC summit trumpets the slogan, "APEC means business!" Since APEC means business, education within the Asia-Pacific zone means preparing workers for business, and little else. The APEC paper explains:

The emphasis on education for itself or on education for good members of a community without a large emphasis on preparations for the future work are no longer appropriate. In other words, the idea that work is only an instrumental part of one's life is no longer appropriate. Such a dichotomic view on education and work cannot be justified in the world where economic development is emphasized.[30]

Once the function of education is defined as preparing workers for business, it follows logically that business should determine what students learn. Predictably, APEC's paper states that "decisions must be taken by a school system for good business reasons with maximum business intervention." It goes on to criticize curriculum designed by "intellectual elites" who favour the teaching of "concepts and theories," and even "learning for the sake of learning" without due attention to "outcomes."

APEC concludes that the remedy is to be found in business-education partnerships. Globalization critic Larry Kuehn says *partnerships* is code for letting corporations shape schools,[31] using tools that are becoming all too familiar. APEC's list of "principles and expectations on a school system that integrates business practices" includes the setting of standards, the acquisition of skills and attitudes "necessary for adjustment into work environments," the teaching of "work ethics," and the development of a common, comprehensive "achievement record" for each student to help employers recruit and select workers more efficiently. System-wide data on the most important features of each economy's education system should be collected and published as "indicators" – benchmarks of region-wide progress towards better-aligned education systems.

One key indicator, according to APEC leaders, is the proportion of students pursuing "non-productive" education. The oversupply of highly educated but underemployed or unemployed youth is a global problem. Supply exceeds demand. Increasing the demand for these young workers would require creating jobs, a cost of doing business that multinationals aren't about to entertain. It is more business-friendly to shrink the supply of some kinds of labour by restricting the number of students who can receive a high-cost and (from APEC's perspective) less productive education, while increasing the number of students who are edu-trained at lower cost. An idle, well-educated work force generates unrest. A poorly educated, poorly paid work force generates profits. The APEC paper complains that, in the Asia-Pacific, "general high schools are highly over-populated compared to vocational high schools. Insufficient numbers of students study the workplace and technology while too many pursue the humanities."

Because APEC hypes globalization as inevitable, and because globalization both seeks and causes cultural integration, APEC believes education should be deemed a "cultural product" – a commodity – that can be bought and sold like any other tradable commodity. The immense implications for the export of McCulture and the "harmonization" of school systems and their curricula may tempt us to dismiss this scenario as extreme and unlikely. Perhaps edu-biz is merely another example of the overextended ambitions of the Asian tigers – a bad idea that will go away.

However, this conclusion would be wrong and dangerous. The distance between South Korea and Canada has never been shorter.

According to the warm and encouraging speech delivered to a Toronto conference devoted to speeding up the privatization of public education, global education marketing is a top priority for the federal government. Speaking on behalf of his minister, Sergio Marchi, Industry Canada official Ken Higham said education exporting will play an increasingly important role in his government's foreign policy.[32] His government is particularly pleased that fifty education marketers were part of the most recent Team Canada trade mission, promoting partnerships worldwide. Higham promised that the APEC region would provide the next growth opportunity for this sector. Success in the Asia-Pacific would be the true test of the federal government's strategy to use "academics as the instruments of diplomacy." (Diplomacy is now governmentalese for trade, which in turn is governmentalese for corporate profit. It was no accident that Industry Canada changed the name of its Department of Science and Academic Affairs to the Information Highway Applications Branch.[33])

To reinforce this message, Minister Marchi signed a statement welcoming participants to the education privatization conference. He wished them well as they discussed what he called "a significant step forward in the advancement of the Canadian education export industry."[34] APEC couldn't have said it better.

The MAI, as it is currently drafted, contains the tools to ensure no nation will be able to develop an education system that displeases any corporation doing business within its borders. The APEC papers, priorities, and frameworks furnish the characteristics of a corporate-friendly education system. Together they contain the words and the vision that are shaping education reform in Canada, used in the same ways and for the same purposes.

This new vision cannot be realized if the schools we have now are allowed to succeed. It cannot be achieved if Canadian schools are allowed to pursue local or even provincially determined goals. The new system cannot be monitored without the regulatory framework of standards and benchmarks, nor without the disciplinary tool of standardized testing. It cannot succeed without national – and, eventually, international – curricula agreeable to education's business partners. Critics of the new vision must be weakened; ideally, they must be divided. The full potential of the education market can be maximized only if minimalist governments reduce education funding, creating new demands that can't be met by the public system. At the same time, obtaining a post-secondary education must become more difficult, except for targeted students in targeted programs. Reforms such as these may be difficult, but they are urgent.

Yet even at the best of times, reforming public education in Canada is complicated and contentious. Since Ottawa has no legitimate constitutional role in determining policy on public education, it may steer but it cannot row. Nonetheless, the federal government's influence on education is felt in many ways, not the least of which is the impact of reduced transfer payments to the provinces. But the power to implement the restructuring of public education resides elsewhere.

At the national level, in the absence of a transparent, accountable body, an organization known as the Council of Ministers of Education, Canada (CMEC) co-ordinates education policy. The CMEC consults whom it wishes, when it wishes. Rather like the supra-national structure of APEC, the CMEC works by "consensus" and exists through the "voluntary" participation of all provinces and territories. Also like APEC, the CMEC is accountable to no electorate, introduces no legislation, and meets behind closed doors. When those doors open, the ministers and deputies turn selected decisions into press releases, and the CMEC announces the new projects it will co-ordinate. "Lead provinces" begin to move on particular priorities, such as cuts to funding, the development of national curriculum frameworks, and the elimination of school boards.

When the same education reform turns up in several provinces, what may look like a coincidence is better understood as a well-orchestrated alignment. Of course, every province and territory wants to convey the impression that its education policies are driven by the unique vision of its citizens and so-called stakeholders. In reality, the vision has more to do with APEC and its clones than with our own priorities for children and their schools. Province by territory, education in Canada is being restructured, in APEC's words, "to meet the strong requirement for flexible and motivated human resources."

Not surprisingly, therefore, using language somewhat more polished than South Korea's, the CMEC announces that "transitions" will be its 1998 focus, and that it will place particular emphasis on "pathways between the various levels of education and training systems to working life, and the match between education, training and the labour market."[35] The CMEC notes that its work will parallel the current thrusts of OECD and APEC, although the council paraphrases APEC's objectives as merely "fostering a linkage between learning and work" – a rather benign translation of capturing education to serve capital.

At issue here is not the tenuous, overstated link between training and employment, nor even how much attention Canadian classrooms should pay to preparing students for the world of work. These are important questions, and they will be explored in more detail in other chapters. But if our national policies on education are to be set by trade blocs bent on globalization, whose actions are in turn determined by transnational corporations, then our national opinions on these questions will become – or perhaps have already become – irrelevant. We may think we elect governments to reflect, in part, our perspectives on public education. However, it is increasingly evident that education reform is not about who governs, but about who rules.

Playing School by New Rules

"The times, they are a-changin," hums the mbanx commercial, one of a series of ads that perfectly captures the intersection of corporate interests, popular culture, and ideas about self and community. "Rules? Why do we have so many rules?" asks a black youth, although without the rules established by governments, he might still be sitting at the back of the bus. "Change is good," chirps a pre-teen girl. "You'd better start swimming or sink like a stone," warns the chorus. Even though we are swimming on our own, we'll be okay – with a little help from mbanx. The public protest over these commercials, such as it was, lamented the corporate takeover of boomers' sacred music, not any overt or subliminal messages about deregulation and individualism. Perhaps mbanx knows what its market wants to hear.

The collapse of traditional, taken-for-granted communitarianism among Canadians has resulted in the election and re-election of governments that champion unabashed individualism. But we are changing, along with our governments. In agreeing to sink or swim in the Darwinian pool, we have changed our expectations of ourselves and our institutions.

Especially among what is left of the middle class, we have developed a harder-edged approach to the values we pass on to our children, what we want them to learn at school, and whom we want them to sit beside. In other times, we looked to schools to sharpen our minds, but also to soften our hearts. Robert Fulghum captured a rather sentimental recollection of these other times in his essay *All I Really Need to Know I Learned in Kindergarten*, in which he recalls learning to listen, take turns, hold hands, share, take a nap after lunch, and flush[36] – small acts that defy measurement and mock the idea of standards. These virtues have become relegated to posters because they contribute little to "employability skills" and are thus redundant, even in kindergarten, especially when we have Barney and Tickle-me-Elmo to take care of children's emotional needs. Today's kindergarten curricula are more likely to refer to career awareness than co-operation; Ontario's minister of education has called for each student's "career file" to be opened in Grade 1.[37]

Said one provincial ministry of education official at a recent meeting: "I think there are two essentials in kindergarten. The first is to get them ready for keyboarding. The other is to get these little kids to start thinking of themselves as 'Me, Inc.'"[38]

Me, Inc. flows directly from "You, too bad," just as surely as it flows from any ministry document. The construction of Me, Inc. is underway in the schools of ed.com. Our schools are being reshaped, and so are the children and adults within them.

"Tell Me What Happened to School Today"

A wise educator once remarked that the only thing that can be done quickly in education is damage. Canadian schools have been under reform – or, some would say, under assault – for the last decade, punished because of their resistance to Me, Inc. Politicians impatient with organic or bottom-up reform have been preparing the ground for change imposed from the top. Seized upon as strategic territory by ideologues and privateers, scapegoated by politicians, ridiculed as bloated bureaucracies by education critics, schools (we are told) are overdue for restructuring.

Schools are not – yet – businesses. Left to their own rhythms, they would never achieve the just-in-time flexibility said to characterize today's successful private-sector organizations. Explanations for the slow and uneven pace of change in schools shift from uninspired leadership and resistant parents to lack of time, money, and accountability. Members of the teaching profession have always argued that when they are excluded from the decision-making process, any innovation is doomed to failure. Teachers can sabotage reform efforts more or less easily, and may do so either as a calling or a sport. Legions of education change experts have written texts on education reform and its implementation, often pocketing enormous speakers' fees in return for castigating teachers at professional development conferences. Their weary audiences return to their classrooms the next day, where things remain pretty much the same.

Our change-addicted society condemns the apparent constancy of the bells, the curricula, the classroom, and its values. Change has become a virtue – a noun, not a verb. A few voices suggest that the enduring structure and resiliency of schools prove their remarkable success. They argue that the core characteristics of schools persist because people – not information, outcomes, or equipment – are at the heart of every school, and that human relationships don't change just because a new minister makes another speech. Perhaps it is as simple as numbers. At school, children outnumber adults, and children show not the slightest interest in anyone's reform agenda. All they want is nice teachers, a good day, something interesting to do.

PREPARING FOR THE work force could start earlier. Junior Achievement (JA) has been teaching entrepreneurship to students since 1955. Lately, the program has gone upscale. Thanks to a $10,000 donation from Microsoft, a small team of Nepean, Ontario, students and teachers went on its own trade mission to Seoul. Canadian JA promoters want to import the U.S. approach where "appreciating how business fits into everyone's life starts even earlier." According to JA's Ottawa organizer, "Why wait until Grade 5 to introduce Business Basics when we can start in kindergarten?"

Source: "What Works: Corporate success in tackling the youth jobs crisis," CIBC 1997

Most children, that is. The disenfranchised global South is showing up in our communities, and its school-aged cohort is turning up for school. The declining quality of life experienced by many students, their diminished capacity and inclination to learn, and the determination of some to drag others down with them have changed schools more than any political reform. Students express their helplessness and hopelessness in aggression towards teachers and each other, hostility towards authority, and indifference to learning. Schools have never had to deal with so many students who couldn't care less, and who have so little reason to care more.

Education's critics blame schools themselves for serving up uninspired teaching and irrelevant curricula, for using industrial-age techniques and even books. If students don't aspire to excellence, surely it is because teachers have tolerated mediocrity or worse, and schools have redefined or explained away failure in the name of self-esteem.

No expertise is required to qualify as an education critic. William Thorsell, editor-in-chief of the *Globe and Mail*, addressed the 1996 National Consultation on Education organized by the Council of Ministers of Education, Canada. Although he admitted that he hadn't been inside a public school in twenty years, Thorsell said he knew how to improve the system anyway.

He began by describing the "lackadaisical" and "crude" characteristics of Canada's public education system as "scandalous and bankrupting," if applied to the design and manufacture of auto parts. He urged "looking to market forces" to leverage systemic reform, and breaking up the monopoly of public education by "establishing and administering system-wide competence tests at regular intervals, and publicizing the results by school. National tests would be the ideal." He liked his speech so well that he published it in his newspaper the next day.[39]

If more is expected, more will be delivered, critics believe. The notion of raising the bar higher so more students will be able to clear it may defy the rules of both logic and gravity, but this strategy is the core of today's education rhetoric.

The code word is "standards," often found in tandem with "outcomes," "quality assurance," "benchmarks," and other phrases imported from the enterprise vocabulary of Total Quality. In educational jargon, the idea of standards is confusing, partly because of the word's two common meanings: "meeting a standard" implies reaching a level of attainment, but "standard" can also mean "similar" and "common." In policy talk, it refers to minimum levels – such as safety standards. In the manufacture of auto parts, processes can ensure the quality and standardization of outcomes – what rolls off the assembly line. If a car manufacturer decides the standard for its hubcaps will be 18-karat gold, no problem.

The trouble with kids is that we can't melt them down and reconstitute them into any kind of standard. Shipments of impure gold can be returned to the manufacturer. Hubcaps accidentally mangled on the production line can be recalled. The assembly line, which created the metaphor of standards, offers only an obscenely inappropriate language to apply to human beings – one that obliges us to refer to students who don't succeed as "substandard."

The language we use to talk about the process of education determines how we think about education's purposes and value – there are no neutral words. To speak of learning as a journey is not just metaphorically different from referring to it as executing measurable outcomes. Yet outcomes – specified, allegedly concrete statements of what all students should know and be able to do at specific points along the journey – have taken over as the focus of education reform in North America and beyond. Ironically, in such a mechanistic and scientistic system, no research base justifies the alignment of schools with outcomes-based education.[40]

Even many people who describe themselves as progressive praise the new focus on outcomes. Because the furies of the religious Right in the United States have targeted outcomes-based education (OBE), it has been associated with liberal approaches to education reform.[41] Surely anything condemned as the work of Satan will sound promising to parts of the Left! Yet OBE is deeply inconsistent with any philosophy that values education as the creation of something personal and unique.

Determining a Grade 11 mathematics standard for non-linear geometry may not be problematic, but this standard won't decide whether every student needs this skill, or what to do with those who fail to jump through this particular hoop. One Ontario ministry document on standards proposes, in all seriousness, applying a five-point scale to grade students on their sense of humour, a graduation outcome that is placed just below "viewing change as a challenge and an opportunity."[42] If students are to exhibit such an Orwellian standard of good-humoured flexibility, what implications flow from setting standard outcomes for the study of history or social studies? To reduce the development of citizenship qualities or the exploration of economic and political issues to "common measurable learnings," we will need the type of ideological conformity that the Soviets once propagated.

The great education philosopher John Dewey, whose thinking shaped the last great wave of North American school reform, called for schools that were laboratories of freedom. Rather than proposing an irresponsible or anarchic vision, Dewey was applying Thomas Jefferson's definition of the purpose of schooling, which Jefferson called learning the skills to live in liberty.[43] The skills to live in liberty must include self-control and self-reliance, but they also include interdependence and responsibility towards others. The new purpose of education – producing and measuring the skills to live in utility – is the antithesis of education for personal development and participation in democratic life.

It is no coincidence that OBE has captivated education reformers devoted to globalizing the schools of Me, Inc. Their goals are well served by a system that sorts the substandard out of the mix while disguising ideological bias as impartial fact. In addition, as we focus our attention on outcomes, we pay correspondingly less attention to the quality of so-called inputs – kids, teachers, and resources. The hard-nosed language of OBE perfectly suits the hard-edged realities of globalization.

Not surprisingly, standards and outcomes are championed by the business sector and adored by the technology sector. An important 1995 American education summit, attended by every state governor and co-hosted by IBM's CEO, Louis V. Gerstner, was set up to "focus on the need for world-class academic standards . . . [to] provide an opportunity for governors and business leaders to understand and experience how emerging technologies can be incorporated into school restructuring."[44] Perhaps the absence of educators at the summit-cum-trade show prompted Nevada's governor Bob Miller to speak plainly. He complained in his keynote address that "too often we seem too willing to accept underachieving standards for a Beavis, a Butt-head, or a Bart Simpson. The nation's CEOs are fed up with passive acceptance of mediocrity."[45]

This kind of criticism of American schools has become familiar fare in the United States, and to a significant extent it has polluted Canadians' view of their schools. Popular media can reinforce the impression. Scenes of violent inner-city American schools merge with local cable broadcasts of school boards debating special education. The television program *Hard Copy* is probably more familiar to many Canadians than their neighbourhood school, as parents of school-aged children compose an ever-shrinking segment of the population.

"IN OTHER WORDS, we have a public system completely divorced from self-evident reality that cannot or will not change. So there can be only one solution: get education away from the public sector and let it be market-driven. . . . The 'professionals' plainly do not know what they're doing."

Source: Ted Byfield, *Financial Post*, February 22, 1997

Not that Canada lacks its share of indigenous education critics and single-minded reformers. The propagation of maliciously misleading statements about the quality of schools, their cost, the performance of students, the accountability and perks of teachers, the idle irresponsibility of school board trustees, and so forth might alone have been sufficient to destabilize public education. Without doubt, the convergence of unrealistic expectations, social upheaval, and reduced funding piled on top of the real and imagined faults of schools has weakened them. By itself, the cult of individualism – so much celebrated by the business sector and right-wing politicians – might have destroyed a system that exists, in part, to teach children that the needs of the group, not the individual, sometimes come first. Together, over time, these forces might have caused public education to "sink like a stone." But some people wanted to go further and faster. One person, in particular, wanted to create a crisis.

A Crisis with a Purpose

Ed.com is not shaped merely by drift and changing circumstances – it is built on concrete political decisions. Former Ontario education minister John Snobelen, speaking to his new staff in July 1995, said, "Yeah, we need to invent a crisis, and that's not just an act of courage, there's some skill involved."[46]

John Snobelen is not the only politician to have seen the value of a manufactured crisis, although he is one of the few to do his thinking out loud while the video camera rolls. Creating a crisis-based window of opportunity to promote otherwise unacceptable ideas is standard operating practice among all radical governments.

To make the most of a crisis, politicians require speed and confusion – and early in the Tory mandate, Ontario's minister delivered both. To the government's advantage, the pace of Ontario's education reforms and the insularity of the education community led many observers to view Ontario's situation as unprecedented, and the restructuring as contradictory and chaotic. But they are wrong. Everything Ontario's ministers and their government have undertaken in education restructuring has been proposed and (in some cases) implemented elsewhere in Canada and in other parts of the world. It is true, however, that with the possible exception of Mexico, where the education system was summarily reformed by the World Bank, nowhere have these reforms been advanced so quickly, so brazenly, and in the face of so much public resistance. Every aspect of the Tory education reform agenda is consistent with every other part, once we understand the purpose of the reforms, and the reformed purpose of schools in "the new Ontario." Canada's largest province is not unique, it is just in a hurry.

Ontario's Progressive Conservatives set out their general education strategy in their pre-election paper, "The Mike Harris Round Table on Common Sense in Education."[47] According to this document, too many students "are not prepared and are dropping out, or even graduating, without acceptable levels of skill in language or mathematics," rendering them unfit to take advantage of the "new technologies and new services leading to new opportunities." To turn around this deplorable drift towards child-centred education, the paper urged a mandated high standards curriculum, more province-wide and national tests, and greater parental involvement. Under "support to teachers," the common sense revolution promised "private sector involvement." In keeping with its "principles of choice and service to the taxpayer," the party proposed options such as charter schools, so long as they fell "within the guidelines of fiscal responsibility and consumer demand."

Despite the leaders' promise to become the government that would act on the wishes and instructions of citizens (or, more specifically, taxpayers), this platform could not be described as populist. The Tory agenda called for schools to provide less of everything except choice, but the Ontario public wanted more, not less, from its schools. The results of the extensive consultations undertaken by the Ontario Royal Commission on Learning had been tabled only months before the Harris government was elected. The commissioners concluded that, despite institutional shortcomings, "there is no serious evidence that our schools are failing our kids any more or less than they ever have."[48] Opinion polls found widespread support for schools, despite the public's constant exposure to exaggerated criticism of them. A 1997 Environics poll reported that 73 per cent of Ontarians rated the quality of education "adequate to excellent."[49] Those closest to schools – recent graduates and parents of students currently in the system – were most convinced of the quality of public education. Like other Canadians, few were ecstatic with their schools, but most were satisfied by a wide margin and prepared to pay more in taxes to maintain them.

Only 4 per cent of Ontarians found "preparing students for the real world" a concern; five times as many (21 per cent) thought "lack of funding" a more pressing education problem.[50]

Although the Tories didn't draw their agenda for education reform from public opinion, neither did they pull it from thin air. Their platform closely followed the recommendations of the Ontario Education Reform Network, which self-published a 1994 tract on schools called *D-: Could Do Better.* This lobby voices a made-in-Ontario version of the critique of public schools imported from the extreme end of the American Right.[51] Bill Robson is the spokesperson for this group, and by coincidence (perhaps) also a senior economist at the corporate-funded C.D. Howe Institute, where the word *public* precedes *debt* more often than *schools.* Snobelen rewarded Robson by appointing him chair of the powerful, unelected Provincial Parent Advisory Council, ensuring a direct link between corporate opinion and education policy. (No doubt Bill Robson also chats frequently with his brother John, who writes the education editorials for the proudly libertarian *Ottawa Citizen.*)

The Tory education platform is also consistent with the views of the Fraser Institute, which has announced its intention to devote greater attention to education.[52] A special issue of the monthly *Fraser Forum* is written by Helen Raham, executive director of the B.C.-based Teachers for Excellence in Education. Raham's organization, which began as an independent group of anti-union teachers, is funded by the Fraser Institute and the Donner Foundation, friend of right-wing causes. Her analysis is familiar if poorly documented: "Our students are emerging without the competitive skills needed to survive in the global marketplace," she writes, and adds that "parents complain of vague reporting methods [and] low academic expectations." Under "barriers to excellence," Raham cites bureaucracy, collective agreements, unions, tenure, regulation, and lack of choice. Her remedy for lack of choice – charter schools – conveniently takes care of the other barriers she identifies.[53]

COMMENTING ON ONTARIO'S new curriculum, which the government boasts links the three R's to increased standardized testing, C.D. Howe economist Bill Robson (identified only as head of the government-appointed Ontario Parent Council and father of three) expressed satisfaction, and said he intended to review the new standards with his daughter, age eight. The government mandated new curricula in all subject areas for nine grades during the summer holidays, four weeks before the 1997–98 new school year. Only a score of teachers turned up at summer meetings called by the ministry to discuss how these multiple changes would be implemented with so little lead time. The *Ottawa Citizen* crowed, "Teachers fail to do homework," but had to eat crow when the ministry confirmed that it had limited teacher participation to a select group of invited teachers. Ordinary teachers who wanted to attend were turned away.

Source: Ottawa Sun, August 3, 1997

The newly elected Ontario government believed it had the right remedies for education, and the Right support, if only it could get its hands on the power to implement its ideas. From its point of view, the enmeshed system of school governance did little but provide opportunities for parents, teachers, and community-level decision makers to thwart the new agenda. Most school boards were evidently prepared to ignore the more radical aspects of the Tory plan, and they were starting to operate as a de facto political opposition with an unexpected talent for mobilizing public protest. The power of local boards to raise taxes, negotiate collective agreements, and set curriculum meant that they could devise and bankroll almost any apostasy. School boards had to go.

Eliminating them outright (as New Brunswick had done) would be politically risky. Instead, the government would marginalize school boards by reducing their responsibilities, by ensuring they had too large an area to govern, and by discouraging candidates. Powerless and out-of-touch, they would dwindle into irrelevancy, and at some point the Tories would easily win public support for their abolition. Thus during the "megaweek" of January 1997, the provincial government announced that it would reduce the number of school boards from 129 to 66, cut the number of trustees from 1,900 to 700, and take over education funding. Furthermore, it would pay each trustee only $5,000 per year – barely enough to fund an election campaign – in return for full-time work, effectively discouraging candidates with community support but without personal wealth or well-heeled backers. Other candidates had second thoughts: who would want to take on such a thankless and toothless role?

This restructuring of who does what (to whom and how often, one wag added) centralized power and decentralized accountability in ways perfectly consistent with right-wing strategy. From Chile to New Zealand, from Alberta to New Brunswick, governments have seized central control of key education "inputs" – curriculum and dollars. They have annulled generally elected (i.e., democratic) governance at the community level, and substituted what amounts to self-selected boards operating at the level of the school. By legislation, some of these school councils must include a representative of the business community, and ideally, each involves the school's corporate partner. The Ontario government decreed that the word *advisory* would be struck from the official title of school councils – their powers would be increased to make up for the loss of the boards' powers.

Publicly, governments claimed that these school-level decision makers would find creative common-sense solutions to everyday problems. Privately, they recognized the political benefits of their strategy: the consequences of unpopular decisions, including program cuts caused by cutbacks in provincial funding, could be downloaded to the parents themselves and their now-powerless, overburdened school boards. Discovering that they would soon be in charge, already overwhelmed volunteers looked up from their fund-raising projects with alarm. While in theory almost everyone supports increased parent involvement, in practice few parents have the time or experience to take on the day-to-day governance of schools.

Take No Prisoners

A take-no-prisoners approach to restructuring either the private or the public sector works best when the reformers advance on as many fronts as possible simultaneously, the better to bewilder and overwhelm the opposition. Ontario's restructuring megaweek of January 1997 also included mandated municipal mergers and the downloading of soft (and therefore unpredictable) costs to municipalities. The government set out only the broad outlines of these changes; politicians evaded the details. As expected, community leaders, the media, the Opposition, and ordinary citizens were shell-shocked.

Accordingly, the little attention that education tax and governance reforms received from people outside the education sector dwindled to "shocked and appalled" sound bites. When six thousand citizens marched in Toronto on February 15, 1997, they were opposing municipal amalgamation, not education restructuring. When John Ralston Saul shouted, "This government is the enemy of the people," he was not attacking the newspeak Education Improvement Commission, but the creation of the Toronto megacity.[54]

Rumours of what was in store for education were reported (on the inside pages) of newspapers almost daily. Focus groups convened by the government early in 1996 had taste-tested a number of options, the better to discover "the public's tolerance for change" and to determine "what messages would sell, how to sell them and which ones it should keep quiet."[55] Public opinion was mixed. A Vector poll found that 28 per cent of respondents thought Minister Snobelen was "on the wrong track" with his education reforms, 15 per cent supported his direction, and 48 per cent thought it was still too soon to tell.[56] They wouldn't have long to wait.

Ontario's education system was about to be reformed from top to bottom. The changes seemed to come down to money – money

A 1996 UNIVERSITY of Toronto survey of Ontario residents found satisfaction with schools to be on the increase, but opinions were not evenly distributed. About 60 per cent of parents were at least satisfied with their local schools, compared with fewer than 50 per cent of non-parents. Two-thirds of those under twenty-five years of age thought schools were doing well, a marked contrast with corporate executives, who had little good to say about public education. Fifty-nine per cent of CEOs said they were dissatisfied with the system in general, 72 per cent said they were dissatisfied with the "value for taxes," and 69 per cent said they were dissatisfied with student discipline.

Source: Ottawa Citizen, September 4, 1997

that was badly needed to finance a promised 30 per cent tax cut. If the government could deliver on this promise, perhaps Ontario's voters would forgive everything else. Yet cutting the education budget would oppose public opinion. A poll found majority support among Ontarians for increased funding to schools and a "willingness to pay higher taxes for education" – except among corporate executives.[57] Perhaps cheered by support from one quarter at least, the government began by cutting the education budget by $600 million, and another billion in cuts was rumoured to be coming. The Tories obviously understood that they wouldn't find this kind of money just by cutting back on photocopying.

To further complicate matters, the minister had already made some new and expensive commitments. He had said that he would lift the existing construction ban placed on school boards, although he promised to limit costs by copying New Brunswick's approach, where at least one school would be "built, owned and maintained by a real estate company that leases it back to the school board."[58] He also had to find $40 million for the Technology Incentive Partnership Program, which would bring schools closer to technology corporations.[59] Snobelen had never withdrawn the commitment he made, soon after the government was elected, to put a computer on every student's desk – at a conservative cost of $1,000 per unit, this promise would cost $1.5 billion for just the quickly outdated hardware. But the hardware couldn't operate without retrofitted classrooms. The *Globe and Mail* reported that for the Metro Toronto separate school system alone, it would cost $100 million simply to rewire ageing schools.[60] Who would train the teachers – or at least those who were left – to use the new equipment? Multiplied across the province, both the cuts and costs of Snobelen's technology promise would be astronomical.

As the opinion polls got worse for the government, the minister tried to build public support for cuts to education by attacking the quality of the province's schools and by taking direct aim at teachers' unions. He launched his offensive at a summer teachers' meeting in 1996 to which he had been invited. Even union officials who had enjoyed a relatively cordial meeting with the minister the week before were stunned by his remarks.

Audience members would have been less surprised if they had been following American presidential politics. Just days earlier, Bob Dole had delivered a televised speech accepting the Republican nomination for president. After insisting that "it takes a family, not a village" to raise a child – a swat at Hillary Clinton – Dole zeroed in on education: "I say this not to the teachers, but to their unions: If education were a war, you would be losing it. If it were a business, you would be driving it into bankruptcy. If it were a patient, it would be dying."[61] According to opinion polls, Dole's speech narrowed the spread between him and Bill Clinton from twenty-one to thirteen points. The Ontario Tories decided to take a page out of the Republicans' book, and set up schools and teachers to take the fall for generalized angst and public debt. Strategists working for both the Progressive Conservatives and the Republicans – political parties that already shared the slogan "common sense" – were sure it was the Right way to go.

But in the autumn of 1996, Ontario public opinion about education was stubbornly indifferent to American-style education politics. Opinion leaders began to defend schools and criticize the minister. Gerald Caplan, who had gained considerable respect as co-chair of Ontario's Royal Commission on Learning, called Snobelen's approach "simply madness," "a bad joke," a "wilfully provocative scheme" that held "a virtual guarantee of failure."[62] "S stands for Shame," cried the pre-Hollinger *Ottawa Citizen*, calling cuts that resulted in an end to junior kindergarten "short-sighted."[63] It itemized the minister of education's "constant criticism": "In recent weeks [he] has called Ontario's school system broken, mediocre, inflexible and overpriced. . . . Snobelen has provided ample proof that he is not the man for the job."[64]

But the minister wouldn't step down; he wouldn't even blink. The mass confusion created by restructuring was loudly protested by parents, teachers, bureaucrats, and school boards who begged for some time and some consultation. Snobelen refused, saying his government "couldn't be frozen by the consultative process."[65] If consultation was out of the question, perhaps confrontation would do the trick. Shortly after it was revealed that his deputy minister's performance contract spelled out another $700 million or so in cuts, Snobelen was replaced by a new education minister, Dave Johnson. New face; same crisis.

Bill 160: The Education Quality Improvement Act

Political historian John Ibbitson has written in depth about the new Ontario under Mike Harris.[66] He concludes that this government is "the most radical in the democratic world." Ibbitson also believes that even if the government lasts only one term, due to a combination of political and economic reasons, many of the changes it is making to the province will never be unmade. If he is right, then the restructuring of public education intended by Bill 160 will continue, indefinitely, along the intended course.

Despite the claims of the Opposition, Bill 160 was not just a strung-together megabill of disparate reforms, but a comprehensive, tightly integrated formula for radically reshaping every feature of public education. Literally, the verb *to reform* means to create a new form – a form that suits a new function. While political debate over this bill focused on the power struggle, on the winners and the losers, it is the form itself, not just the process of reform, that should worry all Canadians. As provinces co-ordinate their education strategies to suit global imperatives, no province can stay out of the loop for long. Citizens of other provinces who believe their geographical or political boundaries will protect them aren't paying attention. Citizens of other provinces who claim they have already experienced what is happening in Ontario are only partly right. Many aspects of Ontario's education act are in place in other parts of Canada, but nowhere else have all the reforms come together, shutting down any opportunity to offset the effects of one reform by using the powers left intact. In Ontario, the new "form" is complete.

More has been written and spoken about Bill 160 than about any piece of Canadian education legislation. New adjectives were in short supply: *draconian* has as few synonyms as *illegal strike*. Those who supported the bill claimed it would improve a weak system that was gridlocked over change. Those who criticized it generally argued that the legislation had nothing to do with education – it was a power grab motivated by political opportunism. A third point of view received less attention, perhaps because its interpretation of the bill was equally plausible but far more frightening. These observers believe the Education Quality Improvement Act may be the legislative blueprint for ed.com – for the privatized, technologized schools of the future that will serve the rulers of the global city.

If we work backwards from this premise, the dozens of seemingly disconnected reforms start to make "common sense." If a government intends to hand over the profitable parts of public education to the private sector, it first needs to control what it wants to give away. Centralizing funding and disembowelling local governance can accomplish that. To create demand for a privatized system, a government must force public education to deliver poorer services and an inferior product. Cutting funding drastically is the quickest way to ensure that schools do less with less. Standardized tests, reported school by school, will document this decline and stimulate demand for alternatives. Taking away the local government's right to compensate for lost funding by levying school taxes ensures that all schools will decline, except those in affluent communities championed by persistent fund-raisers. Schools starved for resources will naturally court private-sector partners, whose demands that students learn employability skills must be respected.

If schools are to be subjected to market forces, ready to compete with each other for students and funding, then they must acquire the stand-alone characteristics of businesses. Parent councils become boards of directors and principals become CEOs. Since businesses require managers who are accountable for results, school principals must adopt managerial allegiances, turning away from colleagues and students to address the interests of owners and directors. The act forces principals and vice-principals out of their unions; their job descriptions no longer mention the words *teacher* or *professional qualifications*. Presumably, an MBA would make a suitable school CEO. Perhaps these new managers would also be less concerned that they and their vice-CEOs would no longer enjoy tenure or collectively negotiated salaries.

Business owners naturally want to control input costs. Since almost 80 per cent of a school's budget is spent on staffing, teachers' assignments and salaries must become more financially flexible. While a government can achieve this imperative by reducing teachers' preparation time (Bill 160 gives high school teachers more classes to teach, thus eliminating seven thousand jobs), this is a one-time-only strategy. The act contains a more permanent solution. Declaring an average maximum class size creates a formula for calculating the number of teachers that will be needed. Then unilaterally determining per-student funding makes the amount available to pay these teachers a simple mathematical equation. When the per-student grant decreases, school boards will not be able to cut teachers because they must maintain the student-teacher ratio. If they cannot employ fewer teachers, they will have to pay those teachers less. If the boards can employ people who are not professional teachers, or if they can find teachers who will waive the right to a full salary, their personnel budgets will stretch further.

Therefore, the first draft of Bill 160 proposed allowing non-certified personnel to teach art, music, technology, and "other" courses, but the government withdrew this proposal after public opinion polling red-flagged the idea. Under the act's amendments, these non-teacher employees – whose necessary qualifications will be determined by the minister – may only "assist" teachers, although this term is not defined. Teachers may find that being cloned will assist them most in carrying out their expanded responsibilities, and over time, the public may well come to prefer pseudo-teachers to school closures.

Although cheaper teachers and other aspects of ed.com may take a while to be realized, all the groundwork has been laid. Businesses will want to know about their customers: conveniently, the act requires that new ID numbers be assigned to each student. In addition to information on courses taken and level of achievement, this electronic file can assemble all kinds of private data about students (including family income, race, religion, and political affiliation of family members) because the section of the act dealing with student information is explicitly exempted from federal and provincial privacy protections. When the money follows the child, as it does under this bill, personal information is invaluable to those who are niche-marketing a school or a product.

Teachers (and especially pseudo-teachers) with larger classes and less preparation time become more willing to teach from cookbook curricula, even if the cookbook is sponsored by a corporation, and especially if the alternative is no cookbook at all. By taking complete control of the provincial curriculum (a pre-Bill 160 measure), the Ontario government created a huge and homogeneous market, not just for core materials such as textbooks, but for curriculum extras such as industry-inspired lessons on global warming. These materials will no longer have to be screened by school boards, parent committees, or teachers: they can become part of the curriculum by ministry fiat.

The ministry will no longer have to waste time persuading school boards to spend more money on technology, nor will technocorps have to pitch their wares board by board. The size of this one-stop-shopping customer, purchasing hardware and software for millions of students and thousands of teachers, will make Ontario's schools a very lucrative industry target. Once technology is built into curriculum standards in every subject and at every grade, the demand for technology will increase at the same rate that decision makers bypass teachers' professional judgement.

In their opposition to the bill and the act, some teachers and their unions tried to point out these dangers to a public that has little patience for abstraction. Most parents were understandably less concerned with the future of public education than with the effect of the changes on their children in the immediate present. Some members of the public understood the risks, but others dismissed the analysis as paranoia. Who would want to privatize education? What's wrong with holding down education costs? Before these two questions could be answered, a third would inevitably arise: Aren't you teachers just worried about yourselves?

Any legislation that diminishes teachers' rights to bargain collectively, or limits the items that can be bargained, will enrage teachers' unions. Preparation time, class size, and the length of the school day and the school year had long been considered negotiable items for Ontario teachers. Under the act, these working conditions became management prerogatives that could be changed by regulation, at the whim of a minister's signature. Naturally, unions protested against these aspects of Bill 160, giving the government the opportunity to dismiss their opposition to other parts of the bill as nothing more than a smoke screen for greedy self-interest.

It was absolutely necessary, from the government's perspective, to ensure that teachers' unions were discredited and not just disempowered. Having already dealt with the boards, the government identified teachers' unions as the only significant opposition that remained, and launched its attack both directly and indirectly. It accused unions of a variety of sins, while insisting that the insults were directed not at "responsible" teachers, but only at union activists and leaders. Other government tactics were more subtle. Removing principals and vice-principals from the unions' rolls, along with reducing the total number of fee-paying teachers, ensured that union revenues would be badly hurt. In addition, the two-week protest that closed the schools, and the media wars that ensued, took millions of dollars out of unions' budgets and reserves. Finally, by targeting the most severe cuts at the secondary level, the government intended to drive a wedge between the unions representing elementary and high school teachers. After two weeks on the picket lines, Ontario teachers went back to their classrooms somewhat embarrassed by the sudden collapse of their united front, and worried about the future of their organizations. Minister Johnson was pleased. There are no unions @ed.com.

Some people date the beginning of Ontario's education "crisis" to John Snobelen's promise to create one. Twenty-nine months later, the Education Quality Improvement Act became law. A lesser-known quote from the former education minister seems apropos: "Power is the rate at which your intentions become reality."[67]

2

OFFICIALKNOWLEDGE@ED.COM

WHAT SCHOOLS TEACH,
AND WHAT THEY TEST

At the centre of all education debates should be the question of
what students should learn. Proclaiming a deep affection for public
education in a democratic society is somewhat hollow unless we
also pay attention to the mix of knowledge, skills, attitudes, and
values imbedded in the curriculum.

Curriculum should be our preoccupation, but when overhaul-
ing government structures, slashing funding, and eliminating jobs
create chaos, curriculum reform inevitably receives less attention. One teacher who waded through all 219 pages of Ontario's
Education Quality Improvement Act tallied 260 references to
either *tax* or *power*, and 154 instances of the word *fund* – but
neither *curriculum* nor *learning* merited a single mention.[1] The
obscure vocabulary of *prerequisites* and *credits* can't compete with
the simplistic rhetoric of political reforms that involve *higher standards* and *tax dollars*.

At first glance, curriculum questions have obvious answers,
even @ed.com. Surely all kids should learn to read, write, spell,
calculate, compute – the obvious, everyday life skills that most
adults value and use? But the next cut at this question gets a little

more complicated. Yes, everyone should be able to read, but how should students be taught to read? Once they *can* read, what *should* they read? Once they can write, should they write business letters, editorials, or personal journals? In what language or languages? Should they compose on a computer, or write by hand? With a spell-checker, or without? Good grammar is nice, but do real adults or real writers ever put one line under the subject and two lines under the predicate? Literacy certainly requires the ability to understand and produce written text, but today's youth (like the rest of us) also need to know how to read between the lines, and to decode and produce information that isn't limited to the written word.

Most parents would like their children to learn history. But whose history? Canadian baby boomers surfed over world (i.e., British and American) history, memorizing (or not) the dates, treaties, and rulers that commemorated the story of events from the point of view of "the white guys who won." Of course, other versions of history should be told, and other points of view need to be considered, complications almost always overlooked in the history curriculum that today's adults once studied.

Adults are quick to condemn any curriculum that omits the parts that they remember or, more precisely, remember memorizing but have since forgotten. What kind of course/teacher/school can this be if my kid doesn't have to memorize the periodic table, the dates of the Peloponnesian Wars, or any of Shakespeare's sonnets? Although only a minute percentage of adults have used these accomplishments since high school, many people measure a good curriculum by its "rigour" – the thickness of the textbooks assigned, the amount of homework required, and the memorization of detail expected.

The curriculum attempts to answer this difficult question: What is worth knowing? While "everything" is a convenient answer, time and other resources constrain what is possible, and opinions differ on what is essential or desirable. A curriculum of compromise results. Parties to the compromise give up their ideal curriculum in exchange for what is attainable. What is attainable is further limited by what students are actually prepared to learn, and fewer students each year find intrinsic value in multivariate equations.

But curriculum has never been determined exclusively by the functional utility of particular kinds of content. As Herbert Kliebard, education historian, writes, "School knowledge, the know ledge that becomes the official knowledge in a society, becomes a kind of prize that is sought by competing groups with varying ideological convictions. . . . The curriculum in any time and place is seen as contested terrain, the battleground where warring parties contend for a kind of official sanctification of their deeply held beliefs."[2]

The history of curriculum reform is littered with wounded academics, disillusioned parents, beleaguered trustees, aggrieved minority groups, frustrated teachers, and, occasionally, outraged editorialists. Yet, like all matters involving public consultation and compromise, curriculum at its best represents our ever-changing collective approximation of what is worth knowing. Over the last decade, provincial governments have conducted ambitious public consultations on education. From *Directions* in Saskatchewan to the *Royal Commission on Learning* in Ontario, from *Year 2000 – A Framework for Learning* in British Columbia to *Excellence in Education* in New Brunswick, each report has restated the need to engage citizens, their organizations, and representatives continually in this never-ending curriculum debate. Specific answers to the question of what is worth knowing therefore remain in a perpetual state of flux. They are outlined in general terms at the provincial level, refined at the local level, further reshaped by the school and the teacher, and finally (although most potently) determined by parents and students, who choose schools, programs, and teachers.

Thus as long as curriculum responds to this interplay of factors, it will be somewhat unstable and non-standard. As the product of compromise, curriculum can never fully satisfy any group's expectations. Governments with aspirations for greater control over education – especially over what is worth knowing – can find irresistible the temptation to use this dissatisfaction to centralize control over the curriculum. A single easy-to-test curriculum appeals to an anxious public. Many people want to believe that today's students, who seem alarmingly less standard each year, can somehow be coerced into uniformity by the requirement that each learn the same material to the same level of mastery at the same grade.

True, the schools of the mythical golden age – readers may select their favourite decade – followed a more standardized curriculum taught in more predictable (and sometimes mind-numbing) ways. This system worked primarily because those who found the curriculum too difficult, meaningless, or tedious were simply left behind to repeat grades until they were old enough to drop out. More than half of the generation that parents today's teenagers dropped out before completing high school. (In 1971, only 52 per cent of Canadians graduated from high school; in 1956, just 30 per cent of eighteen-year-olds had a high school diploma.)[3]

In part, increased curriculum diversity responded to calls over the last two decades for a greater flexibility and relevancy that would encourage more students to stay in school. Although more varied programs and courses did keep more kids in the classroom, a particularly rigid form of curriculum flexibility, known as streaming, continued to sort students on grounds that were only superficially academic. Race and class became the strongest predictors of whether students would graduate with basic or academic diplomas, just as race and class had determined who would drop out.

The paradox of insisting that more students of increasingly diverse experiences, languages, and inclinations submit to an increasingly rigid program of studies has not unduly troubled education's politicians. After all, they can shift the consequences downstream. Ministries in every province – alone and in regional and national partnerships – have pumped out new curricula at an amazing pace, phrased in an incomprehensible edspeak of astounding optimism. Pity the teacher who tries to achieve the following outcome expected of *all* graduates of "the public schools of Atlantic Canada":

Graduates will be able to assess social, cultural, economic and environmental interdependence in a local and global context [by explaining] the significance of the global economy on economic renewal and the development of society.[4]

This is a tall order, given few mortals would claim to have mastered global economics, let alone figured out "the development of society." Nonetheless, every student must meet this outcome, including "students with exceptionalities." Teachers will be held accountable for achieving these results, even though resources to help them teach revised curricula have not been provided: copies of the basic documents, required materials, and textbooks have been held up because of budget cuts.

The imposition of rigid and unrealistic curricula, coupled with declining resources and harder-to-teach students, is reshaping what is learned and how it is taught. In the process, fiat and circumstance are resolving a fundamental debate. Is the point of curriculum the mastery of information that may become quickly outdated, or is curriculum content the vehicle to teach students to understand, value, reflect, and create? Is curriculum about providing marketable skills – assuming such a market exists – or opening minds? Should the individual's potential or the progress of the group receive priority?

These decades-old questions have never been, and can never be, answered once and for all. At best, a compromise accommodates different orientations to the purpose of education, as we try to find a balance that shifts as teachers and students interpret or subvert prevailing points of view. Yet such compromises require the freedom to negotiate among alternatives. An inflexible, obligatory curriculum is easily skewed towards the more concrete and easily measured domains of facts and skills, squeezing out the less tangible goals of schooling that have to do with making a life, not just making a living.

Other circumstances have conspired (or been intended) to limit the extent to which the chemistry of teachers, students, and curricula can combine in new ways. Increased content in certain subjects drains time away from other subjects considered less important. Traditional subjects such as English are expected to accommodate media literacy, proficiency with spreadsheets, and electronic research skills, while remaining faithful to Shakespeare. Expert advice on how teachers might accomplish this task is harder to come by, as curriculum consultants and other specialists at provincial and board levels are let go because of budget cuts. When costs are reduced, they fall victim to political promises to "not touch the classroom."

ACCORDING TO THE University of Toronto's Len Fertak, schools shouldn't be agonizing over empty library shelves. Fertak says books are the past; reading novels and classic literature is not what makes today's students educated, when they can learn more from a CD-ROM encyclopedia than "a stack of books." "We've given too much honour to the liberal arts in general," he says. After inflation, school library budgets have been cut 75 per cent over the last twenty-five years, and half the remaining budget goes to CDs and other electronic resources.

Source: Ottawa Citizen, August 21, 1996

Increases to class size and workload have reduced teachers' opportunity and enthusiasm for the hard work of tailoring curricula to students' interests. It is hard to get excited about curriculum priorities when there is no more photocopy paper and no time left in the day. Teacher-librarians who searched out new resources have been replaced by technicians with little background in education, but then library acquisitions – other than CD-ROMs – have ceased.

Hiring new teachers with new ideas has become unthinkable; when the history teacher with thirty years of experience retires, his assignment will quite likely be handed over to the almost-redundant English teacher. The control that parents and students can exercise over curriculum is further reduced as options disappear in favour of mandated courses.

Fewer teaching assistants and special education aides mean less opportunity for teaching adapted curricula and more time pulled away from following the lessons planned. A mandated emphasis on teaching the employability skill of teamwork mixes keen students with slower learners. Too often, more motivated kids feel exploited by group projects, while those unable or unwilling to do their share of the work learn to coast.

> "HOW WILL YOUNG Canadians know that the utter reliance on the private sector helped lead to the Great Depression if they don't even know there was a Great Depression? How will they know how dangerous it is to blame minority groups for society's problems if they don't know the events that created the Third Reich? How will they know that the erosion of democratic principles in the interests of political efficiency was just what Mussolini had in mind when he said he wanted the trains to run on time?"
>
> *Source:* Angus Reid, *Shakedown*

In the classroom, all these changes threaten to reduce curriculum to frantic and inadequate runs at fragmented topics. Away from the classroom, governments are using this scramble as an excuse to forge new guidelines, based on outcomes and standardized testing. Exploiting parents' confusion over complex and rapidly changing curricula, Ontario's Ministry of Education and Training has promised to create order out of chaos by prescribing "what students should learn year-by-year," so that parents will know what is expected and "whether their kids are meeting those standards." To ensure "rigorous and relevant" curriculum, the private sector will become involved in content, delivery, and evaluation. In announcing that "a return to the 3 R's is long overdue," the ministry has promised standardized report cards to go along with standardized testing, with results reported to the public on a school-by-school basis.[5] The official knowledge of ed.com will not be determined by what is worth knowing, but by what will be tested.

McCredits @ed.com

John Snobelen announced that sweeping curriculum reforms would "move Ontario students to the head of the class." Although the ministry's curriculum staff had been decimated, with fewer than half the employees in 1996 than in 1988, the minister promised an insanely ambitious overhaul of K–12 curriculum by 1998. He floated his ideas in a consultation document that Gerry Caplan called "virtually incomprehensible, so confusing it seems almost deliberately to be making a mockery of the very process of consultation. . . . Should it be 27 compulsory credits out of 37 courses? Maybe 20? 21? Do I hear 25? . . . This is simply madness."

Mad, perhaps, but not without purpose. The intent of the reforms was actually quite transparent. The minister had already proposed that up to a third of high school time and credits could be earned in part-time (but unpaid) jobs, where, according to Snobelen's definition of official knowledge, students would "learn job skills, learn the value of showing up, learn how to work in teams, and learn how to serve people."[6] Math, science, and technology would also be elevated in prestige and receive a much larger share of the curricular pie. These hours had to be stolen from unofficial knowledge: the ministry suggests that "some students might choose to take optional arts or drama courses out of personal interest; others will take extra math or physics courses to prepare for university."[7]

Although a single history class might still be made compulsory at some point in high school, it would come with a consumer advisory: history would require a reduction in the technology component. Alternatively, students would be able to substitute business studies for their single history course if they found it more productive.

Without once mentioning the imminent demise of high school history, over which the Tories would preside, the *Ottawa Citizen* took its own swipe at curriculum and teachers. An editorial called "Sir John A. McDonald's®"[8] praised McDonald's True North Comics for providing superior history curriculum: "Meagre as they are, these tiny morsels of the past will be as filling as the thin history gruel our multi-billion dollar school systems are serving to students." Blame teachers, the paper suggested. "What is actually taught in courses is a reflection of educators' priorities. And in history, social engineering is the goal. . . ." Noting that opponents of education reforms "often paint a dark picture of public education being put under the corporate yoke," the editorial could only wish the critics were right: "Are powerful corporate interests plotting to take over the education system? By Diefenbaker, we hope so."

Do Ontario parents want to kill history, or buy it with their hamburgers? Apparently not. The curriculum reform consultation process consisted of a three-week period during which parents could mail their responses to questionnaires, or attend a scattering of reservation-only hearings facilitated by employees of the Ministry of Agriculture. The inability of education (or agriculture) officials to give concrete answers to practical questions infuriated participants.[9] The private sector wasn't happy either. Although the government had already introduced a co-operative education tax credit that allowed employers to write off $1,000 in taxes for each co-op student,[10] businesses were not anxious to find placements for 700,000 young people, even if doing so would mean savings from laying off some minimum-wage staff. Taking your kids to work for a day was all very well, but putting those kids to work for a semester or so was out of the question. The ministry will have to sweeten the pot if it wants to realize its goal of setting up work-study programs – beginning in kindergarten, as proposed in one leaked ministry document.[11]

The various rationales for these reforms and others like them, implemented in every province and every country of the world, have become mantras. Global competitiveness and the information age have become false excuses for renovating the student by retooling the curriculum. When interprovincial science test results were released, the *Globe and Mail* pontificated that "the shortage of elite science students should be a concern because it could erode Canada's ability to compete internationally." This statement was made with a straight face, even though in the same week the paper announced that the government had refused to grant a stay of execution for the renowned Atomic Energy Commission laboratory research facilities at Chalk River. As our world-class science institution closed (for budgetary reasons, of course), Canadian scientists shed a tear and booked their tickets to the United States.

Whether these expatriates will find jobs is questionable. The *Boston Globe* reports that "at a time when overall unemployment has fallen to around 5 per cent, high-level scientists have been experiencing double-digit unemployment. The American government predicts a surplus of more than one million scientists and engineers by the year 2010, even if the percentage of graduates in these fields does not increase."[12]

These highly skilled workers will join millions of other Americans who have not shared in the rising fortunes of the Fortune 500 companies (whose profits increased 23 per cent in 1996) and of the wealthiest people in the United States (the 1 per cent who now own or control 95 per cent of the nation's wealth).[13] Riding the wave of economic recovery, the United States boasts an enviable unemployment rate of about 5 per cent. However, it can claim this figure only by adopting unconventional labour force definitions, including the omission of "discouraged" workers (those who have given up searching for jobs) from the ranks of the officially unemployed. Other critics point out that if the 1.5 million Americans in jail and the 8.1 million on parole were included in the tally, the official U.S. jobless rate would double. In America's new economy, the only group that has increased its employment rate is low-skilled black youth, who have picked up some of the recovery's effluent – temporary, low-paying part-time jobs. Yet American black men in their twenties still have a better chance of going to jail or living on parole than of finding work. "Corrections" spending is the fastest-growing item in most states' budgets, easily exceeding spending on education.[14]

IN AN EDITORIAL advocating lowering the minimum wage, reducing taxes, increasing deregulation, and removing trade barriers, the *Globe and Mail* found a way to blame unemployment on the employed, especially workers who are unionized: "In reality, the causes of our high levels of unemployment have powerful self-interested friends. High minimum wages help support wages higher up the scale, and protect unionized jobs from some low-wage competition."
Source: Globe and Mail, September 17, 1997

As American-based corporations have responded to global competition and shareholder greed by shedding employees, they have not spared more elite workers. In 1993 alone, the richly rewarded CEOs of the Fortune 500 companies laid off 583,000 high-tech, highly skilled workers.[15] For a compensation package worth more than $21 million, Louis Gerstner moved from RJR Nabisco to IBM, where he embraces both parts of lean and mean. Gerstner has cut another 90,000 highly skilled employees to join the 183,000 that IBM had already dumped from its payroll.[16]

His workload has not prevented Gerstner from being one of American education's harshest critics and a vigorous, if not necessarily well-informed, advocate of its reform. Gerstner knows taking care of business means demanding that schools continue to oversupply the pool of highly skilled workers from which IBM can choose, the better to ensure a disciplined, low-wage work force. Gerstner's approach is less than moderate. He says that when it comes to school reform, the public should be satisfied with nothing less than "a fundamental, bone-jarring, full-fledged, 100% revolution that discards the old and replaces it with a totally new performance-driven system" – in which IBM computers will figure prominently.[17]

Canadian business leaders are somewhat more tempered in their rhetoric about school reform, but not necessarily because they disagree with Gerstner's premise. They tend to advocate school restructuring as a competitive strategy that will reap jobs and prosperity. Canadian federal politicians seize every opportunity to reinforce the links among schools, technology, and jobs jobs jobs, treading delicately around the problem of provincial jurisdiction.

No opportunity to preach can be overlooked. Through Human Resources Development Canada (i.e., Canadian taxpayers), a career guide prepared by the heavy-hitters in the software industry has been distributed for use in Grades 4, 5, and 6 – because ten-year-olds need to know that "Canada competes in a global economy" and "the shortage of software professionals can be overcome [if] more young people . . . pursue a software career."[18] October is Women's History Month, a modest federal project that for a decade has encouraged schools to foster an appreciation of the often-untold stories of women in Canadian history. But in 1997, even this month was retrofitted as "Discovering Women in Science and Technology." At a corporate-sponsored launch, the Honourable Hedy Frye, minister responsible for the Status of Women, told teachers, students, and the business community that "our challenge is to ensure that no Canadian woman or girl is left behind as the country moves forward into the knowledge-based economy of the future."[19]

Mismatched or Misled?

Of course, the minister was not about to mention how many students, including young women, are turned away each year from overfull engineering programs, or to draw attention to the sky-rocketing number of bankruptcies among unemployed graduates with un-repayable student loans. These statistics would contradict a decade's worth of propaganda. The public has been told repeatedly that unemployment is caused by a mismatch between the (terrific) jobs available and the (terrible) skills of the unemployed. Hundreds of thousands of jobs are allegedly available, but Canadians are too poorly educated to take advantage of them.

The current workplace reality differs starkly from the myth of the new knowledge-based economy. Less than 20 per cent of

Canadian workplaces have the defining features of high-tech environments, according to University of Toronto professor David Livingstone.[20] A 1994 survey of Ontarians reported that there are "substantial indications of underuse of existing skills. About 20 per cent have higher qualifications than their jobs require, while only 5 per cent feel underqualified for their jobs."[21] In 1996, about half of all employed workers under thirty-five years of age and about half of all university graduates reported that they possess skills they would like to use but can't in their present jobs.[22] Eighty per cent of service workers claim basic computer literacy – but only 54 per cent say they have access to a computer at work.[23] More than 90 per cent of people eighteen to twenty-four years old consider themselves computer literate; 75 per cent have taken a computer course.[24]

In 1997, the Canadian Labour Force Development Board finally admitted, under pressure, that no more than 20 per cent of unemployment could be attributed to a skills mismatch.[25] Other studies have stated clearly that the unemployed view the lack of jobs, not their lack of skills, as the reason why they can't find work.

The high-tech sector, even as it lays off employees, is fond of drawing attention to jobs it claims that today's workers can't fill. However, the thousands of jobs said to be going begging have never been counted independently. Exaggerating their expanding need for employees makes technology corporations look healthy and ambitious, ripe for new investment. Overstating the demand makes perfect sense if their objective is to stimulate the supply of newly trained, not-yet-burned-out technical specialists, educated at public expense, who will undercut each other to find work.

The high-tech sector's pleas have even won the industry an exemption to Canada's immigration policy, allowing these corporations to recruit and fast-track immigrants with desirable "skill sets." This decision infuriates unemployed Canadian applicants with all the right degrees but with little experience. One frustrated father poured out his anger at corporate hypocrisy in a letter to the editor: "They refuse to hire new graduates in the field. They all want their new employees to have at least two years experience

. . . then they expect the government to relax immigration quotas to solve their management bungling while the country is full of intelligent, committed educated youngsters . . . who are shut out. My heart goes out to these young Canadians. . . . One of them is my daughter."[26]

To the one in three families touched each year by unemployment, the idea that everything would be fine if Mom or Dad had just taken high school physics or computer studies just isn't convincing. Too many adults have sons and daughters with the advanced degrees said to be in high demand in the information age whose résumés are never read. The gap between citizens' experiences and official knowledge has never been greater.

Under these conditions, if education reforms are to be built on the shaky logic of economic competitiveness and employability skills, the public must become convinced that what is false for them in the present will nonetheless be true for their children in the globalized future. It will take some political work – some manipulated data – to convince everyone that ed.com is the solution to all our woes.

Testing the Waters

The exaggerated criticism of schools that characterized the first half of the nineties has been wearing a bit thin, as Canadians persist in giving higher approval ratings to their schools than to their governments. Politicians must find other means to nurture the appetite for education reform, particularly among resisters. In general, the people don't like to see their schools threatened, but they appear open to mild rebukes, particularly if the criticism is allegedly based on facts. Accordingly, a curious, multi-purpose argument is emerging. Either schools are decent institutions, but need reform in order to be better, or they are dismal failures that need reform in order to be better. Politicians can have it both ways: they can adapt this either-or analysis to please any constituency with any set of attitudes about schools. Whether the alleged deficiency is curriculum, standards, or accountability, the strategy is to use data, no matter how corrupt, to leverage education reforms. Thus a key political mechanism is to increase testing – more tests for more kids more often, producing more data, more widely reported and more susceptible to manipulation.

Relying only on newspaper headlines, we could falsely conclude that before corporate leaders and politicians started demanding it, Canadian students were rarely (or perhaps never) evaluated. This has never been true. While policies and practices vary, teachers evaluate the typical student dozens, perhaps hundreds, of times during a school year. Sometimes student evaluation is formal – a letter, a number, a grade – and sometimes it is informal – a compliment, a raised eyebrow, a quiet conversation. These multiple sources of information must somehow be reduced to report cards, the shorthand version of student evaluation.

Many parents complain that they find these report cards too general, or incomprehensible, or lacking in specifics. One parent complained her son was pushed through the system. "I didn't know he couldn't read until his last year of high school," she told the television camera, an admission that might cast as much doubt on her involvement as a parent as on her son's report cards. Not according to the *Globe and Mail*, whose editorial writers called Ontario's curriculum reforms "promising" since, at long last, "if Johnny can't read, moms and dads will finally know."[27]

Still, parents clearly prefer straightforward reports, ideally those that document exactly where their children stand compared with students in other classes, schools, provinces, countries, and perhaps the world. If life is a contest, it is vital to know who is coming out ahead. Meeting this demand means reversing long-standing education policies and practices. While today's students, especially those in higher grades, still write comprehensive exams in most subjects, the trend of the last two decades has been away from the single make-or-break exam that determines how well the student mastered the year or the course. These tests were (and are) well suited as devices to sort and rank students. However, if our educational goals include valuing effort, engagement, curiosity, the ability to work with others, and creativity, then equating success with performance on one final examination is illogical.

WIRED MAGAZINE SAYS teachers are turning to technology to bring objectivity to student evaluation. An American company advertises a device called the "Learner Profile" that scans bar codes and student ID numbers. Teachers who observe #66728 applying poor decision-making skills or using research wisely can just scan the appropriate observation. The distributor claims that ten thousand teachers have bought the device. Presumably, their students become accustomed to the sounds of the supermarket.

Source: Wired, October 1997

Although teachers' formal and informal evaluations have been found to be remarkably good predictors of their students' future success, both in other courses and in life,[28] the value of teachers' expert subjectivity is under attack. As a grade point here or there decides which university programs will accept which students (and soon, perhaps, which elementary or secondary schools they may attend), parents and students demand that teachers defend the accuracy and objectivity of their evaluations. The pursuit of greater objectivity in the name of greater accountability has resulted in a marked increase in the number of formal classroom evaluations – perhaps in the misguided belief that averaging a large number of somewhat subjective assessments delivers a more objective mean.

Until recently, aggregated student evaluations have rarely been used to judge how well a school or system is performing relative to others. The old assessment loop included teachers, students, and their parents, not policy-makers or the general public. It is entirely appropriate for schools to give the public their best response to the general question, "How are students doing?" But providing meaningful answers to this deceptively simple question is very complex. While the growing demand for accountability may be legitimate, meeting it through high-stakes testing has proved hazardous to public education.

In an era of accountabilism, test results serve up a dangerous brew of complicated variables and easy sound bites to critics and politicians with short-term political agendas. The Council of Ministers of Education (or, more precisely, Canadian taxpayers) has spent millions of dollars bankrolling a series of "Pan-Canadian" exams. The most recent is known as the Science Achievement Indicators Project (SAIP-Science), which allegedly reported on science achievement by thirteen- and sixteen-year-olds. "Young Canadians lack elite skills, science test finds," announced the Globe and Mail.[29] The report stated that fewer students than expected had performed above a certain standard, one arbitrarily set by a panel of educators "and the public at large who were asked to spell out what these students should be able to know and do in science." How the public at large concluded how much or little the average sixteen-year-old should know about vectors, the report did not explore – but these tests aren't really about science.

Since their invention as tools to separate officer material from enlisted men during World War I, achievement tests have been refined to better sort one test-taker from another. These tests may accurately determine the nature and size of the gap between individuals or groups, but a test designed to sort can't indicate the quality of a school, a system, or a program. Consider the results of a round-robin hockey tournament. We can easily figure out which team was the best and which one was the worst by looking at the cumulative win/loss records because the score sheet sorts the winners from the losers. What the score sheet cannot tell us is whether the kids played House League C or Triple-A quality hockey, or how individual players performed.

Publishing tournament results in the local paper isn't likely to improve the quality of play, either. There is no evidence that publicly reporting test results or measuring students more frequently improves their competency, yet this faulty logic permeates education reform. Defending his new $14 million testing bureaucracy, the Education Quality and Accountability Office, Snobelen actually claimed, "The more often we assess the system and the

---

AMERICAN TEACHERS WITH time on their hands will soon
have a new way to keep busy. A consortium made up of Vice-
President Al Gore and "about a dozen of the most innovative
minds in the computer industry" has unveiled the Education
Dashboard. The software is designed to improve home and
school communication, according to the industry. As long as
teachers provide the input, on-line parents can have daily
reports on attendance, grades, and classroom events. They can
compare their children's scores with state and national standards, set up on-line tutorials for their children, and participate in chat lines. Critics pointed out that less than 20 per
cent of families are connected to the Internet, and that many
homes don't have telephones, let alone computers. Industry
spokespersons responded that they were working hard on the
solution, "but we don't have the answer yet."

Source: *Los Angeles Times*, June 25, 1997

---

individual students, the better our results are going to be."[30] In
other words, weighing a pig more often makes it fatter.

There are fewer ways to weigh a pig than to evaluate student
achievement. Although they tend to be the most hazardous and
inaccurate, large-scale assessments of students are popular because
of the high cost of attempting better ways of assessing what children know and how they perform. The testing module adminis-
tered to all Ontario Grade 3 students in 1997 required ten full
teaching days. The publicly announced $7 million expenditure for
these tests didn't include the opportunity costs of teachers' and
students' time, the raid on the schools' photocopy budget, or the
translators hired by school boards to provide information in more
than fifty languages to parents.

Predictably, the government found the Grade 3 results unacceptable, and the premier used the scores in his anti-teacher print
and television messages during Ontario's teacher strike – an

"unavoidable delay" meant that the release of the results coincided with the introduction of Bill 160. Writing in the *Globe and Mail*, commentator Jeffrey Simpson used students' "poor results" to justify his support for the legislation.[31] Simpson's column demonstrated a rather naïve faith in numbers that he shares with many of his readers, who have been encouraged to believe that the facts speak for themselves.

Judith Wiener, a professor of applied psychology at the Ontario Institute for Studies in Education, rebutted this conclusion in a letter to the editor: "Mr. Simpson failed to consider another possible interpretation of these results; namely that the test is not a valid indicator of student performance. . . . The test only superficially measured the aspects of mathematics which are typically emphasized in the primary grades. Calculation skills . . . were only directly assessed in one part of one of the 10 sections of the test. . . . The test emphasized areas of irregular figures, interpretations of graphs and data, and two- and three-dimensional geometry – not exactly the core content of grade 3 math."[32] Most adults would find at least one of the key activities challenging: exactly how would you determine the perimeter and area of a zucchini leaf?

According to Dr. Wiener, "The instructions given to the children were frequently confusing. I gave the section on patterning to five university professors who had extensive backgrounds in statistics, none of whom could figure out what was wanted. . . . The children were asked to explain their reasoning process in writing, a task which is difficult for many adults. . . ." Finally, she wrote, the "bimodal distribution" of the results (lots of students at both ends of the curve, few in the middle) tells every expert on large-scale assessment that this test was invalid. By definition, invalid tests do not measure what they claim to measure. Given the distribution of scores, the test would only be valid if its purpose was to screen for children who were mathematically gifted or to discredit the performance of the majority – goals repeatedly denied by the ministry.

Despite the test's limitations, some Grade 3 teachers liked it. They were anxious to appear co-operative with government and accountable to parents, although some complained that telling their young students, "No, I can't help you" and "No, this time you can't help anyone else" all day for two weeks was undoing the relationships they were trying to build in their classrooms. Kids picked up on their teachers' stress, and added it to their own. Many teachers (and parents) reported that their children became increasingly tense and frustrated, especially when they were confronted by tasks they had never seen before and instructions they couldn't understand. One teacher told me she thought the test was a good idea, but that the ordeal got to be a bit of a strain, especially since one of her more anxious students threw up on his test booklets almost every day.

The expensive and extensive Grade 3 module was a marketing ploy, designed to persuade teachers that this exercise wasn't about standardized testing, but about "authentic assessment." In the current environment, $7 million ten-day test modules should be regarded as the political equivalent of supermarket specials – loss leaders designed to hook the customer on the product. Once parents, the media, and the public begin to expect their schools (and teachers, and kids) to be ranked in each subject each year, and once some ministry official calculates that contracting out one-shot computer-based evaluations can save time and millions of dollars, these high-end tests will be quickly replaced. No opinion poll will ever conclude that the public cares whether the tests are criterion-based or norm-referenced, or whether tests are handed out by teachers or downloaded from computers. Perhaps even the vomiting will cease if the tests are disguised as multimedia entertainment. Bimodal distribution must never be allowed to interfere with common sense.

Test Trickery

Despite professional navel-gazing and political hand-wringing, it is not terribly difficult to raise standardized test scores. The tests can be made easier, or else only the more capable students can be allowed to take them. Schools that manage to exclude low-achievers entirely will do better than those that serve a wider group of students. Alternatively, curriculum can be rewritten to match the test. Teachers can spend more classroom time on the areas being tested, and less time on non-tested areas. They can also teach to the test; indeed, this is actually the slogan of one Florida school district.[33] To improve their results, highly motivated students can sign up with a for-profit test-tutoring service.

Hiking the consequences for students – perhaps those who fail particular tests should fail a grade – would no doubt boost scores. Teachers are understandably more concerned with student performance on the tests than some of their students, many of whom tend to coast if they think the tests don't count. Worried teachers might profit from one piece of research that found teachers who plead with their students explicitly – telling them it is extremely important that they do the very best they can for themselves, their parents, and their teachers – get results. One study found the typical student's score increased from the fiftieth to the sixty-second percentile when this kind of encouragement or pressure was applied.[34] But then again, there's the vomiting problem.

A somewhat riskier – but effective – method of improving scores is to cheat. Stratfield elementary school in Connecticut prospered in a nice upper-middle-class community, consistently posting admirable scores on standardized tests. Board officials thought they could mine Stratfield for its pedagogical secrets and implement winning strategies in lower-performing schools. On close examination, however, it turned out that Stratfield's erasure rate – the number of times the first little HB2 pencil marks had been erased and the correct box had been marked – was more than three times the rate of the other schools in the district. Was someone hinting that c was a better answer than d? Retested by suspicious officials, Stratfield's students received lower scores that matched the level of comparable schools. The ensuing scandal shook the town. According to an American education magazine, "the uproar over alleged cheating has resulted in psychological trauma to students, community anger and declining property values."[35] One local resident launched a civil action because the value of his home had declined.

High-stakes standardized testing depreciates more than just real estate. Standardized tests actually squeeze out what is most commonly taught and learned, not because of any nefarious plot, but because of the statistical requirements of data analysis. The type of question that best discriminates among learners is the one that is answered correctly only 50 per cent of the time. Questions that are consistently answered correctly by more than 60 per cent of students are routinely dropped. While these questions may be too easy, they may also represent a core area of content that has been carefully taught to almost every child. To function as they are intended, standardized tests require the evaluation of peripheral concepts, not the common core. Forced to teach to the test, teachers must focus on less important content – the kind of factoids that suit multiple-guess exams – rather than on core ideas or complex understandings.[36]

Since they are designed to determine what only some students know, rather than what nearly everybody knows, achievement tests become aptitude tests. Most of the discriminating questions test the kind of accidental knowledge that some kids pick up in literate homes with money and time to spend on certain kinds of recreation: trips to museums and zoos, hours spent on bedtime stories, computer camps in the summer.[37]

It is impossible to separate what students learn in class and what they learn because of class. Testing cannot avoid social bias, since class and culture can't be eliminated from what we learn. For example, Ontario's Grade 3 tests were partly based on the Robert Munsch story *Moira's Birthday*, a choice that caused some discussion at the testing-orientation meetings. Teachers who risked complaining that many of their multicultural students had never celebrated birthdays or eaten pizza at a party had their names and schools pointedly recorded by Ministry of Education officials. An alternate story turned out to be about horseback riding – that familiar inner-city recreation.

All kinds of class and culture-bound experiences have an impact on test scores. Some children live in test-friendly environments, where parents unconsciously pass on successful strategies. For example, middle-class parents tend to ask their young children questions to which the adults know the answer, and to which they believe their children know the answer. ("How many doggies are in the picture? That's right! Three!") These children learn and repeat the drill of question-performance-reward. Less advantaged children tend to be asked open-ended questions ("Why are you doing that?"), or experience questions as challenges and criticism ("Who do you think you are?"), from which they withdraw. These examples only skim the surface of the thoroughly documented ways in which standardized testing systematically disadvantages certain groups and individuals.[38]

IN AN INDEPENDENT study of the standardized tests adminis-tered to students in Edmonton schools, researcher W. Todd Rogers concluded that "by far, the strongest predictor of student performance is socio-economic status." When this factor is added to school size and parent satisfaction, it accounts for almost half of the variation in school-by-school performance. A parallel study of Calgary's test results found that socio-economic status accounted for 45 per cent of the variation in results: a difference of $50,000 per year in family income translates to a test score difference of 14 per cent.

Source: The ATA News, Alberta Teachers' Association, Septem-ber 16, 1997

A focus on testing achievement conveniently diverts the public's attention from inequality or genuine school improvement. It is so much easier to increase the quantity of testing than to improve the quality of teaching – or to deal with inequality of opportunity. A black education activist speaks for many margin-alized groups when he claims that standardized testing is what the folks on top do to justify their advantages – testing is used as "the central affirmation of American meritocracy."[39]

As public education in Canada becomes a high-stakes, test-driven system, we can expect results similar to those found in the

United States, frequently referred to as the most-tested population on the planet. The average American student takes thirty-five standardized tests during his or her school career, for a total of more than 80 million tests administered annually.[40] In the United States, testing has been promoted from indicator to terminator, determining who can enter the learning society. In Florida, for example, students who want to move from the second to third year in college must pass the College Level Academic Skills Test (CLAST). Those who fail, regardless of the quality of their course work, are gone. The privately owned CLAST administration has refused to release any data on whether students' results predict how well they will do in their final two years; nor can CLAST administrators rebut critics' claims that "passing score levels [are] not determined by any established psychometric means." In 1993–94, 65 per cent of white test-takers passed, but only 30 per cent of black and 40 per cent of Hispanic students made the grade.[41]

Results such as these are typical, not exceptional. Race and class bias are not correctable accidents of standardized testing, but its essential characteristics. Yet each Canadian minister of education has taken up the call and found religion in increased standardized testing, claiming that this method of evaluation responds to calls for accountability. Conveniently, politicians can also use more testing to bolster other parts of the political/educational reform agenda under construction.

Multipurpose Multiple Choice

Following the release of results of the national Science Achievement Indicators Project (SAIP), most ministers of education denounced their province's results.[42] It turned out that the average student had produced average results – an outcome that should not have come as a surprise, but that ministers took as confirmation higher standards were required. Good performance provided no protection, however; commenting on the superior scores of students on a previous national exam, the Manitoba minister concluded that these results just proved how low the standards had been set. In Alberta, where students had excelled in an international test of math and science, the magazine *Western Report* sneered that teachers would use the results as "an invitation to slack off." Education critic and charter-school supporter Joe Freedman first shrugged off the good results, saying the natural bias of such tests "is against high-performance, demanding questions." He nonetheless grabbed the credit for his right-wing crusade: "What would Alberta's results have been if there had been no education reformers?"

Former education minister Snobelen used Ontario's results on the SAIP to bash "science-phobic" female elementary teachers to support his proposal for an "employability-focused" math/science high standards curriculum, and even used testing to call for more testing. Under the headline "Curriculum, teachers blamed for poor grades," the *Ottawa Citizen* quotes him as saying, "We need to have much clearer and much higher standards. And, by the way, standards go hand-in-hand with testing. There has to be common testing so we can have a common measure of what people are doing."[43]

Occasionally, the link between political spin and testing comes into perfect view. SAIP results were released two weeks later than originally planned, apparently because of a hitch: it was rumoured that one or more provinces weren't happy with the results. Days before the release, one minister met with provincial education leaders and proudly announced that "their" students had come out on top. They were number one! A flustered deputy pulled the minister aside, and quickly explained that, as a result of the most recent negotiations, the data had been massaged to show Alberta on top instead of their province. Rarely has it been so clear that high-stakes testing is a political exercise of the highest order.[44]

The public doesn't hear these stories, of course, nor does it hear competing interpretations of the data. While the national and international reports explain their methodologies in detail, the footnotes pointing out which jurisdictions failed to assess a large enough sample of students, or which countries hand-picked their test-takers, never appear in headlines and ministry statements. As well, the media and government press releases rarely explain how the data has been assessed. Applied to test results, the rules of statistics require that scores within a few points of each other should be declared a tie; only significant gaps can be considered meaningful.

Academics generally respect the interpretive and statistical limits that are emphasized throughout the thick international reports on standardized testing. However, politicians and the media ignore the same caveats so routinely that Gerald Bracey, an American who tracks the use and abuse of test results, refers to test-talk as "gratuitous media violence."[45] For example, when established statistical rules are applied, only eight of the thirty participating jurisdictions scored "significantly" higher than Canada in the most recent international math tests, and three of these eight failed to meet unbiased sampling requirements.[46] Only six jurisdictions out-performed Canada in science, and two of these tested inadequate samples. Neither the media nor their masters were about to settle for good news, however. According to critics, Canada's results were dismal, or at best mediocre. Some testing experts, including Canadian professor Philip Nagy, say the blame for spreading false news should be shared by the media and the studies' sponsors – including the Organization for Economic Co-operation and Development, since its reports on the tests also feature the graphs and rank-ordered tables that invite simplistic and misleading summaries.[47] Perhaps, then, mistakes in public interpretation are not intentional; then again, perhaps they are.

Governments make the most of test results when it suits them. The several-hundred-page *Third International Math and Science Study* (TIMSS) reports the scores of students in three different grades from forty-one countries or jurisdictions, tested in two subject areas. The Ontario Ministry of Education, however, manages to condense the results into a single graph, 7 cm square, that can be downloaded as part of its electronic brochure justifying the need for a provincial policy on higher standards.[48]

Using international comparative testing to determine policies on how to reform schools in general, or a curriculum in particular, is an absurd enterprise. The growing stacks of international assessments routinely contradict each other, according to experts

"TWICE A WEEK, Ko goes to cram school to prepare for the crucial entrance exam he will have to take next year. He arrives for class with a tiny knapsack packed with his crayons, lunch box and a diaper. He is, after all, only two years old. . . . About 150 cram schools in Tokyo now cater to preschoolers who are drilled in test-taking strategies. . . . 26 per cent of preschoolers [are] either attending cram schools or following correspondence courses at home."

Source: *Ottawa Citizen*, February 16, 1996

who have undertaken cross-analysis. Copying the "winning" country might seem an easy solution, but it leads to a dead end, since experts say there is high dissatisfaction with the teaching of math and science everywhere. The winners are restructuring their schools and curricula with as much vigour as the losers.

These methods of restructuring are similar, even if the tests do not reveal their direction. American Myron Atkin and his British colleague, Paul Black, are math and science curriculum experts who identify three key international trends driving these reforms.[49] The first is towards "intensification" – teaching more math and science in more complexity to fewer and more elite students. The second trend is the shift away from the general study of science, which Atkin and Black define as our attempt to understand and explain the natural world. This somewhat reflective activity is being replaced by the detailed study of technology, which they define as "how to do things that make life more productive." Third, math and science education is becoming more driven by "relevancy" or practical applications. Although few people would champion an irrelevant curriculum, applying this rule strictly poses some challenges. In North Carolina, for example, the high school calculus curriculum was revised into extinction once state policy required its content to show "immediate application to the real world." Calculus is not the only study put at risk by curricular utilitarianism, of course.

According to Atkin and Black, despite the global convergence of these curriculum trends, nothing found in any international study points to them as the ticket to higher test scores or to a better education, which the reader is reminded are not necessarily synonymous. International test scores may furnish an excuse for these reforms, but they do not provide the reason.

In the political world of education reform, however, reason is a relative term. Politicians and pundits look to international and interprovincial test results to win support for reforms intended to suit other purposes. If test results improve, the better scores will be considered a bonus: handy ammunition to call upon when governments need to justify the next round of reforms.

Meanwhile, Canadians are deluged with the media's version of the link between testing and education policy. Dr. David Ireland, formerly manager of research and evaluation with the Carleton Board of Education, examined TIMSS in considerable detail.[50] He paid particular attention to the opportunity-to-learn factor. Put simply, this factor means that students who are tested on something they have been taught will perform better than students who haven't. This self-evident observation is omitted in most discussions of comparative results. For example, the TIMSS report made much of the fact that thirteen-year-old Canadian students did poorly on solving the following linear equation: Find x if $10x - 15 = 5x + 20$. Only 27 per cent found the correct solution, compared with 46 per cent internationally. Ireland writes:

Wow, they beat us 46 to 27. Freedman and Snobelen are right. We're worse than mediocre. No need to invent a crisis, we have one! But wait a minute! The report finishes the paragraph thus: "It should be noted, however, that this was one of the items which was not considered a match for the Canadian curriculum!"
In other words, grade 8 kids don't do linear equations in Canada! So why is it reported . . . that way?[51]

Would it not have been more appropriate to admire the 27 per cent of students who figured out a type of problem they had never seen? According to the official Canadian report on TIMSS, the overlap between our curricula and what was tested varied from 53 to 98 per cent, but the crucial details – which provinces, which topics – are omitted, leaving more questions than answers.

Maybe we *should* teach linear equations in Grade 8, but do we decide what is worth learning by analysing what is being tested? If we chose to, we could devote half of every child's time in school to algebra and calculus, and feel secure that we had beaten the Koreans at their own game. And then what? Ireland attempts to find any useful purpose for several types of TIMSS questions, including one on the division of fractions: $^8/_{35}$ divided by $^4/_{15}$. Neither Canadian students nor their international counterparts did well on this question, but does it matter? "In what circumstances, except in an arithmetic class, would I want to carry out such calculations? . . . I am at a loss to know why, having divided 8 by 35, I should then divide it again by $^4/_{15}$."[52]

One TIMSS finding received no ministerial commentary, no editorial attention, no corporate posturing. In fine print, with no comment, the *Globe and Mail* noted that the "use of a computer is not a significant factor in achievement. . . . There is little difference in achievement between those who use and don't use computers for written projects and science experiments."[53] How could this be, given that powering up the classroom is touted as the solution to our lack of elite skills? Could this finding be a blip, a testing anomaly, a mistake? Could it also be just a measurement error that the TIMSS study found, utterly unreported in the media: an *inverse* relationship between use of computers and student proficiency in math and science?[54]

In part, these findings have escaped commentary because they contradict the premises of ed.com, but they have also been ignored because these tests are *not* being used to learn anything about improving education. At the level of the student, standardized tests are used to sort. At the level of the teacher and the school, they are used to justify reforms and to supply marketing data. At the political level, they are used to provide leverage. At every level, they irreparably harm our ability to thoughtfully answer the question, What is worth knowing?

Testing becomes the fastest route to ed.com. Poor results will be used to condemn public education in general. Good results from some schools will attract good (i.e., fortunate) students and business partnerships, along with resources. Good parents will be actively recruited. Smart companies will see a marketing niche. Technology companies will promise that they alone can make good schools better and weak students smarter – and investors richer.

Marking Up Profits

Properly exploited, parents' anxiety about their children's future, widespread concern about school quality, and our faith in testing can be turned into profit inside and outside schools. Testing itself is big business – and a business, moreover, with the capacity to generate spin-off markets. Perhaps not many parents would shell out eighty dollars for a paper and pencil do-it-yourself IQ and aptitude test that promises "to maximize your children's potential" and to help parents "take charge of their child's academic development" (especially when the test is designed by a company called Virtual Entertainment).[55] But package a CD-ROM version of this multiple-choice test, and you have a marketing winner.

The promoters claim that "although the test was designed in Texas, it translates well for Canadian children" – at least for those who speak English, use American spelling, and have experience with and access to a high-end computer.[56] Psychometricians may have compared do-it-yourself IQ testing to analysing your own X-ray, but at least some buyers have been persuaded that it's useful. In only four months, the company has shipped forty thousand copies to North American retailers.

Having shelled out eighty dollars, not many parents are likely to mail off a further hundred dollars to receive the technical manual that might – or might not – support the company's claim that the tests are valid and reliable. The booklet accompanying the CD-ROM states the program is based on two well-known standardized tests, but a data base of ten thousand recognized tests provides no reference to either. Nonetheless, if a child's IQ, graphed over his or her achievement index, indicates that the child is not performing at the expected level in Grade 2 – a situation, the authors imply, that is all too common – then parents should book a conference with their child's teacher. Armed with a printout of their child's IQ and achievement as determined by Virtual Entertainment, parents can take charge. "Unfortunately," explains the test manual, "some teachers are not well trained in assessment so it may be helpful to parents to suggest how the test results can be used in schools."[57] Apparently, the test bestows upon the purchaser both psychometric and pedagogical expertise.

Upstart companies such as Virtual Entertainment pose little threat to the big players. The mother of standardized tests is the Scholastic Aptitude Test, known as the SAT. Three million students take the SAT each year – nearly all prospective American university and college hopefuls and an increasing number of Canadian students. The SAT is assumed to predict performance at the post-secondary level, although abundant research indicates that many other indicators, including high school marks on teacher-designed (i.e., non-standardized) tests, are more accurate predictors of success. The tests are notoriously biased in favour of the elites: a recent version required familiarity with such activities as polo, golfing, tennis, minuets, pirouettes, property taxes, violins, melodeons, and horseback riding.[58]

Despite the fact that women slightly outperform men in their first year of post-secondary education, the SAT average for women is 881 and for men it is 926. Black Americans average a score of 740, Mexican Americans 799, and Caucasians 938. The average student with a family income of less than $10,000 per year scores 766; at $50,000, the average rises to 929, and by $70,000, it hits 1000.[59] Despite the fact that SAT scores are better predictors of income, race, and gender than of performance at university, a SAT scale-point here or there determines admissions and scholarships. Not surprisingly, SAT-preparatory courses flourish, in person and on-line, although their average cost exceeds $600 (U.S.) per student.[60] Not many poor students get to enjoy the guaranteed aptitude bonus of 150 SAT points promised by Princeton Review, one of the biggest American SAT-prep corporations.[61]

Educational Testing Service (ETS), the organization that manufactures the SAT and other tests, delivers 9.5 million exams annually and lobbies for the extended use of its products. The self-assigned mission of ETS is to "lead the effort to reshape not only the tests themselves, but also to change the way that people think about testing . . . new opportunities through multiple choices."[62]

Smart corporations can make even more money by becoming involved in selling the content that will be tested. Standardized testing begets standardized curricula, since, for a test to be fair, every student must have studied the same material. To make the playing field of the testing olympiad perfectly flat, we require standardized texts, either digital or print. Enter the big players. Says Harvey Daniels, an American professor of education who specializes in the problems of urban schools,

> Let me tell you an unequivocal fact – every test given in America – the CTBS, the CAT, the Iowa Test of Basic Skills [the model for the CTBS, the Canadian Test of Basic Skills] – every single test is owned by a company that also publishes basal textbooks. What we're talking about here is cross-marketing. . . . It's like Pepsi owning Fritos. You get thirsty when you eat Fritos, right? So drink a Pepsi. It's the same thing in education. The publishers make tests mainly to create markets for their textbooks.[63]

Daniels was speaking in 1993. Only five years later, he might well substitute *software* or *courseware* for *textbooks*. The testing barons have entered actively into new partnerships with other education niche-marketers to exploit technology. ETS has established a partnership with Sylvan Learning Systems, Inc., to create "a nationwide network of computer-based test centres that will expand as demand for computer-based testing grows."[64]

Peter Cohen, president of Sylvan Learning Systems, says Sylvan's mission statement is "to be the world's leading provider of education services to students, families and communities" – in other words, its mission is to replace public education.[65] Sylvan has now franchised 700 Learning Centres (60 of which are located in Canada), 300 testing centres, and 1,500 information technology testing centres. Each pushes "the ubiquity and power of Sylvan's brands," according to Cohen. Sylvan's profits rose 22 per cent over the last four quarters, and it predicts even better results as the corporation moves into China and Singapore.

Cohen claims that Sylvan has succeeded because its partnerships with universities and school systems have generated contracts to carry out education services that the strapped public system can no longer afford: diagnosis of learning disabilities, tutoring, enrichment, and remediation. Sylvan takes quick advantage of turmoil in the public system. During Ontario's battle over Bill 160, Sylvan placed ads in daily newspapers exhorting parents, "Don't let the education crisis become your child's problem" – call Sylvan at 1-800-EDUCATE for further information.[66]

"AS THE PUBLIC becomes more aware of the facts, and the facts themselves become increasingly compelling, support for major education reform will likely continue to intensify, creating a climate for entrepreneurial innovation."

Source: Lehman Brothers, investment advisors

Sylvan's contract with Education Testing Services to become the official testing centres for the all-important SAT, GMAT, and other standardized tests means that computer-based exams are still bringing in the bulk of the corporation's profits. Now that Sylvan tests for Microsoft too, the sky is the limit. "Testing provides the credentials of the education industry," says Cohen. "Testing is the gatekeeper of society. We want to be at the gate."

Sylvan is widening its niche to include upstream content, not just testing and downstream remediation. The corporation has just invested in Jostens, which is moving from indifferent school photographs and pricey class rings to pricey, indifferent software. It has also formed yet another partnership, this time with the National Geographic Society, through which "they will offer an experiential [virtual?] education program for students to attend after school on the premises of public and private schools."

This entrepreneurial gambit both deals with the high cost of renting instructional space and solves parents' day-care problems. The most promising students (whose parents can afford the tuition) will perhaps be directed to "the exciting alliance" formed by Sylvan and Johns Hopkins University "to provide specially designed math and language arts curricula to students in Sylvan Learning Centres across North America." Their joint talent search envisions administering a "pre-SAT" to Grade 7 applicants, a step towards "the eventual [mandatory] use of the SAT in general college admissions."[67]

What of the students who are left behind? They can rely on public school teachers evaluated by the Sylvan Learning Systems' Praxis Series, a "performance-based module" that tests teachers on academic knowledge and classroom performance.[68] Who better to test teachers than a company competing with them for customers? Teachers who fail cast doubt on the competence of the public system that Sylvan aims to replace. Furthermore, since standardized professional competency tests make teachers anxious, Sylvan has discovered a new test-prep market.

So many tests! So many numbers! School boards swamped by testing data can employ the Centre for Educational Assessment, which has hired the former ETS director of assessment to figure out what all the ETS-related tests actually mean, and how to massage the figures for public consumption. The centre will "focus on helping lay people – that is people who don't understand statistics and psychometrics – utilize information."[69]

A little more psychometric sophistication on the part of the Canadian media certainly would be welcome. Commenting on a series of education articles appearing in the *Vancouver Province*, each of which featured a ranking of provincial schools, the British Columbia Teachers' Federation (BCTF) suggested that ranking schools on the basis of a single Grade 12 exam was "misguided."

Their choice of such a tepid adjective suggests damage control in full tilt.

As BCTF's published critique pointed out, the report failed to mention the relevance of each school population's socio-economic status to its students' results. The articles also omitted the size of the gap between each school's average score, an omission "that reduces rankings to guesses," leaving readers unable to tell whether the differences between third place and tenth place were insignificant or substantial. Sample size was ignored – one school that made the top ten in math had exactly seven students writing the math final. The critique also questioned how reliable the report could be, since there was no overlap between the 1996 and 1995 lists of the top ten schools. Could twenty high schools have changed so dramatically in one year?[70]

Someone should have made the point that the schools could have been ranked inversely, based on their average math scores. Aren't schools being told to keep more students forging ahead in math and science, the better to advance our global competitiveness? Schools that are following orders will see their average scores drop: after all, it is not the high achievers we have to persuade to stay in math, it is the kids who are just scraping through.

We can push all students – regardless of inclination and ability – to study advanced mathematics and science, and accept the fact that they won't all be whizzes. Or, like most of our international competitors, we can concentrate our resources on those students with a real aptitude for technical subjects, and reap the benefits of better test results. But to assume that all students can be highly successful in calculus and advanced physics is to deny reality. Sooner or later, critics may realize that we can't have it both ways.

The Council's Counsel

On February 18, 1997, the Council of Ministers of Education, Canada (CMEC) issued two press releases. One reported that the ministers had met with "private sector leaders" – in private, of course – "to discuss partnerships."

The seventeen guests and ten observers represented the technology sector (including Hewlett-Packard and IBM), text and software developers (McGraw-Hill Ryerson, the Software Human Resource Council), telecommunications (Northern Telecom, N.B. Tel), and business lobby groups (the Conference Board of Canada, the Business Council on National Issues). To balance the conversation, real estate developers experimenting with lease-back arrangements with schools, CTV, high-tech employers, private trainers, and bankers also attended.[71]

The "frank, useful and positive" talks centred on "the strengths and weaknesses of the education systems in Canada" and "major obstacles to better performance." They discussed "the extent to which the systems are competitive internationally, and whether they provide the background, training and skills that private sector enterprises are seeking."[72]

According to the *Globe and Mail*, following the meeting Nova Scotia education minister Robert Harrison spoke on behalf of the ministers, saying that "the next step is for business to propose ways to get involved . . . [in] arts education or computer literacy for teachers and students." (This statement alone is astonishing, suggesting that the private sector is currently uninvolved.) Time is of the essence. Mary Anne McLaughlin, director of the Conference Board's National Business and Education Centre, warned about wasting time reaching consensus: "We have to make sure we are moving forward and not going over old ground."[73]

The second CMEC press release of the day reported that, "following a review of the national science tests," the ministers would work for "greater coherence in science education across the country" and "introduce changes in such things as curriculum and teacher training."[74] The SAIP results had provided a convenient excuse to increase the space and priority that certain subjects would receive in testing and the curriculum – demands that had been key in the discussions just held with the private sector.

The CMEC's project to develop a pan-Canadian framework for science education was underway. With the exception of their counterpart in Quebec, education ministers from all the provinces and territories had reached a breakthrough agreement intended to harmonize K–12 science curriculum. The CMEC sidestepped the thorny constitutional problem of curriculum as a provincial matter by declaring the document to be only a framework for curriculum developers, not an actual curriculum. But no one was fooled.

Despite the fact that many provinces (including those that had begun to develop curriculum regionally) had just revised their own programs, all jurisdictions except Quebec embraced the new framework. The national nature of the curriculum is not its only novel feature. For the first time, ministers of education ignored the process of curriculum consensus-building through the active involvement of teachers and their organizations, trustees, science education experts, ministry officials, and representatives of parents and communities. Most provinces limited consultation with such so-called special interest groups to declaring three-week deadlines, within which representatives could respond to hundreds of pages of draft versions of the framework. Those wishing to comment were told that they could question neither the desirability of a national curriculum nor its contentious devotion to outcomes. However, comments about formatting the document to make it more user-friendly and minor editorial revisions would be welcomed.

Every teachers' union and school board organization in the country condemned the process and their exclusion from it. The CMEC shrugged off the criticism, saying that it was in no position to impose rules regarding the consultative process each minister chose to undertake. Meanwhile, those provincial ministries that wished to foster good relationships with their stakeholders could point out that the whole project was being driven from the outside. Their own ministry had only exercised a limited – but nonetheless positive – influence on the final document. In other words, no one was accountable for the process.

But it was not just the dictatorial process that drew fire. A number of Canadian university professors specializing in science education – some of whom have all-star international reputations – joined forces to condemn the content of the framework as well. Charles McFadden of the University of New Brunswick accused the CMEC of an exercise in co-option and micro-management, a process that would lead to "a dumbing down of curriculum and poorer educational results."[75] John Haysom of Mount Saint Vincent University in Halifax reviewed the CMEC's process and the value of his personal involvement. He wrote, "I have begun to wonder if this Project . . . is about science curriculum development at all. I don't believe it is! Indeed, in retrospect I feel that I was gullible and my first response naïve. I now perceive this document to be really about assessment." He then revised his conclusion: "Perhaps it is a political attempt to deflect public concern from such pressing issues as those raised by the recent Statistics Canada report [which found high correlations between achievement and social class], and rising poverty rates among children." Overall, Haysom concludes, "this document charts a dangerous and retrogressive course: it proposes a lock-step, factory model of education. Some students, those who cannot keep up, will be excluded. . . . Teachers will either succumb to a pressure which desensitises and deskills them or attempt to subvert the model. . . . Genuine curriculum development may well be hampered and responsibility for it transferred to publishing companies (and their commercial interests)."[76]

Despite these criticisms, the framework was proclaimed by yet another CMEC press release that announced it will be implemented beginning in 1998.[77] The CMEC's response to the unprecedented intensity of reaction from educators at all levels has been to promise "a process of reflection" to accompany its next foray into national curriculum. The council is widely expected to produce a national curriculum on technology, which will no doubt be accompanied by a standardized test.

Thus ends the national debate over what is worth knowing. What is worth knowing becomes what will be tested; what will be tested becomes the subjects most closely associated with the employability skills of the global economy. These skills are said to be those of the learning society, the information age, and the high-skilled, high-tech work force of tomorrow. Since these skills are for and about technology, they can be taught only through technology.

Perhaps technology can rescue us from the endless debate over what is worth knowing, free us from duplication and uncertainty, partner us out of our expensive obligations to educate children with public dollars. As a CMEC-commissioned paper intended to shape ministers' decisions on information technology says, "All of those in charge, whether of the classrooms, schools, school districts, teachers' unions, homes or governments, are faced with increasingly tough decisions as regards the most thoughtful ways to respond to *another victory of humans over nature – a networked world* [emphasis added]."[78] Perhaps information technology will finally realize the Christian god's promise that man would "have dominion over the fish of the sea, and over the birds of the air, and over the cattle and over all the earth."[79] If technology can help us defeat nature, it should easily help us wrestle education's problems to the ground. Shouldn't we be thankful, and, with the children who share the Methodist Children's hymnbook in Britain, sing:

> Hallelujah!
> For microchips, for oven chips,
>   computer chips, we thank you Lord,
> For floppy disks, for compact discs,
>   computer disks, we thank you Lord.[80]

3

TECHNOLOGY AND POWER

At a 1997 meeting of organizations that consider themselves players in the labour force development business, a new and exciting product was distributed around the table. The booklet, called *Software – A World of Opportunity: A Guide to the Canadian Software Industry and Its Careers for Grade 4 to 6 Teachers*, comes complete with a full-colour poster and an impressive list of corporate sponsors.[1] Who better to pitch the value of getting an early start on career planning than Nortel, Stentor (an alliance of telephone carriers), SHL Systemhouse, and Human Resources Development Canada?

The correct answer is the Software Human Resources Council (SHRC), the industry's "supply management" lobby, charged with ensuring that the wants and needs of the software-manufacturing sector are never far from government priorities or public consciousness. Page two of this classroom guide to software careers is devoted to explaining software's vital importance, not just to the people who manufacture, market, and sell it, but also to the rest of us: "A rudimentary understanding of how software functions will be critical to owning and operating most appliances and machines at home and work in the near future." I think this over. Do I need to know how software functions to stop at the instant teller? Do I need to know how software functions to own a VCR, or even to hook up to the Internet? I read on. According to the booklet,

> By the year 1999, all cars produced in North America will have onboard Global Positioning Systems (GPS). . . . In the near future, call repair centres will be able to fix your car as you drive, saving you time and money. Smart homes, which are now experimental, will soon be affordable to the average homeowner. It is now possible to let your dog out or turn the heat up with a single call from anywhere in the world, thus improving convenience and efficiency.

Well, perhaps I *could* let my dog out by calling from Beijing, but how would I get her to come back in? Why would I turn the heat up if I'm not at home? How much will I have to pay when, in 1999, I can no longer choose whether my car is among the many conveniences reminding me of my global position?

Perhaps it was the booklet's soft, sepia-toned illustration of a teacher leaning over her student's shoulder, touching him with gentle encouragement, that stirred old memories. There was something familiar about that woman on the booklet's cover – and suddenly I recognized her. She had been drawn as the perfect likeness of Dick-and-Jane's mother, the apron-clad woman these perfect children shared with Father, Baby Sally, Spot, and Puff. This unforgettable family lived in the pages of the primary readers of the one-room Saskatchewan school I attended during the late 1950s. It was Mother, all right. Although her hairstyle and beatific expression hadn't changed in forty years, I could detect that in subtle ways she had been keeping up with the times. Sans apron, reincarnated as a teacher/ software spokesperson, she and her student (could it be Dick?) were both gazing delightedly at a computer monitor.

A few minutes later – the meeting *was* a bit tedious – another memory surfaced. My Grade 5 language textbook, called *Language*, as I recall, contained a paragraph that had fascinated me much more than the correct use of dependent clauses. The paragraph was in an article about helicopters, and described how, by 1959, men (*sic*) would be flying to work every morning in helicopters that would land on top of their office buildings. The helicopters would disappear for a while, and then reappear to collect the men at the end of the workday, presumably to return them home to Mother.

What intrigued me was not the thought of flying in a helicopter so nonchalantly, but rather the incontrovertible evidence that either (a) textbooks could be wrong, or (b) there was some glitch in the helicopter scheme. The problem, of course, was that the forecast had specified 1959 and it was already 1960! To a child well schooled in the myth of continuous progress through technology (Better Living Through Chemistry!) that blanketed post-war North America, as well as in the infallibility of official knowledge, the paragraph was a troubling sign that perhaps everything was not quite what it seemed.

Over-predicting the speed of technological innovation and the benefits of its smooth adoption has a long history. Reason was the foundation of science and technology, and honouring Reason above all other human capacities would bring Enlightenment, according to the last wave of positivists. Not so long ago, wide-eyed enthusiasts claimed that it was impossible to overestimate the benefits of the motor car. Not only would streets become "clean, dustless and odourless" once motor cars were generally adopted, but their use would eliminate the "nervousness, distraction, and strain of modern metropolitan life."[2] The motor car would also improve the quality of life of "workingmen," who, after toiling in "cheerful and sanitary factories," would slip away to their little cottages and farms, "healthier, happier, more intelligent and self-respecting citizens because of the chance to live among the meadows and flowers of the country instead of in crowded city streets."[3]

Before that, it was promised that electrical lighting would "make cities green, heal the breach between the classes, create a wealth of new goods, extend day into night, cure age-old diseases, and bring peace and harmony into the world."[4] Ordinary citizens have been promised repeatedly that if we could just free our minds of doubt, adopt and adapt, then we would all enjoy the endless benefits of technology. Yesterday's quaint faith in an automotive or electrical utopia is today's software propaganda. We are still attached to the idea that new, complicated, and poorly understood technology can solve complex human problems.

Again and again, we exaggerate the benefits of technology and overlook the risks. While we view all forms of technology, especially anything electronic or digital, in this infatuated manner, we regard information technology, or IT, with particular delight. IT is useful shorthand to refer to information stored and retrieved by computer, to the hardware and software that house and deliver it, and to the Internet, the highway on which the information travels. We may not eulogize cars or lightbulbs in quite the same way as our grandparents did, but our enthusiasm for IT and its transformative powers has the same gushing tone. Consider, for example, the claim made by the Council of Ministers of Education, Canada (CMEC), included in its official report to a 1997 meeting of the Commonwealth Ministers of Education: "Information technologies help build students' self-esteem, empowering and enabling them, as well as building their confidence and feelings of success." The CMEC promises that merely by being in the presence of networked computers, these fortunate students will "assume more responsibility for their learning, using inquiry, collaborative, technological and problem-solving skills, all of which are required in the global marketplace."[5]

Whether by a politician promising jobs in the future, a bank CEO defending corporate profits and downsizing, or a writer in any issue of The Futurist magazine, technology – its inevitability, its desirability, and its promise – is held out as the way to overcome today's frustrations and pave the way to a better tomorrow. IT, in particular, will rescue us if we just get on-line fast enough.

The same people who summarily toss "You're a Winner!" junk mail into the blue box nonetheless buy into techno-enthusiasm. Leaders and followers alike hype IT and anything high-tech. A handful of experts may admit that IT has a few small glitches – technologically induced unemployment, for example – but they still see technology as capable of solving the very problems it creates, if we just have faith and move quickly. Bill Gates, the world's richest man and owner of the technology giant Microsoft, admits that we may sometimes get a little carried away, but claims that, in the long run, our overenthusiasm will be amusing rather than dangerous. Chuckling over the little mistakes – perhaps he had Windows 95 in mind – Gates told an interviewer that some-day we'll look back and say, "Wow! What a lot of excesses, a lot of things really didn't pan out."[6]

The mainstream media, upbeat futurists, corporate CEOs, and politicians assure us that small detours on the road to better living through technology are just annoying delays, little things that "didn't pan out." It is only outside the mainstream that we can find a different assessment: a body count of lost jobs, an analysis of the loss of community, the consequences of empowering global corporations at the expense of sovereignty and democracy. We also find the pivotal role of technology and its worship in accelerating societal dysfunction.

John Ralston Saul argues that our willingness to be ruled by inanimate objects is one of the conditions of our "unconscious civilization."[7] Not only do we seem prepared to be ruled by the inanimate objects of technology (without so much as a televised town hall meeting to call our rulers to account), but some also suggest that we have taken up idolatry – the worship of technology itself.

One American culture critic, Neil Postman, writes that we have a sacred relationship with technology, not just an infatuation. If we have allowed technology to rule, then the new state is a theocracy. Postman writes that we have deified technology, made it our god, "in the sense that people believe that technology works, that they rely on it, that it makes promises, that they are bereft when denied access to it, that they are delighted when they are in its presence, that for most people it works in mysterious ways, that they condemn people who speak against it, that they stand in awe of it and that, in the 'born again' mode, they will

alter their lifestyles, their schedules, their habits and their relationships to accommodate it. If this is not a form of religious belief,
what is?"[8]

Postman's insights help explain our attitudes and behaviours
towards technology. Techno-positivism, as it is sometimes called, is
faith not just in the power of technology, but in its ultimate goodness. The progress of technology is frequently described in ways
that make it seem inexorable and inevitable, operating outside of
human choice or direction. Yes, we may be sacrificing today in the
name of a more technological tomorrow, but don't all true believers suffer and make sacrifices in the pursuit of a better afterlife?

Technology will shape us into subjects worthy of the future that
it will create once its dominion is fully realized. Postman argues
that the converted often describe this future in language used by
Christians to refer to the second coming: "The technology is here
or soon will be; we must use it because it is here; we will become
the kind of people the technology requires us to be, and whether
we like it or not, we will remake our institutions to accommodate
technology." All of this must happen because technology is good
for us, of course, but in any case, we have no choice. God does not
exist subject to our permission. He – or IT – simply is.

The religion of technology even has its own commandments.

1. *The benefits and value of technology are never to be judged in the
present, but only from the perspective of the future.*
This commandment functions by eliminating the burden of proof.
If the CMEC had claimed that the millions of Canadian students
with routine access to computers were already demonstrating
"empowered self-confidence" and "collaborative problem-solving
skills," the public would expect some citation of the research
leading to these conclusions. But when the CMEC writes the same
claims in the future tense, phrased as what *will* (inevitably) result,
no such obligation exists (and indeed, the council cites no research
anywhere in its paper).

The first commandment is also particularly useful for dealing
with the lost souls who see the quality of their present lives

damaged by technology. The report of the Canadian government's Information Highway Advisory Council (IHAC) applies this com- mandment and spreads the word: "The route to prosperity in the knowledge economy is for workers to make intelligent use of infor- mation. . . . Technology will make that possible."[9] When the real unemployment rate exceeds 15 per cent, with many of the job losses caused by technology, it is certainly convenient to claim that technology will return us to prosperity. It is equally convenient to imply that the unemployed (or otherwise un-prosperous) are either making unintelligent use of information, or somehow lacking what the rest of us have in excess. In either case, however, unemploy- ment is their own fault. Salvation is a personal responsibility.

2. Focus on the positive, and never count the cost.
Applied to automobile technology, this commandment means that a car contributes to the GDP when it is built, when it is bought, when it consumes gasoline, when it is insured, and even when it is surgically reconstructed after an accident. There is no ledger offset for hours lost commuting, automobile-related deaths and injuries, or the accumulation of greenhouse gases. When it comes to information technologies, even the most obvious costs aren't tallied. A recent extensive, multinational review of the number and use of computers in the schools of various nations accumulated thousands of data sets about types, power, applica- tions, and instruction – but contained not one word about how much money had been invested in computer purchases or main- tenance. Apparently, this state-of-the-art assessment had never thought to ask about costs.[10]

3. Shun critics and their critiques.
Despite its religious connotations, the verb *to shun* does not quite capture the disgust and pity directed at those who question the faith. One of modernism's most pejorative terms, *illiterate*, is now routinely applied to those who do not comfortably and enthusias- tically use their computers and discuss their virtues. Computer lit- eracy, in fact, is often defined as the ability to feel comfortable

with technology, or even to embrace technology – hardly stances well suited to critical questioning. In a stunning redefinition of this amorphous term, the *Globe and Mail* claims that thanks to "totware" for babies, "kids can become computer literate before they are literate."[11]

Of course, *Luddite* is the ultimate insult, used to suggest that the doubter harbours the same irrational fear and hatred of machines as the nineteenth-century workers who smashed the machines in textile mills. This use of the word badly misrepresents the true sentiments of the Luddites, but it is such a powerful put-down that people often preface even the most gentle criticism of technology with "I'm not a Luddite, but . . .".

4. The entrepreneurs and high priests of techno-worship are visionaries, not mercenaries.

According to this commandment, we are to revere all technology corporations and their CEOs as our prophets, committed to improving the quality of our lives and our communities, not to making a personal profit. While never denying their worldly success – perhaps because conspicuous consumption of the type practised by Corel's Michael Cowpland or Microsoft's Bill Gates is hard to disguise – these organizations and their leaders assure us that technology fortunes are amassed indirectly. Wealth is merely a by-product of being technologically adept. If we could just be quicker and more positive ourselves, we too would have riches beyond counting.

In *Canadian Technology* magazine, Larry Boisvert, chair of Telesat Canada, boasts that the 1990s will be remembered as the years "when satellite digitization wrought incredible new opportunities as well as formidable challenges; they will be known as the time of expanded consumer awareness about all aspects of telecommunication and broadcasting regulation, and they will be noted as the period when wireless technology opened up the world, making national borders irrelevant. . . . We look forward to helping Canadians take full advantage of the tremendous opportunities of the digital satellite age."[12] In other words, at the small price of ending nation-state autonomy, we are promised "expanded consumer awareness" and unspecified "tremendous opportunities." If the so-called opportunities flowing from the erosion of national and governmental authority favour global profits for Telesat rather than benefits for ordinary citizens, you'll never hear it from Boisvert.

5. *If it can be done, it should be done.*
This commandment, which is sometimes called the technological imperative, defines our relationship with technology as one driven by our collective genetic code rather than by our short-sightedness or greed. If we assume humans are ruled by an uncontrollable urge to climb the mountain because it is there, or to put a man on the moon just to see whether it can be done, we will see little point in debating whether technological adventures are worth the investment or the trade-offs that they entail. If we believe ourselves to be hostages of our own nature, arguments over technology will be limited to determining what is possible, rather than what is desirable.

The technological imperative, or rather our belief in it, has direct implications for public policy. When the Royal Commission on New Reproductive Technologies examined the ethical dimensions of allowing what is possible to determine what is acceptable, the commissioners concluded: (1) that we are grossly unprepared to wrestle with the choices we must make and their implications, and (2) that we are being kept out of the debate.[13] The report's recommendations were quietly shelved. The difficult public discussion that they would have required lost out – not to the argument that there is no point trying to stop progress, but to greed.

We are no longer pursuing technological innovation because it is possible, but because it is profitable. The technological imperative might have applied to Orville and Wilbur Wright's determination to fly, but this urge has been supplanted by the greed imperative, which dovetails nicely with the global imperative. Canadian corporations are well positioned to exploit both. They will profit from a climate that considers regulation on ethical grounds either futile or just too complicated for public debate. They are already exploiting the right to secrecy that scientists claim is essential to protect the economic value of their research. This secrecy relegates public discussion to after-the-fact assessments. Dolly was a mature sheep before she was presented to the world as a clone.

We often blame the velocity of innovation for our inability to get ahead of new developments in time to think about them. But corporate-funded research science – which is almost always underwritten by public dollars through public universities and government R and D grants – has a direct interest in keeping us in the dark. It would be difficult, one hopes, to win informed public support for the Human Genome Diversity Project (HGDP), a transnational corporate venture that is extracting DNA samples, without consent, from indigenous peoples threatened with extinction. This so-called biodiversity project is, in fact, the pursuit of new explanations of resistance to diseases, knowledge that pharmaceutical corporations will use to develop marketable vaccines that they will sell to the non-indigenous peoples who can pay for them.[14]

While the race to patent the genotype of small groups of indigenous peoples might lead to a cure for Alzheimer's disease, it could as easily lead to a virus that could wipe out everyone who shared the same DNA, a scenario that many indigenous peoples living alongside a hostile majority find all too plausible. Understandably, most impoverished indigenous peoples would prefer a little low-tech attention to their need for clean water – less attention to patent rights and more attention to human rights. If the technological imperative was truly what motivated human behaviour, we would have solved the problem of drinking water long ago.

Because IT inspires so much of techno-worship, it is governed by a special commandment:

6. *Access to an increasing quantity of information is the same thing as thinking and learning. Information equals knowledge, wisdom, and possibly virtue.*

Like the other commandments, this one appears so self-evident it hardly requires examination. Surely human progress is the sum total of information gained and distributed. Surely what distinguishes some countries (or citizens) from their more fortunate neighbours is that they are information-poor. The information-rich shall inherit the earth. The same article that promotes computer literacy for eight-month-olds quotes one toddler's proud father: "Parents can beat the rest of the pack in getting kids into computers earlier. . . . It really prepares them." For what?

What do we make of the most difficult and persistent human problems? Do people die of hunger because information is lacking about the exact specificities of their misery? Do we extinguish species because we can't locate data about their beauty or their value? Do kids join street gangs or work in factories or use drugs because they lack a search engine or database? It seems unlikely that many distraught families – surveying their strained relationships, or their lay-off notices, or their credit card balances, or their frantically busy days – conclude that if they just had a little more information, everything would be better. How can we embrace this commandment when our own experience contradicts it at every turn?

The answer lies in the subset of myths that prop up IT. These myths include the promises of job creation, reduced complexity, cheaper and more efficient government services, and benevolent unregulated markets. They also nurture the conviction that more information will make us not only smarter and wealthier, but also happier. For those with lingering doubts, there is the myth of all-purpose, generic "empowerment" – a truly corporate word that reframes power as the possession of a shaky set of coping skills.

There is one last commandment of techno-worship:

7. There are no commandments.
If we acknowledge that commandments exist, then we admit that technology is not value-free, because commandments are expressions of values, not just arbitrary rules. This would shatter the overarching myth of technology – that as a tool it is value-neutral,

incapable of advancing either good or evil unless pointed in that direction. Of course, one of the central contradictions of techno-worship is that true believers must promote the goodness of technology and its neutrality simultaneously. This logical black hole, however, doesn't seem to shake the faith. It just establishes techno-worship as a fitting companion to the other great religions, which require blind acceptance in the face of seeming impossibilities. (It is difficult, for example, to take an eye for an eye while turning the other cheek.)

To see something as both valuable and value-free, it helps to believe that technology is only value-laden when we want it to be, and that when we are unconscious of its value-associated effects, they do not exist. We must also convince ourselves that our intentions – especially when they are positive – determine the limits of what actually happens, so that the only consequences of technology will be those that we intend. These delusions undermine our ability to expose and take responsibility for the effects of techno-worship.

When we cling to the idea that technologies are neutral, it becomes more difficult to recognize their economic, ecological, political, or personal effects. Even when we acknowledge these effects, we tend to become more passive. Often using the same technology that we criticize, we amass yet more damning information, but take no action. By neutralizing technology, we therefore neutralize ourselves, confirming what Marshall McLuhan said: we *become* the technologies we use.

Technology as a Tool

Marshall McLuhan was among the first to recognize that "the medium is the message" – or, in simplified terms, that technological tools have an impact in themselves, apart from the tasks we ask them to do.[15] The most significant aspects of technologies lie not in the content they carry, but in the systemic changes that they bring about. We are just beginning to understand how unpredictable and irreversible these systemic changes are. The early technologies of ocean shipping, for example, were not intended to persuade traditional cultures to abandon their religions in favour of cargo cults, but this is what happened. The developers of the cell phone did not set out to redesign how street drugs would be marketed and purchased, but this has happened too.

Parents know that television and computer games have an impact on their children beyond information or amusement. These technologies change family dynamics. One study even found that a majority of four- to six-year-olds trusted their computers more than their parents.[16] Children quite reasonably come to assume that machines deliver pleasure, and that other activities, such as meals, conversations, and homework, should be rearranged to suit the schedules of these tools.

Some parents are fond of reminiscing to their yawning children about what it was like before television. Their kids are bored not just because their (undigitized) parents have the floor, but because they cannot imagine a world without television. New technologies not only shape the present, they erase the past. Social scientists talk about the monoculture that is emerging – that trade and technology, together, are making the cultural present almost indistinguishable from one country to the next. McCulture, perhaps. But as technology makes unthinkable even the recent past of non-dominant cultures – say that of a previously isolated northern community – a monocultural future is becoming inescapable.

Jerry Mander, an expert on globalization, says that while we often hear about revolutionary technology, we are rarely told whether the revolution is right-wing or left-wing, or perhaps even a coup d'état.[17] Only after the revolution, and after the treaties with technology have been signed, can we figure out who won, who lost, what was being overthrown, and how our families, communities, and culture will be affected. Too often, we don't ask fundamental questions about how the revolution has redistributed power until after the winners have plundered the losers, and it is too late to go back.

All technologies have a political drift, says Mander, but too often we're satisfied to just go with the flow while ignoring where the current is taking us. Our behaviour isn't really surprising: the scenery is quite appealing, at least from a distance. To the individual, most technologies seem either useful or entertaining, or both. No doubt many of the workers downsized by technology are grateful that surfing the Net fills their empty days. When we judge automobile technology only from our personal experience of it, most of us conclude we want a car. Since we are encouraged to judge society's progress from the atomized perspective of short-term personal gain, it isn't surprising that we fail to ask questions about long-term or collective effects.

So, have we just been too lazy and negligent to ask more questions about technology? Are we content to sleepwalk into a future written for the benefit of machines and their makers? If we have responded to technology with a shrug, then perhaps we deserve the consequences. But perhaps our consent has been manufactured and our tendencies towards techno-worship have been exploited. Maybe the terms of the treaties that are distributing the spoils of the technology revolution have been fixed.

The Media and the Message

As products and vehicles of mass culture, the media have ensured that we remain a one-religion state, true to techno-worship in all its forms. The mass media pursue two complementary premises enthusiastically, and they profit directly from our acceptance of these premises as revealed truth.

The first premise is that the contribution of technology to any contemporary problem is doubtful. We might have our suspicions, but we just can't be sure. The jury is always out on the hole in the ozone layer, birth defects caused by computer radiation, the dangers of living beside a kkk-volt generator, and so forth. The evidence may mount, but in the service of "objective journalism," the media can always find at least one naysayer prepared to discount any damning research findings.

Canadians may have been surprised when Thomas D'Aquino, head of the aggressive lobby known as the Business Council on National Issues (BCNI), turned out to be an expert on global warming. He was interviewed often and quoted widely while the

government waffled on setting new targets for greenhouse gas emissions. The BCNI's objective was to pressure the government into
making only the smallest (and most corporate-friendly) commitment to the international effort. But, in addition, the BCNI also
wants Canadians to believe that it is far too soon to tell whether
there *is* any global warming problem, and that, at any rate, the goal
of remaining globally competitive is far more important.

In the event that there *may* be a problem that can't be dismissed, the second premise kicks in. Now the popular media
actively strive to convince us that effective technological solutions are at hand. Certainly, technology improves productivity
and relieves unemployment, they insist, but it also solves our more
mundane problems. Stressed? Oppressed? Living in the feminine
mystique? In a 1970 issue of *Homemaker's* magazine, an article
called "Hello House! I Want to Talk to the Oven" promised that
by the 1980s we would have powerful light beams that would
vaporize garbage, doorway sonic cleaners that would remove dust
and dirt from our shoes, and clothes and ovens that would take
direction by phone. However, such labour-saving innovations,
coupled with our fully automated and paperless workplaces, might
create just one teeny problem: leisure. The same magazine warned
in 1969 that by 1985 "the average North American will only have
to toil six months of the year to maintain his present standard of
living. . . . If we fail to prepare for it, many of us may quite literally
go mad with leisure."[18]

Mainstream magazines are often a more faithful measure of our
attitudes towards technology than specialty pro-tech magazines
such as *The Futurist* or *Wired*. It is in *Homemaker's* and *Canadian
Living* that the minor matters of public policy are debated, at least
when these issues impinge on the well-being of the family. These
magazines cover learning disabilities, breast cancer, childhood
asthma, and the Young Offenders Act. From time to time, they
revive debate on television violence.

Although they have never presented the effects of television as
a problem of technology per se, mainstream print media have
covered criticism of these effects right from the beginning. In

1951, Boston University president Daniel Marsh told *Maclean's* magazine that "if the television craze continues with the present levels of programs we are destined to become a nation of morons."[19] Twenty years later, Canada's Royal Commission on Television Violence, chaired by the Honourable Judy LaMarsh, concluded that violence was a "toxic additive" to children's diets.

George Gerbner, American media guru and professor of communications, told the *Atlantic Monthly* magazine in May 1997 that television presents "a coherent vision of the world . . . [that is] violent, mean, repressive, dangerous and inaccurate. Television programming is the toxic byproduct of the market forces run amok. . . . It breeds what fear and resentment mixed with economic frustration can lead to – the undermining of democracy."[20] As television has become progressively more violent and more American in content and approach, public alarm has grown. In 1993, more than one million Canadians signed a petition demanding that the federal government reduce violence on television, and 72 per cent of the surveyed public wanted federal laws to restrict the amount of violence aired, not just to limit the time of day it could be shown.[21]

The government acknowledged the public's grave concern, and tossed the issue to the Canadian Radio and Television Commission. The CRTC, the arm's-length agency charged with regulating the industry and representing the public interest, responded by encouraging Canadian broadcasters to develop a set of voluntary self-regulating guidelines on the portrayal of violence. These guidelines were accompanied by a bewildering and inaccessible public complaints process. As a result, not only did the industry set its own rules, but it could decide when they had been violated – which almost never seemed to happen.

Despite an expensive (government-funded) public relations campaign undertaken by broadcasters, Canadians were not satisfied. The industry redoubled its efforts to align itself with responsibility, if not regulation, in part by founding and funding organizations that promote media literacy through schools. The same *Globe and Mail* story that described Gerbner's analysis of how free-market television was "undermining democracy" and disguising neofascism as "amusement" reached a predictable conclusion. According to columnist John Haslett Cuff, "The only way to effectively and democratically counteract the more pernicious effects [of television] is through media education." In other words, government should add media deconstruction to the crowded curriculum, and have schools take on (perhaps alone) the responsibility for restoring democracy and thwarting the rise of neofascism. On the other hand, to expect the CRTC to actually carry out its mandate to regulate television in the public interest would be undemocratic, no matter how many citizens desired it.

Media literacy deserves an important place in the curriculum but, as advocate Brian Burke writes, it should be understood for what it is: "a struggle to arm our children against a foe who no longer respects their rights."[22] However, media literacy is teaching students to assert their rights not as children or citizens, but only as consumers. Giving students skills to become more critical consumers will restore neither their civic rights, nor those of their parents. Teaching media literacy will not force broadcasters to fulfil the public obligations they have undertaken in exchange for access to the airwaves.

We can now understand the industry's enthusiasm for media literacy: it is the equivalent of telling kids, "Smoke, just don't inhale." Rather like the tobacco companies that long denied the link between smoking and lung disease, the television industry and its apologists had spent years fighting off regulation by dismissing any link between real and televised violence. But as research findings mounted and methodologies became more sophisticated, the industry's position was no longer credible. Just when denial ceased to be a plausible strategy, and just when political pressure for real action began to mount, technological advances appeared, apparently making public interest legislation impossible. The uncontrollable one-hundred-channel universe had arrived (or would soon, depending on the legality of the family's dish). Even the rarely modest Keith Spicer, then chair of the CRTC, felt obliged to bow to the invincible forces of technology – or, more precisely, to the giant industries profiting from these technologies and the governments they influenced.

Meanwhile, in the United States, hearings about television violence were underway. A swing to the right, fuelled in part by television-induced paranoia and political posturing, demanded that politicians get tough on crime. Although their governments had doubled and redoubled prison sentences, and had even introduced chain gangs, American voters were not satisfied. Exposed as they were to real and synthesized crime on television every night, the public ignored reports that youth crime was actually declining. Citizens wanted their governments to act, and citizens cast ballots. Since the First Amendment to the U.S. Constitution left little room to manoeuvre, the mere thought of applying meaningful controls to television was political suicide. But the administration couldn't afford to look helpless, either. Technology to the rescue.

Manufactured Consent: The Story of the V-Chip

A thirty-four-year-old Canadian professor, Tim Collings, applied his engineering skills and his conscience to the invention of the V-chip. On specially equipped televisions, this computer-chip device reveals information encoded on the "vertical blanking interval" – the blank space between each frame of video.[23] Once programs are rated, the V-chip responds to a remote-control device that prompts an on-screen display. Collings's V-chip would allow parents – or anyone, including children – to determine acceptable levels of violence, profanity, nudity, or any other encoded characteristic, and to block programs containing scenes that exceeded these levels. If adopted, this technology would present the perfect political compromise: it would avert industry accusations of government censorship while still allowing vigilant parents to ensure that Barney was never eclipsed by Beavis and Butt-head.

"Parents need all the help they can get. That means information and technology. . . . The V-chip is probably the sexiest, most telegenic aspect of the strategy. It's very hard to dramatize a voluntary code, but a V-chip is a little piece of magic," said the CRTC's Keith Spicer in 1996.[24] Master of the art of vigorous rhetoric in public and smooth compromise in private, Spicer recognized a god-sent technology when he saw one. He began to promote the V-chip, although he cautiously pronounced that it was "only 10 per cent of the solution." (He had already declared that 90 per cent of the solution was to teach media literacy in schools, so his figures added up.)[25] To ensure that he wasn't mistaken for a prude, he confessed that he liked to warm up his audiences by saying, "We need less violence, but we could probably use a bit more sex on TV."[26] Spicer's name and position gave his ideas a certain credibility in Canada, but the dominance of U.S.-produced television meant that his "little piece of magic" would be meaningless, and the political payoff negligible, unless the Americans bought into the V-chip solution.

Spicer headed to the United States. In Washington, he was stood up by American network executives who were unanimously opposed to regulation in general and the V-chip in particular.[27] Nonetheless, the V-chip caught on with some politicians, who began to promote its virtues to sceptical reception. "So typical of liberal Democrats," sneered Majority leader Richard Armey (Republican, Texas), speaking before the National Press Club. "First, let's make sure we advocate something that is not currently available – it's probably ten years away – that's going to be very costly, and then make it mandatory."[28] Media stars came out in force to condemn a rating system of any kind. Dick Wolf, producer of the prime-time favourite *Law and Order*, even played the gender card. Wolf claimed that the survey conducted by the American PTA, which had found strong support for regulation, wasn't representative: "Ninety-eight per cent of them [the returned surveys] were from mothers, not fathers. And frankly, I feel that fathers should be heard in this area too."[29]

Bob Dole – soon to be the Republican presidential candidate – was sensitive to television and telecommunications industry sentiments and opposed the measure. An NBC spokesperson claimed the V-chip could become an all-purpose hidden censor, and that government involvement in a rating scheme would be "totally inconsistent with the values of this country." "However

108 NO MORE TEACHERS, NO MORE BOOKS

well-intentioned," said the National Association of Broadcasters, "legislative programs to restrict violence or access to programs deemed to contain 'objectionable' content mean government control . . . and violate the First Amendment."[30] It looked as if the V-chip was dead in the water.

But few of the players had assessed the family values electoral potential of the V-chip. Bill Clinton's superb political nose smelt a winning issue, and he began endorsing the V-chip as a pre-emptive strike against Dole and the House Republicans. Indeed, the V-chip and everything it stood for were to become key planks in his 1996 presidential bid, an issue well positioned to take full advantage of the "soccer moms" and their electoral clout. Clinton promised the V-chip would "become a powerful voice against teen violence, teen pregnancy, teen drug use and for both learning and entertainment."[31] (Showing a bit more restraint, in his state of the union address Clinton merely proclaimed the V-chip to be "a very big deal" and "a technological fix.")[32]

The industry that only weeks earlier had ridiculed and denounced the V-chip suddenly came on board, promising support as long as it could control the rating categories and do the ratings itself. An unprecedented meeting took place between Bill Clinton and the men the *New York Times* called "the titans of the entertainment industry" – more accurately, perhaps, the titans of the telecommunications industry. The newspaper's front page story claimed that the event "showcased the persuasive powers of the Presidency."[33] Not only was the industry now 100 per cent behind the V-chip, but it dropped plans to challenge V-chip legislation in the courts. The industry promised that the rating scheme would be in place by January 1997 – a date conveniently close to, but not preceding, the American presidential election.

What had happened on the road to Damascus? Had the industry suddenly taken public interest to heart, and chosen to reduce its toxic programming voluntarily? Only days earlier, a spokesperson for Ted Turner, Rupert Murdoch, Disney, and the other networks and cable providers had insisted that a "moral shield, fortified by the commandments of God," was what the country's children needed, not a rating system.[34] Had President Clinton's powers of persuasion been irresistible?

The *New York Times* speculated that something very different was going on. True, on the issue of television violence, public sentiment appeared virtually united, and if the industry tried to argue that TV violence was harmless, it risked being hung out to dry. Without industry support, Clinton's aggressive marketing of his V-chip solution would be a political liability, not a vote-getter. The president needed the industry, and the industry apparently needed him too.

When the first discussions on the V-chip were getting underway, the television and telecommunications industry had a lot on its plate. Under consideration was a bill that would determine whether it would be required to pay for extra channels for high-quality digital television. To be spared these additional costs, the industry needed some political favours. Even more important issues were pending: new telecommunications policies were about to be decided that would change the way TV and telephone services would be delivered, and how much Americans would pay for them. Potentially, millions of dollars was at stake, and so was a presidency.

Early versions of the Telecommunications Act of 1996 had Republican backers – the legislation looked as if it would champion the regional Bells and other small providers, which might then end up dominating the lucrative delivery markets at the expense of the big players. Hollywood, the major networks, and media companies decided to protect their interests by pouring contributions into the Democratic party's election fund. Thomas Ferguson, who tracks political donations and favours, concluded that "the best-kept secret of the election is that it was the telecommunications industry that rescued Bill Clinton."[35]

The strategy paid off, not only because Clinton was re-elected, but because the final version of the Telecommunications Act would be "tilted in favour of Hollywood, the networks and newspapers."[36] It would be so tilted that Brian Burke, director of the Center for Educational Priorities, wrote that the act offered "unprecedented gifts to broadcasters, including six megahertz of public spectrum and a bountiful largesse of 'deregulatory pro-competitive' opportunities for the entire telecommunications industry."[37] Burke concluded that tucking the V-chip into the act was little more than staging a distraction, intended to keep the public from understanding the act's other implications. The industry needed Bill Clinton to come through, Clinton needed votes, and an industry-controlled V-chip rating scheme, while annoying, seemed a modest price to pay to ensure that the president would continue to be grateful for four more years.

It began to dawn on the industry that the rating system might even be to its commercial advantage. Rupert Murdoch, master of TV raunch, was quick to grasp the possibility. Burke notes that Murdoch's network produces *The Mighty Morphin Power Rangers*, described by critics as the prime example of "sinister combat violence" packaged as children's entertainment. Murdoch has said that he intends to use the "global" popularity of the *Power Rangers* to front his penetration of TV markets in Latin America and the East. Writes Burke, "Murdoch supports the V-chip because he understands the joke, a joke the rest of the national networks were slow at first to get, but then after a wink and a few knowing jabs of the elbow . . . within weeks [they] were heartily embracing the idea." The joke is that the industry is now free to produce whatever it wants, and those who complain can be directed to the nearest V-chip distributor, where someday soon – perhaps – there will be V-chips on the shelves.

Back in Canada, Spicer completed his term as CRTC chair in a flurry of goodwill. He called for yet more hearings on violence in television in August of 1995, despite the fact that after forty years of government-inspired public consultations, further debate was scarcely necessary. The announcement of the hearings specified that those who wished to appear should be prepared to speak to the possibility of "technological solutions," especially the potential of the V-chip. At the conclusion of the hearings, Spicer announced that the V-chip had everyone's blessing.

A review of the submissions to these hearings suggests otherwise. Advocates of responsible television – although few organizations are not funded by the television industry itself – unanimously refused to accept the V-chip as a transformative tool in the pursuit of less violence on television. They pointed out that the majority of kids do not have parents affluent enough to purchase TVs with V-chips installed – to replace every ordinary TV in the house. They questioned how many parents were sufficiently vigilant to use the device consistently, to put up with their children's complaints, and to keep the programmer away from technologically adept kids.

Television watchdogs argued that rather than reducing violence, the V-chip might actually inspire broadcasters to increase it, since they could claim that the V-chip let them off the hook. Certainly, the industry will not stop producing violent programming as long as advertisers believe violence is a magnet. (They may well be right. A University of Western Ontario study found that teenagers were more likely to watch a TV commercial if it aired during a program carrying a violence warning.)[38] Activists denounced industry self-regulation as an abject failure, pointing out that only one program – *The Power Rangers* – had ever fallen victim to complaints and public pressure. They argued that industry-controlled regulation was incestuous, and that the mathematics of advertising dollars and market share would skew program ratings. Perhaps most important, these groups argued that government and the industry were dumping the problem of televised violence in the laps of parents. This downloading of social problems to the smallest possible unit – the individual and the family – was further evidence, they said, of the downloading of societal responsibility from the collective to the individual. Furthermore, this transfer of responsibility profited a collection man in the middle – the industry itself.

Not surprisingly, people appearing on behalf of the public interest – who were significantly outnumbered by industry delegations – thought the hearings were about children, or television, or even about the V-chip. But public hearings are better understood as the way Canada covers up backroom deals, when everything that matters has already been divvied up.

Anti-violence activist Patricia Herdman, who heads the Coalition for Responsible Television (CRTV), agrees with this analysis. Says Herdman:

> To my knowledge, no one other than the cable companies pointed to technology as the only solution. Who wanted the V-chip? The cable companies did. Most notably, Rogers Cable really, really wanted the V-chip. At the hearings, their team of well-coiffed lawyers (Canadian and American), consultants and high-powered employees sat before the CRTC commissioners in Ottawa while the volunteers and average citizens sat and waited. And waited. And waited. . . . Rogers Cable had so much to say about the wondrous V-chip and its potential for 'empowering' parents that the commission fell behind schedule by a mere four and one half hours. Just enough time to push (other) perspectives out of the day's news deadlines, and out of the news altogether.[39]

The *Globe and Mail* did cover the hearings – if one editorial belittling public concern over TV violence, one essay from the head of an entertainment lobby, and a summary of the presentation made by Rogers Cable constitute coverage.[40] The editorial reminded readers that "no one is forcing us to watch," and at any rate, "the V-chip will soon sort things out." The essay warned that "personal freedom" would be at risk if "innovative advertisers" were discouraged by a rating scheme that victimized "challenging and stimulating programs." At stake were not really children or the social fabric, but "the vulnerability of advertisers and broadcasters."[41] The submission from Rogers commended the CRTC at length for its "vision," and promised its full co-operation in developing and distributing the V-chip, which it claimed (in August 1995) "works well technically, and users like it."

What was in the V-chip solution for Rogers and the other cable companies? There are several possibilities. Certainly, Spicer's proposal (which had Intergovernmental Affairs sweating) to scramble offensive American programs risked cable revenues, but most saw this threat as typical Spicer bluster. A greater threat was the possibility – in both Canada and the United States – that government might become involved in the ratings scheme or its implementation plan. If the self-interested cable companies lost control of the V-chip, activists might press for new regulations that were not quite as illogical and spineless as the industry's voluntary guidelines. (These guidelines spurn "gratuitous violence," but define *gratuitous* as concerning material not related to the story line. Therefore, depicting the severed heads of raped and murdered women is not gratuitous if the plot is about the decapitation of raped and murdered women.) Tougher – or at least more rational – guidelines would result in fewer people watching some programs, with obvious consequences for ratings and advertising revenues.

As far as Rogers et al were concerned, this possibility represented a negative incentive, but another matter of much greater long-term importance was looming. Spicer had been an ally of the industry throughout his time as chair, but his term was about to end, just as negotiations with the CRTC were starting to heat up. A series of decisions would determine how soon, and under what conditions, the giant American and Canadian telephone companies would be allowed to compete for the opportunity to cash in on delivering television and related technology to Canadian homes. The cable companies badly wanted this date to be pushed back as far as possible, allowing them time to position themselves most advantageously, and they needed both CRTC and government goodwill.

The Liberal government (much like the Clinton administration) had quite a lot of political coin invested in the V-chip. Sheila Copps, minister of communications, had personally piloted an early version of the device and was publicly championing it. If a little more insipid self-regulation was the price the industry had to pay for gaining future considerations from both the CRTC and the government, the V-chip would be a bargain. (A Rogers executive vice-president promised that the technology would be available to the public by September 1996. More than eighteen months later it was still in development, still a promised technology. Meanwhile, each season's television lineup is described as the bloodiest and most violent ever.)

Although it was still pretending to wait for the V-chip, the Canadian television industry was moving right ahead on a parallel initiative in tandem with its U.S. counterparts. This initiative was the rating system that the American networks had once opposed so vigorously, then endorsed once they were promised control of it. In Canada, the CRTC put the Action Group on Violence in Television (AGVOT) in charge of the rating game. AGVOT, cleverly named to sound like a public interest group, is actually made up of the broadcasting and cable industries. Predictably, the group claimed that the new system, implemented in September 1997, made Canada "number one in the world among countries that classify or control programming."[42]

This claim of "control" is gross misrepresentation. The classification system that AGVOT devised turns over the unqualified right to rate programs to the networks themselves. News, including tabloid-type programs, sports, talk shows, music videos, documentaries, and advertisements – no matter how offensive – are exempted from review.

The little icons that indicate "viewer suitability" – much smaller than the networks' logos – appear for exactly fifteen seconds at the beginning of hour-long programs. The C (for children) and PG (for parental guidance) are almost unreadable on smaller TV screens, and disappear in a flash. These symbols do not control programming, as the industry claims, and they are not likely to control viewing. Unless parents are looking closely at the screen for the first few seconds of a program, they will know nothing more than they did before about any program's suitability. These limitations do not deter AGVOT's Trina McQueen from claiming that "no other country has the kind of involvement by viewers in the content of programming."[43]

Press reports on the new rating system were positive, although they noted that "the ratings are a temporary measure." The icons would disappear, they said, "once household control falls into place – through the V-chip," the device that has been temporarily delayed by "technical bugs."[44] As if by magic, the subject of television violence has disappeared from the pages of North American newspapers and magazines. No one is calling for the regulation of the industry, or interference with the market. This time, no one has needed to promise that technology will solve a difficult and complex modern problem; all it has taken is the promise of a promise. At last, the television and cable industries can get back to their number one objective: figuring out how to make money by providing Internet services, in what Rogers calls the global era of "ME TV."

The story of the V-chip is instructive on several levels. It underlines not only our naïve faith in the power of technology to solve the problems that technology causes, but also our willingness to put experts in charge of solutions. As it turns out, the experts invariably have an interest in the business of technology and politics. The V-chip story tells us exactly what role the public interest plays in these debates. It suggests that many forces are at work, and huge stakes involved, in getting the public onside with technological innovations, and that, if necessary, our consent will be manufactured. It reminds us that techno-worship requires us not to assess the impact of technology in the present, but to have faith that in the future all will be revealed and resolved. It illustrates the downloading of technologically induced fall-out to the least powerful level – that of the individual, who alone bears the blame if he or she cannot apply the prescribed remedy. It teaches us that we are expected to feel powerless to do anything except mitigate the damages of technology's impact. Finally, it tells us what happens to heretics.

Patricia Herdman has been a thorn in the side of the television industry – and the CRTC – for a long time. She has another history of which she is equally proud, as a foster parent and as an advocate for abused and murdered women and their families. As it happens, she is also a software consultant. During November 1996, her name appeared often in the press because her group was mounting a well-planned boycott of advertisers who sold their products on the bloodthirsty Canadian-filmed series *Millennium*.

The media regularly dismiss Herdman as a representative of the religious Right or the amorphous do-gooders who refuse to get with it. Alternatively, she is vilified.

The *Globe and Mail* columnist Rick Salutin, dismissing criticism of *The Power Rangers*, wrote in 1994: "Activist Patricia Herdman on *Prime Time News* cut off another woman on the show and talked icily right over her: you felt she was ready to kill to get those shows off TV. In fact, you sometimes sense not just a violence out there but a fury within, and even towards their kids. Think of last week's story about a mother who said her sons had been kidnapped but who's now been charged with killing them herself."[45] This leap from impolite conversationalist to child-murderer is stunning – but no less illogical than the remarks about Herdman made by another *Globe* columnist two years later.

John Haslett Cuff, at the end of a quite creditable review of two televised documentaries on rape as a war crime, segued awkwardly into a few gratuitous Herdman insults. "Vis-à-vis the above," he wrote, "it is with some amusement that I noted the triumphal remarks of Patricia Herdman [on the *Millennium* boycott]. . . . Ms. Herdman . . . why don't you watch *Rape: A Crime of War* and then tell me, if you still can, that the world is not a uniformly terrifying place."[46] Obviously, Cuff believes that anyone who thinks television might be contributing to this terror – and that ordinary people might consider fighting back – is out of touch with the real world.

What really bugs Cuff, Salutin, and her other media critics, according to Herdman, isn't her stand on violence, but her insistence that citizens should not always accept something just because it can be technologically delivered and commercially profitable. Her very public accusations that the CRTC has become not only an apologist but a bagman for the telecommunications industry are dangerous. Her heretical position opposing technological fixes for human problems is also dangerous – she had better be careful, or next they'll be calling her a Luddite.

The Luddites Revisited

In 1812, so the story goes, Ned Ludd began breaking machines. He and his fellow workers in the English Midlands were encountering the first industrial revolution, the mechanical technologies that left workers out on the streets and resulted in widespread misery and even starvation. Actually, Ned Ludd never existed; he was created by the last workers not to have their response to technological progress shaped and manipulated by ideology and experts. For more than a decade, the Luddites and their sympathizers broke machines and interrupted the advance of the industrial revolution.

Orthodox history books cast the Luddites as a backwards mob, the symbol of foolish resistance to progress. But some historians argue that their resistance was legitimate, widely supported, and in many ways successful. They say the Luddites' opposition played an integral part in a protest against the social, economic, and political changes that accompanied technology. Power looms were not the only enemy. Unemployment, the lowering of wages, the declining quality of products, and the intensification of work that accompanied the mechanized looms were equally important targets. While smashing machines proved an effective means of direct protest, the Luddites also demanded political leadership on matters such as piecework, unfair competition, and market conditions. Above all, says historian David Noble, the Luddites demanded a social policy on technology, including a tax on power looms, and other legislative measures to protect the lives of the weavers.[47]

The response to the Luddites was both political and ideological. Political economy as a discipline and the idea of market forces emerged as theoretical constructs to explain society. Indeed, society as an abstract entity, separate from people themselves, was making its debut. Says Noble, "Society as a human artifact, a human endeavour, composed of people, was lost in the wake of capitalism." The hard logic of the market and the machine arose, replacing human values with "the abstractions of constant technological progress and endless pecuniary gain."[48]

Social progress, defined as progress towards justice, fairness, equality, and reason – the rallying cries of political revolutions in Europe and America – had been overthrown by the idea of progress through technology. An influential clergyman of the day, George Beaumont, summed it up when he said that "in my opinion, machinery ought to be encouraged to any extent whatsoever" because the inventors of machines were, after all, "the true benefactors of mankind."[49]

In the background, however, the management consultants of the day speculated that the true beneficiaries of technology would be those with control over manufacturing standards and labour processes – the owners and managers of factories. In 1835, a treatise extolling the virtues of technology as a means of disciplining labour concluded "that when capital enlists science in her service, the refractory hand of labour will always be taught docility."[50]

This power shift in favour of owners and managers was precisely what the Luddites had foreseen. Yet most observers dismissed this link between technology and the disempowerment of workers. The fashionable political movements of the day, both left and right, endorsed the wonders of machines and the progress they would guarantee. Marx himself argued that technology would emancipate workers and provide the economic base for the classless society.

Thus experts comfortably removed from first-hand experience with technology denounced the Luddites' resistance as dangerous and demented. Similarly, latter-day Luddites, those who criticize technology almost two centuries later, are condemned as being out of the loop. By today's standards, this fate is harsh, but not as severe as that which befell Ned Ludd's fellow workers. In 1812, the British parliament enacted a law extending the death penalty to those convicted of breaking machines. Eighteen Luddites were hanged.

Unconscious, or Unconsciously Manipulated?

The Luddites were sentenced to death for ideological treason. Their resistance broke the rules and risked exposing the new regime of technological efficiency for what it was – an ideological victory of profit over people. As history teaches, ideologies survive by exacting conformity in everything that matters to the state and its rulers, but successful modern ideologies must achieve this control while maintaining the illusion of free choice. Just as we live by the techno-commandment that there are no commandments, so we are taught to believe that there is no ideology – that we left such crude kinds of thought control behind when we abandoned Marxism and fascism. It is this illusion of independent thought that blinds us to the dominant ideology of our time, the worship of what John Ralston Saul calls "a new all-powerful clockmaker god – the marketplace and its sidekick, technology."[51] Perhaps the Luddites were our first human sacrifice to this new ideological god, the one we pretend does not exist.

Those who doubt – or even name – this ideology or who break the commandments will face ostracism and ridicule. Politicians, both left and right, face political suicide if they challenge the orthodoxy of trusting the free market or embracing globalization. Ordinary workers face their manager's disapproval, or worse, if they resist the introduction of technologies that serve these goals. Activists face ridicule. Everyone is told there is no alternative. Those who benefit from this passivity nurture it by divorcing the source of problems from the fall-out. Around the world, citizens are encouraged to pursue personal industry and family values, not to consider why work and family have fallen victim to global competition, or whether we might find sustainable alternatives to the ideology of individualism and markets.

We encourage this shift from concern for the welfare of the group and matters of public interest to the pursuit of personal advantage (or, for increasing numbers, personal survival) when we cast government as the problem and propose individualism as the solution. When we relegate minimalist government to performing only those functions that the private sector has no interest in (i.e., cannot profit from), we relinquish the power that democracy can give us. "If the citizenry agree to exclude themselves from any given area, they are automatically excluding the possibility that in that domain the public good could have any role to play. . . . The citizenry might well wonder why they should put artificial limits on their only force," says Saul. "The power we refuse ourselves goes somewhere else."[52]

As we can see in the software industry's propaganda packaged as curriculum and through the saga of the V-chip, when this power goes "somewhere else," it serves corporations, which use the power to promote private, not public, interests. We have to awaken from the unconscious notion that Microsoft or Rogers Cable or any other corporate entity exists to serve the public good, rather than to maximize private profit. To wake up, however, we must recognize how our unconsciousness is induced. Technology is not only the conduit that drains power from citizens to corporations, but also the religion that keeps us in a coma.

Rather than consolidating our accomplishments and re-examining our strategies in pursuit of the public good, we are assuming that the technologies of a self-interested market will pursue these same goals. In homage to our demanding gods, we have eroded the quality of our lives, our jobs, our incomes, our health care, our communities, our social safety net, and public education. As we strip the assets from the public space – sometimes enthusiastically, sometimes with a regretful nod to inevitability and the market – we are committing what Saul calls "slow, masochistic suicide."[53]

What we fail to notice is that the market is hardly a disinterested spectator on the suicide watch.

4

ON-LINE@ED.COM

TECHNOLOGY IN THE SCHOOL

When Microsoft launched Windows '95, it orchestrated what the media called the biggest product roll-out ever. Many of the thousands of promotions that took place around the world featured the Rolling Stones hit "Start Me Up," to which Microsoft had bought the rights for $12 million. Although Bill Gates appeared via a worldwide satellite conference, perhaps more Canadians got started up by seeing a 160-metre banner for Windows 95 hanging from Toronto's CN Tower.[1]

New technology is welcomed into education without the fanfare that more exciting techno-launches enjoy. Only regular readers of the *Times Educational Supplement* would have caught Malaysia's announcement that eighty-five "smart" schools would be linked to the Internet by 1999, and that all its schools would be on-line by 2010. Since nearly 1,500 Malay schools don't have electricity, this goal may prove a bit tricky.[2] This story reminds us of the pathetic aftermath of Bill Clinton's declaration that all U.S. schools would be on the Net by the year 2000. He made the announcement in a poverty-plagued inner-city school in Washington that enjoyed the limelight until the cameras left. Then the crew unplugged, unwired, and undisked the school, and everything returned to dismal normality.

Most Malaysian – and inner-city American – students may be out of the loop and out in the cold for some time to come, but they can look forward to another techno-innovation that gets to the bottom of the high cost of heating classrooms. Electronically heated underpants may improve students' school marks, according to the European Parliament. "The pants exist in prototype form in America, and are an illustration of the way things are happening in educational technology in ways you would never dream of," said an EU representative.[3]

Back in Canada, a small news item reported that the principal of Sudbury's Lasalle School has decided to have Sotheby's auction a signed Andy Warhol silkscreen. The school bought the print for $250 in 1970, back when hanging the real thing was thought a good way of exposing kids to art. Apparently, things have changed now that art can be viewed on the Internet. "It sounds crass," said school principal Bert Brankely. "But when I looked at that piece of art, I said to myself, 'That's the better part of a computer lab.'"[4]

Is Mr. Brankely a hopeless Philistine, an art critic, or an astute educator? He did exactly the right thing if what he has heard about computers in schools is true, although he might not be around long to enjoy the product of his insight. Consider the following:

From the heart of the New Right, on doing away with teachers:

Information technology is at least as capable of displacing and transforming labour requirements in education as any other business. . . . This is the greatest opportunity since Rockefeller struck oil.
  – Lewis Perelman, the Hudson Institute

From early techno-visionaries, on encouraging the end of schools:

There won't be schools in the future. . . . I think the computer will blow up the school. . . . The whole system is incompatible with the presence of the computer. . . . But this will happen only in communities of children who have access to computers on a sufficient scale.[5]

 – Seymour Papert

From the thoughtful deliberations of Ontario commissioners, on what is real:

Information technology can become the link between the school and the real world of Ontario's men and women – the component that makes schools, at long last, seem relevant to their lives, and that provides the motivation to rethink their attitudes to learning and the education system.[6]

 – Ontario Royal Commission on Learning

From a school's "CEO," on how it's all about students:

Education is obligated to make changes in keeping with change in society and the business world. . . . The inability to make sufficient changes to have a natural merge of technology and education could be quite detrimental to the appropriate education of our students.[7]

 – Principal Gerry Smith, on his school's partnership with Apple Canada, Northern Telecom, Dupont Canada, Sony, Bell Canada, DEC, Hewlett-Packard, Claris and Telesec

From high-tech marketers, on magic bullets:

Traditional classes and curriculums, which often prove to be inefficient and troublesome, can be drastically reformed and invigorated through the educational use of electronic mail, the World Wide Web and other InterNet capabilities.[8]

 – Symposium flyer

From a futurist, on choices:

> You're going to have to commit to a complete changeover. You won't have the budget to finance both paper-based tools and computer-based tools. . . . This mass customization concept may work best within the charter school model. . . .[9]
> – Richard Worzel

From the lobby of Canada's technology sector, on inevitability:

> These skills will not result from special classes in computer technology, but rather from a restructuring of the classroom curriculum. . . . Technology in education is not an option for institutions and government to choose or reject.[10]
> – Information Technology Association of Canada (ITAC)

From government/business/technology think-tanks, on doing more with less:

> More than incremental change is needed in order to improve the educational system. The Information Highway is a primary educational tool that can reduce costs, yet at the same time improve the educational services available to Canadians.[11]
> – Information Highway Advisory Council (IHAC)

From academics, on trying harder:

> Unless the new technologies become typical and usual . . . everyone involved will be less likely to attend to the technology with the same vigour as the "important" parts of the curriculum.[12]
> – Jeffrey Hecht, University of Illinois, trying to explain research that found student achievement dropped after home/school technology links were built

From students, on options:

Find an area to pursue, and figure out how technology can get you there and you'll see school paying off.
  – A Grade 11 student who used his school's partnership connections to land a part-time job that paid $12,000 in stock options[13]

From Wall Street, on ripe opportunities:

There's nothing sacrosanct about schooling that says we can't make money off it. Education is ripe for investment today. The rewards could be great, but so could the losses.[14]
  – Editor of the *Education Industry Report*

Some telling themes run through these statements. It seems possible that technology could be used to revive public education, but corporate dollars will change hands even if we abandon public schools. Although most techno-corporate investments are parked (at least temporarily) in public education, they don't have to stay there. Investors have choices. The fate of public education will depend on the investments (or "philanthropy") of high-tech speculators. In interpersonal relationships, when one person needs the other in order to survive, we call the relationship dysfunctional. In nature, when one biological organism feeds off another, we call it a parasite. In education, we call this relationship a partnership.

Note that none of the people or groups quoted actually claim that the use of information technology will improve student learning. Supposedly, this outcome is too obvious to need stating. There are occasional exceptions, as when Bill Clinton tucked the following statistics into a 1996 campaign speech: "The facts speak for themselves. Children with access to computers learn faster and learn better. Scores on standardized tests for children with computers, according to Apple Classrooms of Tomorrow [ACOT] . . . caused scores to go up by 10 to 15 per cent. Children mastered basic skills in 30 per cent less time. . . ."[15]

President Clinton's exuberant claims were posted on Apple's Web site, directly above an item that asked: "Who rules in schools?"

Here Apple boasts that its market share of personal computers in American schools has grown "four full share points" to 63 per cent.

Who Rules in Schools?

The battle over technology sales to schools is heating up as the global shakedown of high-tech providers gets serious. Billions of dollars in direct sales will accrue to the manufacturer of education's software platform of choice. Winning over this market will also ensure a competitive advantage in lucrative home computer sales. Families with children are almost three times as likely to own a home computer as single adults,[16] and compatibility between home and school systems is important to parents. The type of operating system that schools use will also determine the size and profitability of educational software sales and spur demand for compatible home software. As Intel executive Pat Foy boasts, "What we do isn't really philanthropy, which is giving something away. This is about making an investment. . . . If we don't make those kind of investments, we're going to go out of business."[17]

The demand for personal computers (PCs) in the private sector is shrinking – increasingly, it's limited to the upgrading of existing systems – and most businesses have met, or exceeded, their IT needs. Consequently, the education technology market is becoming more important. *Business Week* explains the new marketing strategy: "Penetration of PC's in American homes is stalled at about 40%. . . . Where do you get new users? Enter the education market."[18] It is almost impossible to estimate the amount of money at stake. Obviously, deep penetration (or computer immersion, as it is sometimes called) is more lucrative than limited use. If just 10 per cent of the money spent educating American and Canadian children each year was spent on technology, the market would reach $60 billion annually; calculations of the real costs of technology-rich classrooms suggest that 30 per cent or 40 per cent of total spending would be a more realistic estimate.[19] "The education market represents only 10 per cent of total sales for computer manufacturers. But what a tenth it is," says *Globe and Mail* reporter Andrew Tausz. "This market is most influential in educating

neophytes in the benefits of high tech. And students, once converted, will remain active buyers of computer gadgetry for life."[20]

The push to hook up every child, teacher, and classroom is
intense, but the great marketing plan has a small glitch. Even
with principals selling Warhols at a brisk pace to finance technology purchases, the public remains unconvinced of the schools'
wisdom. A 1996 Vector poll found that only 10 per cent of the
Canadian public thought new education dollars should be spent
on more computers in classes. Survey respondents were more
than twice as likely to prefer smaller class sizes and three times as
likely to choose "upgraded teacher training" as better ways to
improve schools.[21] With a building momentum and so many sales
at stake, lukewarm public opinion is a problem. The public needs
to be convinced that computers can solve the education crisis.
The industry has a huge investment in demonstrating that Bill
(Clinton or Gates) is right, that computers really do improve
student achievement.

Student performance is the new rationale. The old saw about
how computer literacy will guarantee today's students great jobs in
a prosperous global, information-age (etc., etc.) economy looks a
bit weak in the face of widespread youth unemployment. The
IT/education connection needs to show concrete, immediate
results that will move today's opinion polls as well as tomorrow's
market share. From a sales perspective, it is just as important to
show that greater access to computers works better than limited
access, and even better to find research proving that particular
types of computers, using particular types of proprietary software,
boost student success. The industry needs this proof so badly that
it has been tempted to cut a few corners chasing it.

Retrofitting Reality

Educational technology is a perfect example of an outstanding
dual use technology where the defense department can undertake collaborative activities that will push to the forefront the
application of technology in education.[22]
    – U.S. deputy secretary of defense

This statement is just a twist on an old story. Money or politics – usually both – has driven what technology historian Douglas Noble calls "the political history of computer-based education," including "its military roots, its early commercialization, and its widespread adoption."[23] Post-war peace created a hitch in the expansionist plans of the American military-industrial complex, which needed to find new horizons. Thanks to a billion dollars from the American taxpayer, entrepreneurial ventures such as the General Learning Corporation (made up of General Electric and Time Warner) began as early as 1967 to exploit what they hoped would be an exploding knowledge industry. Other Fortune 500 firms, buoyed by wildly exaggerated notions of what technology could accomplish, dived in. One by one the companies failed, unable to come up with either the killer application or the public and teacher enthusiasm they needed to succeed.

Governments and techno-corps stepped up their marketing efforts in the 1970s, but Noble claims "the ideological leavening of the education market had not yet set. . . . The rhetoric of the information age had not yet fully conditioned the schools to welcome the gadgetry into classrooms."[24] Noble correctly pins this reluctance on schools (i.e., teachers), but the time when adopting education reforms depended on teachers' approval was drawing to a close. In 1983, the American corporate-sponsored education critique *A Nation at Risk* damned America's schools and called for computer literacy – even computer programming – as a new basic skill that every student needed to acquire.[25] Timing is everything; the scathing report was released within weeks of *Time* magazine's selection of the personal computer as "Man of the Year." The courtship between corporate America and information technology, which had begun in America's boardrooms, was about to be consummated in its classrooms.

A Nation at Risk coincided with that magical marketing moment when consumers become convinced that they need, not just want, a particular product. The public thought it needed computer literacy, an amorphous phrase invented by the National Science Foundation (NSF); what it got was computers.[26] "We started computer literacy in 1972," says Andrew Molnar, then head of NSF. "It's sort of ironic. Nobody knows what computer literacy is. Nobody can define it. . . . It was a broad enough term you could get all these programs together under one roof. . . ."[27]

Computer literacy, even without a definition, caught on. Primitive military-derived software such as LOGO were repackaged as educational essentials. Featuring a cursor called a turtle that plodded relentlessly across computer monitors, LOGO was praised for teaching "thinking skills," a new edu-buzzword as vague as computer literacy. Today, nostalgia conferences billed as LOGO retrospectives gaze back over its heyday, when LOGO was used all over the world. In 1989, I met ten-year-old students in Costa Rica, studying in open-air schools without running water, who squealed "Tortuga! Tortuga!" as they proudly showed off their Commodore 64's to visiting teachers. Today, only a handful of classes anywhere still uses LOGO. Talk of higher-order thinking skills has long since disappeared.

The extinction of these once-ubiquitous digital turtles tells the archetypal story of the endless cycle of edu-tech hype and disappointment. Even the American Office for Technology Assessment admits that teachers' cynicism is easy to understand. In 1983, teachers were told to teach students to program in BASIC because it was the language that came with their computer. In 1984, they were told to switch to LOGO and to "teach students to think, not just to program." In 1986, they were told to focus on computer-based drill-and-practice that would "individualize instruction and increase test scores." By 1988, drill was out in favour of word processing, but in 1990, teachers were told to forget word processing and keyboarding, and get into simulations and databases that would "integrate computers into the existing curriculum." In 1992, teachers were told to teach hypertext multimedia programming because "students learn best by creating products for an audience." In 1994, they were told to get on the information highway so that students could be "part of the real world."[28]

Therefore, today's teachers require a substantial amount of persuasion to embark on yet another excellent adventure with technology. In order to circumvent these cynics, corporations are directing much of the current techno-hype at either parents who have no personal or corporate memory of previous edu-tech follies, or governments that are more interested in byte-sized claims than facts. While disco-dancing computer chips, prime ministerial speeches, and multi-million-dollar software launches are useful in maintaining IT momentum, they could be insufficient from a marketing perspective. Sooner or later, someone will ask: "Where's the proof?"

Getting Down to Business

All the corporate players agreed that successfully launching the digital school would require a flashy and empirically convincing investigation. The definitive study would become the benchmark of education reform and would finally secure the future of the computers-in-education industry. The corporations themselves would fund the research, design it, conduct it, and report on its results. While corporate-funded education research was unusual, the approach met limited opposition from the education sector, which had never seen a strong link between theory and practice, and was learning to accept partnerships with appropriate levels of gratitude.

Apple Computer took the lead. Apple had dominated the emerging computers-in-education market with Apple II's and II-E's, and had staked out its turf against its only early competitors, TRS and Commodore. In 1985, Apple announced an ambitious and expensive research project that would follow five Apple Classrooms of Tomorrow (known as ACOT sites) for ten years. The experimental model was described as computer saturation – Apples were to be given to every teacher and student, at school and at home, in order to test what happens when students have "total, unlimited access to technology."

(This was the first giveaway that pure educational research was not Apple's priority. Classroom research for educational purposes is usually conducted within the parameters of possibility. To my knowledge, no one has spent ten years finding out what would happen if every student had "total, unlimited access to teachers," although it is a provocative idea.)

The ACOT project was ambitious on all fronts. Although the budgets for setting up the project and conducting the research have not been released, Apple was not the only funder. Recognizing that more was at stake than just one corporation's fortunes, other friends of technology came on board, including the National Science Foundation and the New America Schools Development Corporation (NASDC). NASDC members, including AT&T, IBM, and the American Stock Exchange, had already pumped millions of dollars into other corporate-friendly school reform projects. To call these efforts philanthropy, however, would be inaccurate. Since the organization was created by George Bush, NASDC's agenda has been to ensure the "better alignment of American schools with American business objectives." ACOT fit right in.

Technology corporations have been lead players in NASDC, and welcomed in all the major American school restructuring initiatives. Wisconsin governor and Republican presidential hopeful Tommy Thompson presided over the March 1996 Education Summit, which consisted of high-tech business leaders and state governors, but everyone knew he wasn't really in charge. The event was convened not just symbolically but geographically at Louis Gerstner Jr.'s IBM headquarters, a suitable forum to make the transition from the corporate school-bashing typical of previous summits to the corporate rescue mission that would fix what was wrong with America's schools.

The first step would be to wrench a political commitment to higher standards from the governors – standards that would reflect business priorities. As the American corporate lobby known as the National Alliance of Business puts it, "Standards have 'revolutionized' business in recent years and schools need to follow suit." Since the declaration of a deep attachment to higher standards is the cheapest way for politicians to pretend to reform schools, this commitment was not a tough sell. Gracious in victory (no matter how predictable), Gerstner declared the standards debate to be over as he announced the second step. He vowed that business would do its part for education by developing "products, services and software to support teaching."[29] Stanley Litow, president of the IBM Foundation, concurred: "Our strategic focus has been to figure out the ways you can use technology to systematically fix the flaws in the school system. We decided to treat education as if it were a very important and sophisticated business problem."[30]

The Apple's Core

Apple pledged that research on its ACOT project would be separate from its other philanthropic and promotional ventures, and independent of its sales and marketing division. Apple would release intermittent reports as findings warranted.

In 1997, with considerable fanfare, it published *Teaching with Technology: Creating Student-Centered Classrooms*, the definitive ten-year report on ACOT that was actually a summary of previously released findings.[31] Among the periodic (and copyrighted) reports produced during the ten years, Number 7, "ACOT Evaluation Study: First and Second Year Findings" (1990), is of particular interest. As research reports go, the absence of data or anything else that could be evaluated independently is striking. Even more intriguing is the footprint of Apple's public relations department on the study's results.

The whole purpose of this evaluation study was to measure the effects of computer use on student achievement. The researchers set out to "secure appropriate comparison classrooms for all sites" (find control groups); "re-apply measures of student achievement and attitudes" (give standardized tests to the ACOT groups and control groups); and "administer measures of ACOT's impact on teachers and parents" (collect surveys).[32] The widely used tests that ACOT administered must have yielded numbers, but curiously this report does not disclose them.

Class, deconstruct the following example of damage control: "Recognizing the imperfections of existing measures . . . [the research] has since shifted focus to the development of new . . . technology-based tools . . . that can better capture the diverse and complex outcomes of ACOT."[33] Full marks for figuring out that this is a convoluted way to blame the test when results are disappointing.

The most encouraging ACOT research findings were barely tepid. Even with the help of Apple's spin doctors, the report could only conclude:

> Results showed that ACOT students *maintained* their performance levels on standard measures of educational achievement in basic skills, and they *sustained* positive attitudes. . . . The ACOT program was *at least as effective* in promoting commonly measured student outcomes . . . and in at least *one site* there were indications of advantage for ACOT students [emphasis added].[34]

In other words, after two years of total and unlimited access to technology by carefully selected students, whose parents had chosen the program and whose teachers had unlimited amounts of technical and instructional support, the best that Apple could say about the achievement and attitudes of ACOT students was that they *hadn't declined.*

Don't make hasty judgements, urged the report's authors: "Any conclusions from [these findings] about the effects of ACOT on students and other outcomes would be premature." There were research design problems, after all. For example, student characteristics showed "extraordinary diversity," according to the evaluators, and so did their homes (surprise!). District regulations created unidentified barriers to "consistent administration of each measure." Comparison non-ACOT classrooms, needed for a control group, were said to be reluctant to participate. Again, Apple blamed the limitations of standardized tests in evaluating outcomes such as "complex thinking." While it is true that standardized tests do not measure higher-order skills effectively, these more sophisticated ways of thinking generally build on basic skills, such as reading proficiency, which can be measured. Students are unlikely to master complex thinking in their absence.

But fair enough – this was only year two. Given ACOT's objectives and the deep pockets of its sponsors, future ACOT reports would surely revisit student achievement – basic or complex – and student attitudes. The subsequent research reports discuss topics such as "partnerships for change" (Number 12), "the relationship between technological innovation and collegial interaction" (Number 13), and even "the negotiation of group authorship among second graders using multimedia composing software" (Number 14). But the straightforward question of whether technology-rich classrooms result in increased student learning was never again addressed. If ACOT students were evaluated systematically over this period of time, Apple did not publish the results in their research reports. Perhaps the company was waiting for maximum market impact. Surely the final report would dig up *some* empirical research to justify the huge public spending on Apple technology that the company hoped for and needed badly.

Yet the final report contains exactly two references to measured student achievement, and neither is accompanied by data.[35] The first states that some ACOT students "scored significantly higher" on the California Achievement Test, but cites only a Memphis school newsletter as the source of this important claim. The second reference says that "less time spent on basics . . . did not have a negative impact on student performance"; this finding is attributed to an unpublished paper read at an education conference in 1989. We can safely assume that if better numbers and better sources existed, Apple would not only disclose them, but trumpet them during every sales pitch. Bill Clinton's claims to parents, teachers, and governments (better results! in less time! for all students! courtesy of Apple!) made for good copy, but came from bad data.

Those outside the ed-tech loop may find it hard to believe how much influence ACOT's transparently weak research has had on decisions with multimillion-dollar implications. "Apple Classrooms of Tomorrow – What We've Learned,"[36] written by Apple's David C. Dwyer, who directed the ACOT project and the research, is probably the most frequently cited article promoting computer technology in education. It makes some extraordinary claims. Dwyer boasts that ACOT students "were doing as well as they *might* without all of the technology" (emphasis added). He writes that researchers in the ACOT program observed increased student and teacher enthusiasm, significant changes in the ways ACOT students thought and worked, and improved teacher collegiality. "We watched technology profoundly disturb the inertia of traditional classrooms," Dwyer says. He goes on to promise that providing "an array of tools for acquiring information and for thinking and expression . . . will enable students to live productive lives in the global, digital information-based future they all face." Wow.

Dwyer does not provide any documented evidence to support his conclusions; he simply states that they flow from Apple's research. A glance through the small print at the end of the (Apple-copyrighted) article is most enlightening. Dwyer cites ten sources: he was the principal author of two, six refer to "unpublished" (i.e., unavailable) reports, one is the Memphis newsletter, and one is U.S. labour force data. In an undergraduate term paper, such a weak patchwork of sources to support such sweeping claims would be rejected. From a Distinguished Apple Scientist – an honorific bestowed by Apple, of course – it is a joke.

When Ontario's Royal Commission on Learning recommended that technology should become one of the "four pillars" of education renewal, it used a powerful statement to introduce its proposal: "Technology stands out in our classrooms as a symbol to teachers, parents and students that schooling can and will change, that classrooms may have some bearing on the 21st Century after all." The quotation is lifted directly from David Dwyer's article on ACOT's "success." Imagine a royal commission on the future of health care using the sales pitch of a transnational pharmaceutical corporation to explain why using more drugs more often should become "a pillar" of our health care system. Health care watchdogs would jump all over it. But this is technology; this is education. Not a word of protest was heard from any quarter.

Even if the commissioners (and the public, journalists, the Opposition, and teachers) missed this travesty, reasonable people might expect to find vigorous arguments about ACOT and techno-education going on somewhere, perhaps in mainstream education journals. They aren't. The sidelining of critical comment about technology in general is even more pronounced in the discussion – debate would be too strong a term – of the purposes and effects of information technology in education. The summative paper on the merits of technology in the classroom prepared by the Council of Ministers of Education does contain a section on "concerns," but these are limited to getting enough funding fast enough, ensuring no one is left "behind," and dealing with the perplexing problem of copyright.[37]

Edu-tech's few critics are generally ignored or dismissed as ill-informed, paranoid, or self-interested. Yet outside the mainstream of obligatory enthusiasm, there is a growing critical literature. The criticisms come together around a set of philosophical and practical issues associated with redesigning schools to suit technology. They do not argue that technology has no role in the classroom, only that its role should be chosen, not bought as silicon snake oil or as educational or economic redemption. Perhaps Neil Postman comes closest to summing up the critics: "I am not arguing against using computers in schools. I am arguing against our sleepwalking attitudes towards it, against allowing it to distract us from important things, against making a god of it."[38]

Most critics begin their analysis with an extraordinarily important conclusion derived from empirical data: *There is no independent research support for the extensive use of computers or information technology in education.* That is, there is no independent research that meets generally accepted standards for controls, accuracy, transparency, replicability, sample size, and validity. There are claims, inferences, arguments, and assertions. And, of course, there are promises.

However, the critics are not content simply to point out the lack of research linking edu-tech to student achievement. They find evidence of effects that are at least as important, even if less quantifiable. Most of them believe that we *may* find an important, useful role for technology in education. They insist, however, that as long as the promises are receiving all the attention, the critics will place their emphasis on unresolved – perhaps unresolvable – problems.

EXPERT OPINION THAT challenges compulsory enthusiasm for edu-tech is difficult to hear against the babble of boosterism. Well-informed individuals have, however, spoken out. "None of this material has been developed or tested for its effectiveness," claims Carl Cuneo of McMaster University's Network for the Evaluation of Education and Training Technologies. York's David Noble writes, "There's no pedagogical evidence to show that learning improves with computers." The most thorough review of evaluative studies to date concludes that "no long-term supporting empirical or qualitative evidence shows that technology has made schools and teachers more effective or significantly affected the lives of their students."

Source: Bernie Froese-Germain and Marita Moll, "Bridging the Gap Between Research and Rhetoric"

These problems are present wherever technology is found, but they flourish when they are denied or dismissed. Environments intended to condition children and teachers to embrace technology, not just use it, are not environments that foster critical thought about technology – or any other subject. Critical theory invites us to step back and make sure our enthusiasm for computers in the classroom is not just collaboration with the urban planners of the global city.

Technology – The Tool Shapes the Task

The tasks of education have never been simple, and we have never agreed on the best ways for schools to accomplish them. Canadians certainly agree that education is more than just information without skills, or skills without common sense, or common sense without critical thinking, or critical thinking without creativity, or creativity without . . . and so on. The many tasks of education compete daily, not just in the minds of education ministers and parents, but for time and attention in the classroom. Technology intervenes in this competition in particular, predictable ways.

Since information technology is the tool that seeks, finds, stores, organizes, communicates, and packages information, it is hardly surprising that information tasks jump the queue in technology-centred classrooms.

The tool shapes the task. As philosopher Ursula Franklin, master of social and technological metaphors, says, "Somebody gives you a Cuisinart or one of those machines that slice and dice. Suddenly you find yourself slicing and dicing and not using your old recipes any more. When you get a new tool, it affects your task."[39] A Nova Scotia school district technology co-ordinator said the same thing when he grumbled, "I dunno. When you're carrying around a hammer, everything starts to look like a nail."

After we've sliced, diced, and hammered, we discover that the results may or may not have been as satisfying as we expected. If we are buoyed by success, we look for yet more opportunities to apply our new tool. If we are disappointed, we assume we lacked sufficient skill or didn't follow directions properly. Often we conclude that we need more functions on our Cuisinart or a bigger hammer. Unintended outcomes – at least, the unpleasant ones – are seen as either worth the price (in the event of success) or avoidable next time (through more sophisticated tools and more practice). If we wish, we can even repackage negative effects as important educational tasks. Frustrated by your computer? Relax. You are learning patience. Overwhelmed by information? You are learning its management.

We frequently hear people citing technology's awesome ability to access information as its most important feature, and using this feature to promote technology's obvious relevancy to education. What slips between the lines is the assumption that the purpose of education is primarily, or even exclusively, to acquire more information more quickly. According to this assumption, learning *about* something is an adequate substitute for learning *from* something – or someone. The dramatist Max Frisch once defined technology as "the knack of so arranging the world that we do not experience it."[40] Increasingly, the difference between virtual and real experiences disappears.

The teachers who participated in the ACOT project were probably typical in every way. We are all in info-thrall, so we shouldn't be surprised that ACOT teachers were awed by the information that their students could access through computers. They appeared to waste little (recorded) time worrying about whether the information their students encountered was of value. They may have been impressed to find that middle-grade students could work with "a professional scientific visualization tool developed by the National Institute of Health," but this activity is not, by definition, any more purposeful than reading an encyclopedia entry.

ACOT teachers can be forgiven this oversight; they're in good company. Bill Gates says Microsoft's overall vision for technology in education will be achieved when all children have access to all the world's information all the time.[41] But Neil Postman asks, "What is the problem to which more information is the solution?" and "Whose problem is it?" Postman makes the point that children, like the rest of us, are suffering from information glut, not information scarcity. Not only are we swamped by information we have no control over, but we don't know what to do with it. He writes: "If children are starving in Somalia, it's not because of insufficient information; if crime terrorizes our cities, marriages are breaking up, mental disorders are increasing, and children are being abused, none of this happens because of a lack of information. These things happen because we lack something else. It is the 'something else' that is now the business of schools."[42]

The "something else" is infinitely more difficult (and certainly less profitable) than accessing yet more information. But the tool shapes the task – and since the computer is much better at adding to the information landfill than dealing with the emotional, social, and other intellectual needs of students, we are redirecting schools to teach students how to acquire more information faster, and leaving other goals behind. Info-critic Lowell Monke says that "quiet contemplation was once held up to students as a key cognitive process needed to develop and understand ideas. . . . Ideas don't require much information. . . . Will quiet contemplation give way to frenzied net-surfing as the most esteemed intellectual process?"[43] Will all teaching goals be reduced to improving data management?

ACOT itself provides a perfect example of how easily the pursuit of information pushes other tasks aside. ACOT teacher Mr. Tate submitted his unit plan on "The Twentieth Century" to the ACOT staff, who returned it with suggestions for "expanding the role of technology by using portable computers for data collection." These suggestions led to additional data collection on "leisure activities in the 1940s," which Mr. Tate hoped would help his sixth-grade students understand why television was welcomed so enthusiastically. Mr. Tate was impressed with how the technology promoted collaborative problem-solving:

> As soon as the students had about four rows of data entered, they began to mess around with the Venn loops and axes. As they did so, they realized that some of the attributes they were entering weren't appearing in the loops. They investigated: "Let's check to see if it's in the database again. There it is, but it's spelled wrong." They began to realize that spelling was important but capitalization wasn't. I simply confirmed what they were discovering.

If Mr. Tate's (ACOT-approved) goals for students had not been "to become proficient with the equipment" and "to access, understand, interpret, find and assemble information," he might have tried more meaningful activities, such as having students talk to their parents and grandparents about their leisure activities pre- and post-television, and compared these stories with their own experiences. The results would not have fit so neatly into a database, but students' understanding could have been much richer. Mr. Tate had nothing (recorded) to say about what his students had learned about television in the 1940s, their families, or themselves.

When we glorify information, we also tend to treat it with elevated respect. Under the heading "Changes in Student Attitude," Apple reported that ACOT teachers were thrilled with the high quality of their students' work. ACOT students put together what the report called a tabloid publication. "I'm very happy with the work we're doing on this publication," said their teacher, "40 pages, tabloid size, three colours, borders, colour separation with clip art, over 300 advertisements with very detailed proofreading required. The man at the press is very impressed with the quality of the work. He has offered summer jobs to some of the kids. . . ."[44] This teacher said nothing at all about the content of the tabloid, which we might assume to contain articles, essays, or other student-generated writing. However, squeezing three hundred advertisements into forty pages would have left little room for any other copy. Perhaps the tabloid contained nothing but ads, and students devoted all this technical effort to the production of a glorified flyer – the junk mail version of official knowledge.

Like the man with the hammer, ACOT teachers began to see every classroom situation as a nail to be struck with their computers. Take the unlikely topic of cheating. Wherever there are classrooms, from kindergarten ("He copied my picture!") to graduate school ("That's my research!"), questions of honesty and respect for others' work arise. The ACOT report deals in some detail with cheating, less as a moral problem than as one of computer skill. The "task" of honesty was reshaped as a technical problem, subject to technical solutions. One teacher handled pervasive cheating on tests by "scrambling to learn more and more about the software," finally "assigning a global variable to the scoring portion of the test that he felt confident would keep students from cheating." Other teachers decided to "not have the computers on before school, during lunch, or for study hall . . . as a punishment for illegal copying." Note how cheating became a matter of the illegal violation of intellectual property rights. Note how a human problem was avoided – or, perhaps, made worse – through technology.

ACOT teachers reportedly dealt with other thorny tasks by choosing to do what technology made possible, even if the approaches were pedagogically questionable. One teacher explained that since she had access to a spreadsheet application, she had begun testing students more often because calculating marks was so easy. Another appreciated being able to extend the students' school day, since assigning and checking homework became so much more convenient. A third teacher realized that she could give students "immediate feedback" (or, to be more exact, an immediate number) by ensuring that all their tests were conducted on-line, even though evaluation had to be restricted to questions with a single correct answer.

Technology became the filter through which every task had to pass. One teacher wrote, "You start questioning everything you have done in the past, and wonder how you can adapt it to the computer. Then, you start questioning the whole concept of what you originally did."[45] Whatever the teachers knew before became less important than what they were learning. As they became more computer-adept, ACOT teachers used their skills to pursue technique and teach it to their students, who quickly mastered applications that dazzled adults. The task shifted again, from pursuing information for its own sake to manipulating its display.

The collection of information and its management can be endlessly diverting. Technique impresses adults especially: many of us will sit transfixed before an animated PowerPoint presentation, no matter how banal the content. Brian Alger, vice-principal of Ontario River Oaks School, admits that adults who have seen eight-year-olds using charts, animation, and hypertext during the well-rehearsed school tour are more impressed with "the razzle dazzle of technology" than with content.[46] The task of creating substance is replaced by the task of shaping it.

Even some of those who understand the gap between the gee-whiz of the package and the value of its content aren't above using others' confusion to their advantage. The same York University article that quotes Brian Alger also quotes Stan Shapson, York's dean of education, sounding appropriately cautious. "Getting the hardware into the schools is the easy part. How it becomes meaningful is the real challenge. . . . Knowing how to use the technology is not enough. . . . Teachers must question its effectiveness." On the last page of this article, the editors placed an announcement for York's new SCoOl: "An explosion is about to happen! It won't involve dynamite, but it will involve knowledge. Or, more specifically the way that knowledge will be delivered to those who need it most – Ontario's students." The ad says that delivering courses through e-mail, computer conferencing, and the Web constitutes "a major paradigm shift," quoting the very same Dr. Shapson, whose reservations about touting tools over content apparently don't apply when advertising his own dynamite empire.

Note how the task has changed again, from using technology as a tool to give students an education of value, to attracting students to the tools they enjoy, which allegedly emit knowledge.

This verbal slide from *data* to *information* to *knowledge* isn't limited to advertising copy. These different concepts have merged, making the redesign of education around the pursuit of information that much easier – despite critic Theodore Roszak's warning that people who think these words are synonymous have no idea what either education or information is.[47] The casual interchange of these terms is not just a matter of semantics. Once we become accustomed to equating the pursuit of information – on any topic, of any quality, in growing quantity – to knowledge, those opposed to the aggressive search for more information become opposed to knowledge, which is even more heretical than being opposed to progress.

Our culture's assumptions about progress, about our helplessness in the face of a technologically predetermined future, underlie the last shift. Now the tool of technology rewrites the task of education in both philosophical and concrete ways by redefining what knowledge is of value. This knowledge is not just more technical or utilitarian, but more valuable than other kinds of knowledge. People who possess it are more important people, and nations that pursue it are more advanced. We let this ideology remake us and our schools without any idea of what we are losing, or how much more will be asked of us. It would not be difficult to support these conclusions with quotations from curriculum reform documents, compilations of spending on technology, or speeches from bank presidents. Instead, consider these two stories.

"THE MAIN THING KIDS learn from computers is how to use computers. Absolutely nothing kids learn about using computers in the first grade today will make them more employable when they leave high school."

Source: Theodore Roszak, *New Internationalist,* December 1996

The first comes from a reformed technophile who spent the greater part of his career building his reputation as an expert on technology in the classroom. His advice (which, of course, changed regularly) was followed by hundreds of school districts. A number of events led to his disillusionment. Now, when he is invited to tour high-tech schools and expected to be suitably impressed with the new computer lab, he asks only one question: "What did this room used to be?" Invariably, he says, he is told it was the music room, the stage, the art room, or the teachers' workroom. The answer gives him the only metaphor he needs.

In its own way, the second story blames us rather than technology. When ministries of education rewrite curricula to meet the demands of a global, competitive, information-driven (etc., etc.) world, one of their targets has been to revise the list of prose works that students are expected to read. What task should reading serve? Perhaps research holds the answer.

The nationally syndicated American columnist William Raspberry reported "a study" that found ten- to twelve-year-old students could read VCR manuals and set their VCRs better than eighteen-year-olds. The reason given was that "in high schools, students read literature, not technical manuals." Intrigued, intrepid education researcher Gerald Bracey tracked "the study" back to Willard Daggett, promoter of Total Quality Management and self-styled education guru.

Asked for his source, Daggett backtracked, claiming the reference was an old one he no longer used. Then Bracey heard Daggett elaborate on the same theme in a videotaped speech to edu-crats and politicians. This time, Daggett claimed not only that ten- to

twelve-year-olds were better at using "consumer-friendly technology" because they were able to "read short passages and
respond," but also that a (nonexistent) national reading teachers'
organization had proved that reading novels is a right-brained
process that adversely affects the left brain! Furthermore, Daggett
claimed that eighteen-year-old drop-outs read manuals and used
technology better than high school graduates, who in turn bet-
tered college graduates and those with masters degrees. His point
was not just that time was being wasted on literature (or perhaps
on school), but that the same study, conducted in every state and
in six (or, in some of his references, twelve) different countries,
found only Americans and Canadians were reading-impaired.
Other nations, Daggett claimed, required "four years of technical
reading" in high school; this explained their competitive global
(etc., etc.) advantage.

Bracey continued to press Daggett for citations and sources. He
received neither, but did hear from Daggett's lawyer, who wrote,
"As I am sure you know, Dr. Daggett is vitally interested in research
in educational issues. However, his international schedule prevents
him from consideration of matters outside the scope of his projects."[48] In retelling the story, Bracey invites readers to imagine the
research Daggett describes. By Bracey's calculations, 700,000 individuals would have been required as test subjects in the United
States alone, and many times more to conduct similar research in
six (or twelve) other countries. It isn't just Daggett's reputation
that makes this absurd claim live on in curriculum reforms that
stress the need for business English at the expense of literature. It
is our willingness, through our devotion to a tool, to "re-task" education to serve the needs of technology and commerce.

But surely tools only do what their makers and users demand?
What of the hands that set the tools to work?

The Tool Shapes Its Users – Part I: Students

Since Apple promised that student-centred classrooms would be
the end-product of technology-rich environments, we would reasonably expect students to feature prominently in ACOT's final

report. They don't, although this oversight is hardly unique to Apple; other than as undifferentiated "learners," students are absent from many education documents. Still, ACOT students and their opinions are conspicuously absent from the 193-page report. Where they are mentioned, they exist only in relationship to the classroom's technology. There are eleven photographs in *Teaching with Technology*. In each, students, teachers, or both are staring at information on a computer screen, but not one photograph shows people relating to each other without the computer as their focus, and not one shows people face-to-face.

The report insists that students seemed never to tire of their constant engagement with computers. Apparently, no ACOT adult entertained the thought that an over-attachment to computers could be a problem. The ACOT researchers boasted that students "chose to use the computers during free-time and after-school hours." A sixth-grader, having mastered spreadsheets, became bookkeeper for his mother's import business. Students found field trips an annoyance, since they were separated from their machines. Grade 2 students cut short their Halloween party to get back to the keyboards. "At one site, after a number of indoor recesses due to rain, students became upset when the teacher announced outside recess. . . . The students indicated that they had hoped to stay in and work on their computers."

If the ACOT teachers saw the signs that virtual relationships were eclipsing human ones, they didn't seem worried. Parents were reportedly delighted with their children's new obsession. One parent told researchers, "Instead of wanting to always watch television or go outside and play, John can be found at his computer a large part of the time."[49] A student wrote in her (digital) journal that "a computer a day keeps the blues away."[50] Her world view was being altered by her relationship with technology – a tool that, in Theodore Roszak's words, is not interested in "the full resources of the self," but only the part that is most like the machine.[51] Other ways of knowing – through intuition, physical contact, emotional and spiritual experience – become irrelevant, and even impede us from adapting to suit the technological universe.

As educator and philosopher John Dewey wrote, "Perhaps the greatest of all pedagogical fallacies is the notion that a person learns only the particular thing he is studying at the time."[52] The peripheral learnings about what matters, where ideas come from, and even the attributes of people and machines are constantly changing. By their nature, children are driven to form relationships – with people, certainly, but also with objects. When children name their stuffed toys, the family car, or their printer, they are acting out this drive. Sherry Turkle's six-year study of kids in a computer-immersed classroom found that, even in less interactive environments, younger children saw computers as "sort of" alive because killing them, crashing them, or interrupting programs running on them became taboo.[53]

Does their attachment to computers prove that children themselves are changing, and if so, what do these changes mean? Techno-boosters would have us believe that students will morph into atavistic consumers of information, reprogrammed by their computers to buckle down and produce results. Yet teachers who supervise computer labs admit their chief activity is trying to make sure kids are doing something serious on the Net, not surfing chat groups. Firewalls designed to keep kids from accessing the more offensive content are being expanded to keep out anything that might be considered trivial – which, given the nature of the Net, is no small feat. Somehow, we can feel encouraged to know that cyberkids are still human enough to prefer fun over the hard work of learning.

Some people, however, would like to see childhood rewired entirely. In a clever essay on education and technology, Neil Postman quotes a speech by Diane Ravitch, former U.S. assistant secretary of education.[54] Waxing eloquent about technology and the "new world of pedagogical plenty" in which children and adults can learn "at their own convenience," Ravitch invented a couple of new children, Eva and John:

> If Little Eva cannot sleep, she can learn algebra instead. . . . She will tune in to a series of interesting problems that are presented

in an interactive medium, much like video games. . . . Young
John may decide that he wants to learn the history of modern
Japan, which he can do by dialling up the greatest authorities
and teachers on the subject, who will not only use dazzling
graphs and illustrations, but will narrate a historical video that
excites his curiosity and imagination.[55]

Postman says Ravitch's vision is a mite unrealistic.

Little Eva can't sleep, so she decides to learn a little algebra?
Where does Little Eva come from? Mars? . . . Young John
decides that he wants to learn the history of modern Japan? . . .
How is it that he never visited a library until now? Or is it that
he, too, couldn't sleep and decided that a little modern Japanese
history was just what he needed?

What Ravitch is talking about here is not a new technology
but a new species of child, one who, in any case, no one has
seen up to now.

As the tool changes the tool users, some teachers are seeing a
new species of teaching assistant. Kids who find technology particularly fascinating tend to acquire exceptional computer competency outside the classroom, so every school has some students
much more knowledgeable about computers than their teachers.
Few people will admit the extent to which these kids are exploited
– asked to fix the school's computers, install new programs,
unscramble applications, and revive crashed systems. Every high
school has at least one student who acts as a high-tech technician,
not paid and often not present in his classes because he (and
usually it is a boy) is on duty in another classroom. Business offices
routinely train and assign technical-support people, but schools
with many more computers (and more mischievous users) rarely
have access to trained adult technicians. Teachers who know
enough to fix computers also know enough to keep their knowledge to themselves.

ACOT admitted no problems when it came to using students to

fill roles adults should be expected to play. The only role-shift problem the final report acknowledged was "teacher insecurity." "As teachers became less threatened by some students' exceptional abilities on the computer, they reframed their views about teacher roles and used these students as peer teachers. . . . The teachers themselves drew upon these students' expertise when problems occurred."[56]

Similar references to peer teaching appear frequently throughout the report. ACOT calls it student empowerment, and cites many examples of students' expert technical knowledge being used by other students and teachers. Without doubt, students will find the occasional opportunity to be the teacher a positive experience. On the other hand, most experienced teachers (and some annoyed parents) will admit that certain kids are exploited because they possess skills that are in all-too-short supply in the classroom. Bright and dependable students are routinely recruited to become assistant teachers starting in kindergarten. Athletically talented kids are called on to demonstrate the new skill or organize the tournament. Kids with good social skills are recruited as peer helpers. Reliable kids become crossing guards. The list is endless.

ACOT teacher Mr. Erikson used his student Sam to help him screen every computerized test to see if it was well designed, since Sam knew how kids could "beat the test." Did Mr. Erikson have an assessment problem, a technology problem, or a problem with his students' honesty? Did Sam have a problem? Teachers seemed to think Sam and his ilk presented only solutions. Frieda was called on to produce the class newsletter and to teach others how to help; in no time at all, the kids were also "instructing younger students, administrators, retired community members, non-ACOT teachers . . . and even substitute teachers." Students began offering formal in-service programs to teachers, and community firms hired them as technology consultants.

The tool of technology was changing roles and behaviours, and soon teachers were giving technology the credit for every positive event in ACOT classrooms: "Rather than sitting quietly and waiting for their teacher to help them . . . students began to take the

initiative and ask each other for assistance or volunteer information to one another." According to the authors, "This sudden
increase in peer interaction disturbed teachers, such as Mrs.
Bennet (fifth grade), who were accustomed to children raising
their hands for permission to speak or leave their seats."

No doubt there are still some Mrs. Bennets in charge of Grade
5 classrooms, but they are far outnumbered by their colleagues
who abandoned the role of prison warden some time ago. Kids do
not need high technology to ask for or offer help – all they need
is permission. In an amusing British study, a researcher followed up
on claims that computer use fostered "joint authorship" and "collaboration" among young writers. He gave two students one piece
of paper and one pencil to share. They also collaborated. Not only
were their written products of equal quality to those that were
word-processed, but the students spent more time on content and
much less on formatting. Furthermore, no "mouse-wars" ensued.

The students who were writing with computers may have been
having more fun, particularly when it came to getting their
product ready for display. For the adept, learning *how* is a thrill-a-
minute dazzle, much more exciting than the less spectacular work
of learning *why* and *whether*. The attraction of technique is closely
associated with the merging of education and entertainment: the
edu-tainment industry rests on disguising shaky content with
colourful images, hectic motion, and upbeat music. Activities that
kids might consider boring on worksheets take on a new appeal
when they turn up on an interactive videodisk. The bells and
whistles disguise the content, which can be equally pointless in
any medium.

The future of the edu-tainment industry depends on convincing adults that all learning can and should be fun. Here, adults are
a step behind their children, most of whom already believe that
anything not fun is close to worthless. Clifford Stoll (author of
the techno-critical book, *Silicon Snake Oil*) says this is one of the
reasons why kids "love computers and multimedia. They'll sit
there and click on icons for hours. . . . They love this precisely

because they don't have to work. . . . It's a terrific way to avoid learning in the same way that filmstrips and educational movies were. . . ."[57]

Theodore Roszak says playing around with the computer is fun, all right, but that "learning is another kind of fun, often related to long intervals of dogged attention, persistent questioning, strong doubt, memorizing things, looking things up, being bored, over-coming frustration. Games and learning have their own kind of joy. Confusing the two is the worst lesson to teach kids."[58]

In defence of students, we should note that the number of adults who pursue learning for its own sake may be rather small. Even Prime Minister Chrétien, speaking to students at the Ottawa launch of Cable in the Classroom, a project designed to give class-rooms greater access to television broadcasts, recognized the greater appeal of entertainment over work: "I wish we had these things when I was a student," he said, pointing to the television monitors. "If we had a system like that, and having the teacher to shut up, it would have been great."[59]

Computer-based edu-tainment may control not just what our kids think about, but how they think. Print-based media stamp us with their linear and sequential orientation. We apply this one-thing-at-a-time rule not only to reading, but to how we operate in the real world. Our linearity shows up in everything, from how we lay out city streets to how we follow recipes. With the horizontal skip-and-click of videogames or searches on the Net, it is entirely possible that new cultural and neural pathways are being laid down in computer-users. Try convincing a child to read the instruction manual that comes with a new videogame – he or she undoubtedly prefers trial-and-error, a method that better suits computer-based learning. Reboot, undo, delete, and escape pro-vide consequence-free opportunities to recover from mistakes. Intuition, risk-taking, a good memory, and quick reflexes lead to the mastery of videogames and new computer applications. The cautious linearity of logic is not only of little value in manipulat-ing technology, it is a hindrance.

Robert Bly, who writes about how adults have abandoned their responsibilities to children, claims that overexposure to entertainment-based technology is toxic in other ways. "TV was the mental thalidomide of earlier decades, and multimedia computers are the thalidomides of the 1990's," writes Bly.[60] Brain function specialist Sherry Dingman explains the physiological basis for Bly's concern: multimedia technology is filtered through the receptive, emotive right brain, not the more analytical and critical left brain that processes print.[61] Parents who have seen their otherwise alert toddlers mesmerized in front of a television screen, slack-jawed and blank-faced, have witnessed the left brain on vacation. Parents who have seen their children choose TV or Nintendo over playing with a real person have also witnessed a shift. They are watching the tool change the user.

The Tool Shapes Its Users – Part II: Teachers

Teachers are the other IT tool-users in schools. Computers change not only how individual teachers see themselves and what they do, but how the educational system is redefining their role by valuing some skills over others. The ACOT research suggests that the overlay of technology on what had been people-rich rather than technology-rich classrooms changed teachers' relationships with their students more than anything else. Skewing relationships means skewing the very guts of education.

Stanford educator Larry Cuban emphasizes what every teacher knows: classrooms are built around relationships, and they aren't important only to students. "The touches, smiles, warmth, and even the frowns, annoyance and anger that pass between teacher and student cement ties that deepen learning and give gratification to teachers."[62] Cuban warns that computer-dominated classrooms dry up this emotional life by unravelling the bonds between teachers and students, and creating false liaisons between students and machines.

Ironically, at the onset of the ACOT project, newly recruited teachers feared that their computer-crowded classrooms would become technology-centred, just as many critics had warned. But halfway through the project, these same teachers claimed that despite (or, from Apple's perspective, because of) an overwhelming array of technology, the classroom actually became more student-centred. ACOT's final report presents the statements of two ACOT teachers as evidence of the primacy of students over technology. Said one, "That computer has become so much a part of my body that I just don't seem to be able to work without it."[63] The second told a story: "The power was not working in our classroom, and we had no computers. But the class had to go on. We had to go back to the good old days of pencil and paper. . . . I had the feeling I was in a different classroom, and I didn't like that classroom."

Weren't the students still there, even in the absence of technology? How could anyone deny that these classrooms (and teachers, and perhaps students) had become technocentric when one teacher said he couldn't work with students in the absence of his digitized body part, and the other didn't like her classroom when there were only people present?

In ACOT classrooms, the drama of the interpersonal adventures of childhood and adolescence either disappeared or were considered irrelevant to the story of so-called student-centred classrooms. The reports give no stories of children with problems at home, of playground bullies or sick grandmothers, or even shared laughter and practical jokes. The "ethic of care" that bonds teachers and students either didn't exist, or wasn't seen or valued by ACOT researchers.

The ACOT teachers assumed a distant, third-party way of talking about the emotional life of their classrooms. After commenting on students who were "ecstatic" and "absolutely beside themselves," one teacher reflected: "Their enthusiasm is well worth the effort it has taken to set up a file server." For ACOT teachers, frustration appeared to shift from intractable students to intractable printers. Success became technical mastery: "I have already solved a problem that the district technician could not solve!" said one proudly. Dreams centred on adding yet more technology: "It just seems that what you've got is never enough."

Computers became the classroom focus. When the tool shapes the task, the tool itself becomes the goal. Tool-users bend to new specifications, seeing themselves and others in terms of how they relate to the tool. As students became unpaid teacher-technicians (and unpaid Apple advertisers), ACOT teachers changed too. "I find myself being more of a facilitator," said one teacher. "I am sure that I will change even more as I learn new techniques." This teacher seemed content in her new role as facilitator rather than teacher, but by definition, a facilitator is neutral, unbiased, not critical. A classroom without a critically engaged teacher is just as unhealthy as a family in which parents practise benign neglect. When she predicted that techniques would determine the teacher she would become, she was admitting that the tool was taking over.

Some see the increased technical sophistication of teachers as pure progress, a role-shift wrapped up in words such as *empowerment*. But like other post-modern euphemisms (downsizing, re-engineering), *empowerment through technology* hides diminishment and deskilling. It has become fashionable to speak of redefining the work of teachers, but the greater the role of technology, the more likely that even the label will be discarded. Says Michael Master, co-founder of a techno-centred "non-profit private school" in Vancouver, "We don't even call our teachers 'teachers.' We call them 'learning consultants.'"

Perhaps ACOT teachers would like this label. The reports give little evidence that they objected to how technology had changed them or their classroom activities. One teacher did leave the program early, citing classroom management as her chief concern. We could easily speculate that ACOT researchers suppressed or failed to report the opposition of the other teachers, or that Apple teachers, having volunteered for the project, were different from typical teachers.

Yet their enthusiasm could be entirely authentic. Teachers' alleged resistance to technology tends to be practical rather than philosophical. Lots of teachers like lots of technology; those who don't tend to think they should. Given the kind of technical

IF LIFE IN THE classroom was serene for ACOT teachers, was it the technology or was it the rarefied environment? At West High School, "widely reported as the most successful ACOT site," nine teachers worked with just 120 high school students. These teachers enjoyed a full half day, every day, for co-operative planning (i.e., prep time), and they were excused from all other non-instructional duties. These ACOT teachers spent additional days, all expenses paid, pursuing professional development that explored constructivist teaching and learning.

Source: "Technology and Education Reform," U.S. government Web site

support and unlimited resources that the ACOT teachers enjoyed, practical problems became much more manageable.

Those few teachers who might want to protest technology on principle risk being dismissed as Luddites. For teachers to join the pro-tech forces may be merely sensible, given the real world in which they are trained, selected, and evaluated – and not just by adults. A survey of one group of Canadian high school students found them "unforgiving about the apparent lack of computer expertise their teachers possessed. Many students openly scorned teachers for the fact that they did not know how to use a computer."[64]

The Council of Ministers of Education appears to be similarly scornful: it claims that teachers' resistance is caused by age or motivated by self-interest, not generated by any substantive critique. Like frightened children, teachers require reassurance. The CMEC's statement on technology in Canada's schools tells the rest of the Commonwealth that "many teachers do not embrace the new technologies, and are sceptical of their application in the classroom. The fact that there is an aging teacher cohort exacerbates the problem. . . . Ways must be found to ease their anxieties, assuring them that the role of the teacher is still an important one."[65]

Teachers who avoid or speak ill of computers therefore risk being seen as showing their age or covering up their own inadequacies or even committing heresy. One Ontario teacher told me that the day after she had expressed reservations about spending community-raised funds on new computers, she was summoned to her principal's office, tongue-lashed, and told to write a letter of apology to the parent council, recanting her low-tech biases. Compulsory enthusiasm silences teachers, but something else is also at work.

In their study of teacher and student attitudes towards computer literacy in two Canadian high schools, Ivor Goodson and Marshall Mangan found that both groups had "taken the ideology of computer literacy at face value."[66] This observation is hardly surprising, since the Ontario Ministry of Education defined the term in 1984 as a means to "develop in the general population some degree of psychological 'comfort' with and acceptance of the new technology and the need to apply it."[67] The deputy minister of the day talked about "attitudinal conditioning" as one of the purposes of computers in schools – making the use of the expression "ideology of computer literacy" hardly excessive. (Today's CMEC doesn't call it attitudinal conditioning, but "developing comfort through training.")[68]

Only one teacher in Goodson and Mangan's study – Mr. Harvey – expressed any reservations: "I don't care about this age of computers and everything else, I – excuse me for being old-fashioned – but a student should be able to sit down and write. . . . They should be able to communicate," he said. Nonetheless, in the same interview, Mr. Harvey talked about how he should learn to use spreadsheets: "They sort of grabbed me, and I'm really weak on that. It took me – when I was practising – a long, long time, but I just haven't worked at it, and I've just gotta, next fall, buckle down and start – start doing it. . . ." Such contradictions led the researchers to conclude that some teachers believe expressing their opinions might be not only politically unwise, but professionally illegitimate. More post-modern Pogo than Luddite, Mr. Harvey identified himself as the problem, someone in need of remedial attitudinal conditioning along with a new spreadsheet program. Whatever confidence Mr. Harvey may have had in his other skills, he was beginning to evaluate himself in terms of how he used machines.

Once the Tool Shapes the Task and the Tool-Users, It Takes Over

One of the commandments of techno-worship is that if it can be done (profitably), it should be done – the technological imperative, revised version. Why employ bank tellers when we can have money machines on every corner? Why deprive ourselves of state-of-the-art military helicopters in times of peace? Why pick up the phone when we can use e-mail? These techno-driven decisions, of course, have both intended and unintended consequences. We forgo jobs, other ways of spending public money, and different kinds of relationships, not just because of the profit or convenience involved, but because we get pulled into a vortex of techno-inevitability driven by profit. No self-respecting corporation that wants to be seen as competitive can afford not to have a Web page (even if it has never generated a sale), any more than self-respecting parents can afford not to buy their child a computer (even if it is hardly ever used). No school system would think of promoting itself without a photo of a child facing a computer on the cover of its annual report.

At work, at home, and at school, once we have the technology, we become obliged to use it, seeing new applications to justify either our enthusiasm or our expenditure. We begin to interpret both problems and solutions in terms of technology. Is interest in elections fading? Start electronic discussion groups. Is the economy faltering? Invest in the high-tech sector. If education has a problem, then technology must be the solution.

No discussion of education reform in North America is complete without an obligatory mention of three gaps: the achievement gap between the children of the wealthy and the poor; the gap between "good" kids and "other people's" kids; and the gap between what our children know and what the children of the

THERE IS MOUNTING evidence that studying the arts, especially music, enhances students' ability to learn. California researchers have determined that listening to Mozart before exams boosts performance; they call it "The Mozart Effect." A news item reported that preschoolers who had music instruction scored 34 per cent higher on tests of "temporal-spatial reasoning" than their classmates who were only exposed to "computer training." Quick to frame their findings in terms of today's priorities, the researchers claimed that "even those headed for a career involving computers would probably be better off with art instruction in school."

Source: Globe and Mail, November 17, 1997

Asian tigers know. Not surprisingly, technology (the lack of it) is the culprit in all cases. Also not surprisingly, technology (more of it) is the solution each time – the specifics vary only by the source of the software.

Microsoft proposes closing these gaps by ensuring twenty-four-hour-a-day access to technology. Through Anytime Anywhere Learning, Microsoft's flagship education initiative, students still in primary school lug laptops loaded with "Microsoft Office Professional and other productivity software to help prepare [them] for the work force."[69] The pitch is persuasive. Microsoft's press release boasts that after young Jacobo got his own laptop computer to use as his "personal learning tool," his attitude was "transformed." As a computer have-not, this Grade 5 student "wasn't interested in school, didn't want to do his homework and wouldn't work collaboratively." But now that he can learn anytime, anywhere, Jacobo "does all his homework and classwork, loves working in groups and goes out of his way to be helpful to other students."

With such miraculous turnarounds just a Toshiba laptop away, who could resist Anytime Anywhere Learning? The choice of the portable computer may backfire, however, since the 90,000 New York City youngsters who do without desks are also without laps. Ontario is more fortunate when it comes to desks, and may therefore beat New York to the punch. In its report, Minister Snobelen's "Round Table on Technology in Learning," which concluded that schools were no longer necessary, states, "The Ontario school system, and its graduates, will arrive and transform Ontario into an information-based economy with the new 'Microsoft' of 2005. . . . Learners will learn at their own pace, anytime, anywhere."[70]

It comes down to priorities. Microsoft boasts that it has helped convince even poor parents that the investment in computers is worth it: "In New York City's Community District 6, where more than 90% of the students live below the poverty line, parents share the leasing costs for the laptops with the school district." Interest from other districts has picked up since the federal government gave schools permission to use Title I funds (earmarked for programs for the most disadvantaged students) to buy the computers.

Even when loaded up with technology (although, perhaps, still light on breakfast and somewhere to sit), these students still do not seem to be taking either childhood or their schoolwork seriously enough. Perhaps the problem lies with the teachers. IBM's "efforts in philanthropy," as described on its Web site, include a $2 million grant to develop an application that gives school administrators the tools to assemble "easy-to-read portraits of educational problems": "An elementary school, for example, can call up a list of 4th graders who were taught by a specific 3rd grade teacher."[71]

If the problem doesn't lie with the teachers, perhaps we can blame it on the decline in family values. ACOT's cyber-evangelist David Dwyer likes to cite a Carnegie Council warning that "half of America's children engage in behaviours that place them in serious risk of alienation, even of death." These are children who recognize "that they are not wanted and are of little value in this society. Technology is the only vehicle we may ride as we work to engage more children in the excitement and life-enhancing experience of learning."[72]

Having dealt with the poverty and alienation gaps, technology must tackle an even more serious problem: international competitiveness. During his 1997 state of the union address, Clinton invoked the "bipartisan foreign policy" that was "the greatest source of strength throughout the Cold War," and called for politicians to take on a new "critical national security issue": connecting every school to the Internet. "But we cannot stop there," the president warned. "As the Internet becomes our new town square, a computer in every home – a teacher of all subjects, a connection to all cultures – this will no longer be a dream, but a necessity. . . . Every eight-year-old must be able to read; every 12-year-old must be able to log on to the Internet."[73] Clinton went on to talk about the democratizing effects of trade with Asia, and the need for free trade agreements to ensure fair competition with emerging economies such as South Korea. He also declared that standards, testing, and technology would make American students "first in the world."

The president is playing catch-up. Canada's efforts to connect every school to the information highway by the end of 1997 were only somewhat behind schedule, thanks to what the CMEC calls "collaborative partnerships with the private sector"[74] – meaning computer, telephone, and cable companies. If the Internet is going to help students vault to the performance levels of South Korean students, it had better come with an unlimited-use contract. According to two American educators working in South Korea, Thomas Ellinger and Garry Beckham, student success comes at a high price. High school students attend classes from eight A.M. to four P.M., but they return to study hall for four hours during the evening. Afterwards, they watch educational television or continue to do homework until midnight. Other students attend evening hak gwan – private institutes where they can receive supplementary academic lessons. Yet the international gap consists of more than just the hours these students put in. According to Ellinger and Beckham, "South Koreans view education as they view the rest of life: a process of winning and losing."

Where do the Korean students learn this approach? The Korean mother and corporal punishment make the difference. "Mother ensures every moment of a child's life, from preschool on, is scheduled; she ensures her older children get no more than four hours of sleep a night by reminding them that while they sleep, others are studying."[75] Both the school and the home use corporal punishment. Ellinger and Beckham write that according to the Korean Protection Agency, 97 per cent of children have been beaten. The most common offence is fighting with siblings; the second most common is not studying hard enough.[76]

Most Canadians probably have no desire to replicate the political, economic, or educational characteristics of South Korea, nor do many of us wish to trade school systems with the United States. We've become convinced that closing the education gaps will require no sacrifice, no societal change, no reordering of our priorities, and no public investment – only technology. We fail to see schools as organic parts of a nation's culture. Technology has been sold as an enlightened, inexpensive, and surprise-free tool that can lift students to personal excellence, moral certitude, and international competitiveness at the same time. The promise has all the credibility of a time-share brochure, and much of it is written in the same language.

One of the more troubling parts of the ACOT report is its foreword, written by Larry Cuban, a highly respected Stanford professor who has previously written very critical essays on technology in schools. His apparent defection to the Apple camp will buy the ACOT project – or, more precisely, Apple Computer – exactly the kind of professional credibility it has been looking for. In 1996, Cuban ridiculed America's Netday (hooking schools to the Internet) as "another fantasy" foisted on schools by those who worship access to information. Cuban had destroyed the suggestion that computers in schools would lead to good jobs. He had warned that "virtual experiences making the fake more compelling than the real" was just one of the many unintended, negative effects of computers in schools.

Yet, in his ACOT foreword, Cuban now writes that the lessons learned from ACOT are "straight-forward and mundane, but powerful." He gives no indication that he has ever visited an ACOT classroom or independently evaluated ACOT's claims. Nevertheless, says Cuban, "No reform-minded technophile, after reading this book, can ignore these important findings. No sceptic, after reading this book, can ignore the solid evidence [of] lasting change in teaching practices – the Holy Grail sought by reformers."

If Cuban wants to employ clichés about the cost of chasing myth-imbued objects at any expense, he's certainly entitled to do so. However, he invites us to consider a few other clichés: pig in a poke, Trojan horse, Pandora's box.

And let's not forget another old saw: He who pays the piper calls the tune.

5

EQUITY@ED.COM

Upgrading Reality

"2000-Plus" is a series of techno-boosting fillers that airs twice daily on CTV network stations. Most are gee-whiz in tone; all feature technology in a starring role. Will we survive the year 2000 turnover? See how women can overcome years of wage discrimination and patriarchy by accessing investment advice on-line! "Closetware" and its promises began airing in 1995.

VOICEOVER: They call it Closetware! More than a million discarded Canadian computers are being dusted off and put back to work helping children to learn – and may reduce school drop-outs, juvenile crime, and even unwanted pregnancies.

The ideal is one computer for ten pupils, but we can afford only one for twenty. So volunteers are drumming up donations.

Computer literacy has become the fourth R of education and if you don't have the basic skills you're in grave danger of becoming one of the world's have-nots. . . .

More important, the computer is emerging as social worker. In New York inner-city schools, 125 semi-literate "high-risk" juveniles were given computers to use at home:

GIRL'S VOICE: I get higher grades because I use a computer and printer.

VOICEOVER: Three years later the average drop-out rate was 51 per cent, but over 90 per cent of computer kids sailed on to high school.

In Dallas they opened computer rooms in housing projects and school grades soared while crime dropped. And at this Toronto home for unwed mothers, the computer may provide new skills and interests that reduce the risk of return visits.

GIRL'S VOICE: I can do something in the future, like typing.

CO-ORDINATOR: Using computers really helps. It gives them opportunities for success in the sense that they're in control.

VOICEOVER: Recycling technology is a new philanthropy. . . . yesterday's technology is now helping build tomorrow.[1]

The claims of "Closetware" – that drop-out rates, crime, and unwanted pregnancy can be reduced by sending broken, outdated computers to schools – rest on the teenaged mother's shaky dream: "I can do something in the future, like typing." This young woman, her parents, her teachers, her school system's trustees, and the employers who won't hire her have all been seduced by the same messages, not just about technology, but about the role of education.

Like all scams, this one has a purpose: to deflect and redirect blame. Rather than blaming those who control our economy for the lack of meaningful work and the sad lives of these kids, we are told to focus on the young people's relationship with technology. Instead of asking ourselves about technology's role in creating an underclass of the unemployed and the disengaged, we are invited to blame the victim for not being computer literate. We are informed that the only way schools could help would be by reducing the student-computer ratio, but we are told that we can't afford this cure-all, at least for poor kids.

Instead of asking how education might diminish the distance between those who live in the different quarters of the global city, or better yet, asking how we can challenge city hall, we are asking our schools to fall in line. Perhaps the most profound consequence of technopoly's appropriation of education is that the next generation will learn to blame themselves for being disenfranchised, for having missed opportunities that supposedly are there for the taking.

"Closetware" was retired from the 1997 CTV line-up, not because its propaganda had become stale, or because girls still became pregnant even after the Canadian student-computer ratio dropped below ten to one, but because recycling low-end computers no longer created a buzz. This idea had limited philanthropic or educational value, and even less economic value – the tax write-off for an old computer is hardly worth the effort. Besides, only new computers have enough power to access the new wave of edu-tech – the Internet. And equity has been upgraded.

The On-Ramp to Equity

Much of the money being spent on educational technology is destined for the Internet and the industries behind it. Propelled by the media, politicians, and the info-barons, the drive to connect everything in sight to the information highway – including toasters, Coke machines, and laptop-toting students – seems unstoppable. Canadian info-culture critic Marita Moll points out that the manufactured education crisis created by corporate America provided an excuse and an opportunity for bold initiatives with big payoffs. Even before it was built, the information highway furnished American politicians with a value-added response to education's critics, one that would return political favours to the powerful telecommunications lobby at the same time.

The command for connectivity was issued from the highest level, writes Moll:

In January 1994, U.S. Vice-President Al Gore issued the challenge to connect all schools, hospitals and libraries to the information highway by the year 2000. But his speech was not about schools, hospitals or libraries. It was about competition between the telephone and cable industries and about the Clinton administration's political commitment to "clear from the road the wreckage of outdated regulations and allow a free-flowing traffic of ideas and commerce for the benefit of all Americans," as Al Gore put it.

American-based communications and information industries yearned for an ever-widening dissemination of the American dream through an information highway as ubiquitous as the television set, but now ready to take order for everything from blue chip stocks to running shoes. The strategically- placed nod to schools provided the appearance of public benefit, while regulations designed to maintain some public presence in the vital communications and information sector were being dismantled.[2]

The payoff would be hidden in the promised benefits to "every child."

Neither Gore's challenge nor Bill Clinton's ode to technology in his 1996 state of the union address provoked much in the way of protest from either the Right or the Left. Polls found cross-party support for any candidate who would promise to make computers and information technology in schools a top priority.[3] The Right was happy with deregulation and new business opportunities. The Left heard the part that was ostensibly pro-child, and in general, the American (and international) Left welcomes information technology as either an apolitical tool or a blessing. When the president pledged that "by twelve years of age, every American student will be able to log on to the Internet" – a skill of modest proportions but huge business implications – America applauded.

The U.S. Telecommunications Act of 1996 eliminated the roadblock of regulations that Gore deplored. No longer publicly owned and funded, the Internet infrastructure became a for-profit venture, and traffic became mainly commercial. Writes Moll, "The Net was suddenly the hot advertising medium of the new millennium. Its interactive features are guaranteed to entice, cajole, manipulate and plug directly into the personal data stream of a new generation of consumers."[4] The Net's commercialism has not diminished support for it as an appropriate, even essential, medium for education's content. Nor has the inevitability of steeply increasing user fees curbed enthusiasm. If schools became hooked *on* the Net, as well as hooked up, the tollbooth would become a money machine, financing the expansionist business plans of the communications transnationals. But the whole scheme would depend on convincing the right people that schools should – must – get connected.

SchoolNet Scores

Just as Al Gore was pitching connectivity in the United States, Industry Canada's Science Promotion Directorate was spinning off a little-known product called SchoolNet. As the corporate wing of the federal government, Industry Canada must make sure that the competitive global marketplace is kept front and centre in policy considerations of all types. It set up SchoolNet to ensure that education was onside by providing "Canadian students and teachers with exciting electronic services that would stimulate and develop the skills needed in the knowledge society."[5]

Captivated by the rhetoric of job creation in knowledge-based (etc., etc.) economies, or perhaps by political opportunism, the federal government saw in SchoolNet the synergistic promotion of science and technology, jobs, growth, payoffs to the information and communications industries, and cutting-edge links to the provincially guarded education sector. All these benefits would be accomplished by linking 16,500 schools, libraries, hospitals, and universities to the Internet and each other.

SchoolNet was to be guided by an advisory board that represented public education's stakeholders and industry experts, along with the usual cast of interest groups to ensure equity and access were not overlooked. SchoolNet had attracted a likely set of

MICROSOFT'S BILL GATES likes the way we do business in
Canada. Visiting Ottawa as part of his Windows 95 tour, Gates
was enthusiastic: "It's very exciting to see what's going on here.
... SchoolNet is the leading program in the world in terms of
letting kids get out and use computers." His words reappeared
in the Liberal Red Book II, 1997.
Source: Ottawa Citizen, November 26, 1995

corporate partners too, including Stentor (the alliance of Canada's
largest telephone companies) and Unitel, and both helped
promote the idea that hooking schools up to the fledgling information highway was an inspired use of public dollars. It was only
a coincidence, they implied, that such a scheme dovetailed so perfectly with their business plans.

The telephone companies, which together control an $800
billion long-distance carrier market, are increasingly important
players in determining domestic communications policy. The
globalized world without borders has immense appeal to communications transnationals. They demand recognition of their right
to manage the movement of knowledge in the knowledge society.[6]
Obviously, the more that knowledge depends on their systems,
the more that these companies will enhance their profits, but the
Canadian market and psyche are both too small to accommodate
their ambitions. The deregulation of markets and the disconnec-
tion of communications from public policy are key goals of the
telecommunications lobby. Its interest in education is only a
subset of these objectives. Our schools may end up connected, all
right, but to corporations that hardly consider Canadian content
a priority. SchoolNet launched its Stentor/Unitel-funded public
relations campaign by asking, "Is *your* school connected?" Marita
Moll asks, "Connected to what?"

Furthermore, we should inquire, at what cost? Since 1993,
Industry Canada has spent between $25 and $35 million on
SchoolNet, all the while insisting the project is not a government

operation, but a new-wave public-private partnership. According to Doug Hull, the Industry Canada bureaucrat in charge of SchoolNet, nobody did the math. "To my knowledge," says Hull, "no one has ever sat down and calculated what it would mean [in dollars] for all schools to get connected."[7]

Digging Deep

SchoolNet is not the only black hole in the edu-tech accounting department. Have we spent hundreds of millions? Certainly. Billions? Without question. Yet there are no published data that document how much money provincial ministries and school boards have spent on technology during the last decade, no record of what amount is currently set aside, no real indication of how much will be spent from their increasingly limited budgets in the following years. In a harsh climate of fiscal accountability for schools, this careless accounting is a truly bizarre anomaly. There is also no record of how much hardware and software parents have bought in a frantic attempt to keep up.

No matter how much we spend, it seems we will never be spending enough. In a widely quoted American study, Henry Jay Becker concludes that the "exemplary" use of computers requires class sizes reduced to twenty, approximately $1,000 (U.S.) per pupil per year for extra personnel and support costs, and a further $500 (U.S.) to fund hardware and maintenance costs.[8] If he is right, the "exemplary" use of technology would eat up at least one-third of every education budget every year. "Poor" use would cost less, of course, but only in dollars.

Yet Canadian schools staggering to absorb cuts of $928 million in 1996–97 alone, and anticipating perhaps twice this amount in 1997–98, can't spend more on technology without making deep cuts to other programs. These programs (and the students who would have benefited from them) are techno-casualties, but no public accounting system measures the opportunity costs – the acquisitions of people and resources forgone to spare technology budgets. In per-student spending among the sixty-three jurisdictions of the United States and Canada, our ten provinces

THE RAND IS AN important American research centre/think-
tank that regularly advises government on public policy. Its
report entitled "Fostering the Use of Educational Technology"
is predictably pro-tech, but it does point out that investing in
ample technology for each school may cause "significant and
potentially painful restructuring of school budgets." RAND says
that the obvious solution is "reallocation" – in other words,
cutting other parts of the budget in order to pay for the computers. However, it notes that convincing communities to
"reallocate" has proven to be very difficult. Government, RAND
concludes, should sweeten the rhetorical pot: "Such reallocation will be possible only if the public and the educational
community come to feel that technology is essential to
meeting their objectives for student learning. Information
about and demonstration of the importance of technology are
critical to continued growth in technology's use."

rank from thirty-ninth (Quebec) to sixty-third (Prince Edward
Island).[9] Technology purchases are no longer an add-on, but an
instead-of.

The dearth of information on how much our techno-projects
cost is without doubt deliberate. The Canadian public has repeatedly told pollsters and politicians that spending on computers is
far down on its list of priorities. In 1996, only 10 per cent of the
Canadian public thought that "more computers in the classroom"
should be their priority for spending any new education dollars. By
1997, although support for funding more technology had risen to
15.5 per cent, almost twice as many Canadians preferred to see
class sizes reduced.[10] This poll is of particular interest because of
the marked regional variations it found: in British Columbia,
where the 1997 economy was doing well and unemployment was
relatively low, only 6.3 per cent would make the purchase of more
computers an education priority, but in Atlantic Canada, still
deep in recession, 24.4 per cent of those polled chose this option.

Surely, Atlantic Canadians could be rescued from joblessness and poverty through computers!

Even people who thought more computers should be in the classroom didn't necessarily see the value of connecting them to the Internet. The announcement of SchoolNet's ambitious plan to connect every school created very little enthusiasm. As Marita Moll notes, "In late 1993, very few schools had ever heard of such electronic services, let alone tried to connect them." Given the public's general reluctance to see computers as the solution – especially when most people continue to doubt that schools have any overwhelming problems to solve in the first place – the government would have to work hard to sell SchoolNet and everything it represented. The Vector poll served up some broad hints: if technology could be linked to employability, perhaps the public could be persuaded to reallocate education spending.

A 1997 SURVEY OF six thousand computer co-ordinators, librarians, and teachers in American schools found that 87 per cent believe the Internet has no beneficial effect on classroom performance from third grade through twelfth. However, in another recent American poll, teachers ranked computer skills and media technology as more "essential" than European history, biology, chemistry, and physics.

Source: Todd Openheimer, *Atlantic Monthly*, July 1997

Other players were called in to impress upon schools their opportunity and responsibility. The Information Highway Advisory Council (IHAC), mostly hand-picked Industry Canada advisors drawn from the upper ranks of the communications and information technology industries, obliged by claiming, *without a shred of evidence*, that using the information highway in the classroom "would result in an immediate improvement in the high-school drop-out rate leading to savings in the order of $16 billion by the year 2000."[11] The Telelearning Research Network received 13 million federal dollars "to figure out how technology can be designed to transform Canadian students into hooked-in, lifelong learners."[12] Adding the stick to the carrot, a techno-insert in the *Globe and Mail* warned that "everyone within the education system has to be made to realize the importance of . . . the Highway. What is needed is a major mind shift."[13]

Making Minds Shift

Although SchoolNet began as a connectivity project, it gradually acquired the pretensions of an on-line content provider. Yet aside from a handful of teacher- and student-designed units that offer little competition to the commercial curriculum available on-line, the content is thin. Even *Canadian Business* magazine's *Technology Quarterly*, an unlikely critic, concludes that there's more spin than substance to SchoolNet.[14]

Writer George Emerson found the chemistry news group short on equations but long on "chain letter come-ons, pyramid schemes, and offers for dubious services." Another SchoolNet user group posted a message from two hard-working college students: "We are real live sluty [*sic*] little whores who just cannot get enough." It isn't news, of course, that chat groups encourage libidinous conversations. Indeed, most concerns about children's access to the Net focus on this point.

Some people – but perhaps not the editors of *Technology Quarterly* – find SchoolNet content problematic for other reasons. SchoolNet has become a handy publicly funded vehicle for corporate propaganda, for pitching in the guise of learning opportunities not just products, but corporate-friendly ways of seeing the world.

When the SchoolNet menu brings up half a dozen main categories, click on Business and Economics. Then (beside a Canadian flag icon) find "Global Vision's Global Classroom." (Some market-segment analyst must have reported that adolescents identify with the word *global* – but twice in a four-word phrase?) The global classroom turns out to be a corporate training centre, dedicated to "giving tomorrow's business leaders a solid understanding of the marketplace." The site is sponsored by "a non-profit organization dedicated to helping shape today's youth through science,

A BACK-PAGE ITEM in the *Ottawa Citizen* says it all: "Teen-aged students come face to face with Destiny." Destiny 2000 is an Ottawa high-tech trade show that has adjusted its target audience from Grade 9 students down to Grade 7. "It seems to be a good age to influence them," the organizer states. High-tech companies say their aim is "to cultivate a crop of high-tech labour" by courting twelve- and thirteen-year-olds. Participating school boards say their objective is not to force all students "into scientific or purely technical careers." Other jobs will require "at least an appreciation of science and technology . . . such as marketing." That's Destiny.

Source: *Ottawa Citizen*, May 14, 1997

technology, business and entrepreneurship." The "non-profit" board is made up of senior executives from Brascan, Laidlaw, Mitel, CIBC, Canadian Airlines, and Nova Gas, among others, who thank the Canadian taxpayer (via SchoolNet and Industry Canada) for assistance with their site and the opportunity to reach 3.9 million students.[15]

Here in the global classroom, students can find out how to win Global Vision's contest to become part of Junior Team Canada. As is only fitting in "Canada's Year of the Asia Pacific," winners will join other young entrepreneurs "acting as advocates for companies and institutions" while touring Indonesia, Malaysia, the Philippines, Singapore, and Thailand. To win the contest and make the team, kids enter their marketing plan to exploit emerging economies. To understand the cultures and economies of these countries better, click on the APEC economy-sponsored sites to read all about these harmonious, democratic, and human-rights-respecting regimes.

For further information, click on Partners, a list of corporations (and a few schools) proud to be part of Junior Team Canada. Click on A-wear and order a catalogue, confident that you will be purchasing clothing from a company "devoted to making individuals of all ages more a-wear," and to helping us "wake up to all that we have to offer ourselves, and asking the right questions."

Anyone astonished that the "neutral" tool of technology (and millions of SchoolNet tax dollars) is being used to promote APEC's agenda in our classrooms has not looked closely at SchoolNet's business plan. The plan expands on goals that go well beyond connectivity right to the heart of official knowledge: SchoolNet will "develop a positive image within Canada's corporate community. Through its sponsorship program, SchoolNet hopes to generate significant financial resources . . . and to sustain a mutually beneficial relationship with associated companies." Just under the win-win rhetoric comes the fine print of the SchoolNet Communications Plan.[16] This document identifies pressing issues, including how to ensure that provincial curricula are rewritten "to include a SchoolNet component" and how to "motivate educators to embrace the new technology."

"Media must be approached to convey the importance of information technology and the Electronic Highway to our school systems and to the redefined fundamentals of learning," School-Net is advised by its communications consultants. "Partnering must be further developed to match marketing forces to the target audience." Because competition for sponsorships is fierce, the report warns, SchoolNet must accept trade-offs and recognize that "objectives for sponsor and property are not always the same." In other words, when what students need conflicts with what sponsors want to push, the choice is obvious.

The SchoolNet advisory board trashed this 1995–96 communications plan, thanks to Marita Moll, who organized the revolt. Perhaps as a result, Industry Canada convened the board only once during the following two years, leaving the technocrats free to implement their campaign and to expand the marketing of their empire without having to answer to anyone unconnected to either the government or corporate interests. The new SchoolNet plan positions SchoolNet to leverage "virtual product" – otherwise known as on-line curriculum – that will be treated as an

TUCKED IN WITH the other back-to-school flyers that arrived with the daily newspaper in the fall of 1997 was one advertising "Computers 4 Kids." It told parents that "with a Patriot family computer available in your home, your children's creativity, intellectual growth and interest in learning will increase. ... The possibilities are endless." Each purchase would earn one point that could be donated to a school; fifteen points would net the school a new computer. What distinguished this pitch from the others was the signed endorsement from David Dingwall, then minister of health, who said the project "offers families, schools and businesses a creative way to help each other achieve their goals."

export commodity. SchoolNet/Industry Canada has already signed agreements with Mexico and New Zealand that "hold the promise of significant economic activity for Canadian Educational Software Firms," according to director Doug Hull.[17]

It was inevitable that the propaganda machine pushing the information highway as the tool to restructure education would claim a casualty. SchoolNet, Phase Two, no longer needed the pretence of public input, so the advisory board was officially disbanded in November 1997. "Retiring" board members will be replaced by what Hull calls the "can-do" types of the telecommunications industry. Questions about educational value and access have been tossed to the CMEC, along with a rumoured quarter of a million dollars.

Board members were dismissed with a letter and framed certificate of appreciation recognizing their "generous contribution, dedication, creativity and wisdom."[18] The letter thanks them for their efforts to "ensure all Canadian learners have access to the opportunities presented by the information highway and to ensure our youth is equipped with the skills they need to compete in the knowledge-based economy. The gains we have realized have helped schools, libraries and educators connect more quickly and make more objective use of the InterNet and, coincidentally made Canada's SchoolNet a world leader in educational networking."

Net Losses

The zeal of SchoolNet promoters and other investors in the Internet industry is understandable. No one expects Bill Gates to quote Theodore Roszak, who writes,

> The Internet is a free-for-all, as enjoyable as any conversation one might strike up in a saloon or coffee house. But it is hardly governed by the critical safeguards and intellectual structures that have been developed across the centuries to discriminate between honest thought and rampant eccentricity. Used as a teaching device the Web is an expensive way to distract attention and clutter the mind. . . . I'm not sure I understand why we should, at the behest of entrepreneurial elements, now decide to retire those skills in favour of 'Yahooligans.'[19]

A growing number of critics share Roszak's opinions on the relative worthlessness of the Net, but most of these dissenting voices see the information highway as tedious rather than toxic. A few hopeful activists on the Left still look to the Net to foster a cyber-populist democratic revival, believing the highway to be free from the elitist speedbumps of other media. Stewart Brand, editor of the *Whole Earth Catalog*, claimed in 1996 that "information technology has done what the New Left never actually accomplished, which is to give power to the people. . . . The Net is a gift economy. It is completely based on sharing rather than exchange," he told an international futurists' conference. "It works like gangbusters, and it's changing the world. . . . It's obviously good for education. . . . There is a globalizing that has come with information technology, which is also to the good."[20]

Maintaining the Net's populist glitter requires the simultaneous application of all the techno-commandments, with special attention to "Focus on the positive, and never count the cost." Early techno-enthusiasts such as Howard Rheingold, author of the 1993 bestseller *The Virtual Community: Homesteading on the Electronic Frontier*, saw and named the dangers, but talked himself out of them. Rheingold concluded that the Net would befriend progressives who sought equity and greater democracy, even though he admitted that community-friendly technologies were rare: "The odds are always good that big money and big power will find a way to control access. . . . [They've] always found ways to control new communications media when they emerged in the past."[21] History has repeated itself. It hasn't taken long for a gated community to spring up around Rheingold's homestead, complete with a corporate tollbooth policing access.

MICROSOFT TV COMMERCIALS ask, "Where do you want to go today?" Whatever your virtual destination, your passage will never be commercial-free. Bill Gates says it's an insignificant inconvenience, considering the benefits: "Citizens of the information society will enjoy new opportunities for productivity, learning and entertainment. . . . Whatever problems direct access to information may cause, the benefits it will bring will more than compensate."

Source: Bill Gates, *The Road Ahead*

Much as we are encouraged to believe that access to all that information is worth the price, the unregulated, indiscriminate nature of the Net makes it more suitable for entertainment than student research. Give a sophisticated researcher a few days on the Net to find out information on climate change, for instance, and thanks to skills he learned elsewhere – recognizing key sources, separating fact from opinion, identifying bias – he can produce a detailed and credible overview. Give the same assignment to a twelve-year-old with only a couple of hours of on-line time and undeveloped analytical skills, and her report is likely to be either a recapitulation of an on-line encyclopedic entry or a restatement of the points of view of Environment Canada, Friends of the

Earth, or even doomsday millennialists. The Net does nothing to help the student separate reputable sources from flaky ones, because it gives all information the same status, and all points of view the same legitimacy. For students already overwhelmed by information, greater access to more of it is compounding their problems, not solving them.

Couldn't we simply teach kids to sort out what is valuable from what is flashy or faulty? This task would be less difficult if adults showed a little more discernment and checked their own impulse to see all techno-possibilities as exciting learning opportunities. We gush better than we think. *For the Love of Learning*, the 1994 report of Ontario's Royal Commission on Learning, is long on examples intended to impress readers with the promise of technology, but short on thoughtfulness. Why is it so exciting that a classroom in one Ontario community is using computers to communicate with students in Kentucky, New Orleans, and Maryland? What are students saying in these communications? Why?

More to the point, at what cost? What else could they be doing with their minds, their time, and their school's resources? There is always a price. The report praises the technology initiatives of Lambton County schools, although the commissioners sincerely regret that Lambton's music program had to be sacrificed to get the system up and running. The commissioners hint that these trade-offs are inevitable as long as schools have to rely on public dollars. They contrast Lambton's sacrifice with the bounty of River Oaks school in Oakville, where technology-rich classrooms are "apparently made possible only through donations from the private sector." River Oaks has close ties to Apple. It was at this school, not in Lambton County, that the commissioners chose to release their report, the better to underscore the link between technology and partnerships.

True, technology both enables and demands new kinds of communication among partners as well as students. But what problem does this kind of communication seek to solve? In the report, one teacher tells how he has watched his students communicate

ONTARIO'S ROYAL COMMISSION on Learning claimed that its proposal to transform schools through technology was based on solid research. Yet one-fifth of the references that follow the commission's chapter on technology came from a single issue of *Educational Leadership*, an American magazine that contained only short articles chosen to promote the theme "realizing the promise of technology." Like most education magazines-cum-trade journals, *Educational Leadership* is subsidized almost entirely by advertisements paid for by the technology industry. When the commissioners conceded that "it is not entirely facetious to say that Sega and Nintendo are in control of our children's educational future," they might as easily have added, "and Apple and Microsoft are in control of the contents of this report."

enthusiastically by e-mail with students in Kuala Lumpur, taking part in the kind of activity that outsiders assume will develop students' appreciation of other cultures. His students enjoy this virtual contact, but they still avoid the real thing. The teacher notes that his students have shown no increased interest in their classmates who have themselves lived in other cultures – the "tribes" within the schools are as exclusive as ever. Should tribal hostility break out in the schoolyard, the school system will likely have found it too expensive to keep experts on staff to prevent and resolve this kind of conflict.

Net Worth

To pay for technology, governments have declared education experts of all kinds redundant – even though, ironically, access to expertise is one of the possibilities of technology that convinces us to swallow the price. It is nice to know that the author of a Grade 8 math text has offered to help students with their homework on-line – another example given in *The Love of Learning* –

but how many students will be helped and for how long? Have the international experts, who are supposedly available to teach and advise the world's billion children, signed unlimited use contracts?

Students may be stuck if they think NASA will be on call the night before their report is due. However, the Net does make other kinds of research easier. Research skills have taken on a new dimension, as students have learned how to access sites with names like "Cheat Factory" that advertise ready-made term papers on-line.[22] The term-paper factories are set up as mail-order businesses, able to customize papers on "Imagery in MacBeth" or churn out themes in any of forty categories. The price runs to ten dollars a page, although freebies, "including tips on how to cheat while taking an exam, and which porno Web sites are most entertaining," are thrown in at no charge. All major credit cards are accepted; delivery is guaranteed in two hours or less. One entrepreneurial Harvard freshman laughs it off: "Hey, if they are copying my 'MacBeth' papers and handing them in as is, they are in for a surprise when they get them back. They totally suck."

We may be tempted to dismiss such stories as the unavoidable but low-impact cost of Netting educational benefits. But our accommodation of Net-cheating provides another useful example of how the tool shapes the task. Technology's characteristics are shaping the curriculum itself, not just supporting how the curriculum is taught and learned. At universities, the rate of Web-cheating is rising so quickly that professors are rewriting courses to leave out term papers that require research in favour of assignments that settle for personal experience.

It isn't difficult to criticize the Internet – the hype, the advertising, the cost, the decreased worker productivity, the wasted time, the outdated information, the garbage e-mail, the snarls and bugs, the hate propaganda, the child porn, the addictions, and the substitution of virtual experience for the real thing. All these vices and more have been amply described by others, even if they have usually been dismissed as merely the growing pains of a technology that will change the world, presumably for the better. In the classroom, however, all these problems and others are magnified –

"FRANKLY, I'M NOT concerned about the world whiling away its hours on the information highway. At worst, I expect, it will be like playing video games or gambling. Support groups will convene to help abusers who want to modify their behaviour."
Source: Bill Gates, *The Road Ahead*

partly because students are vulnerable, but particularly because, unlike adults, some have no memory of a pre-technocentric world. A mother whose child is in Grade 2 told me how, on parents' night, her daughter had tugged her over to "the Internet computer" by saying, "Look, Mom, I want to show you the most *important* thing in the room!" She had walked right by her teacher, her friends, and the classroom bunny in its cage.

Does the Net have redeeming features that offer us educational gifts waiting to be unwrapped? Of course it does, but so do local museums, libraries, and senior citizens' centres. Learning how to find information is important, but not nearly as important as learning what to do with it. It is not impossible that any technology, or lots of technology, or particular types of technology applied to certain situations with certain kids and teachers will do whatever they were intended to do – reinforce basic skills, keep kids from getting disruptive, please industry, or get ministers re-elected. But all available evidence suggests that the indiscriminate use of the Net makes achieving educational goals of value and substance more difficult.

Economic and political payoffs are easy to track through the stock market and public opinion polls. The social, cultural, and educational effects of technology are harder to measure – easy to exaggerate when they look positive and convenient to deny when they don't. Unless we recognize the purposes and dangers of classroom techno-worship, our students will be easy prey for those who want to keep a generation entertained and edu-trained, ready to fit into an allotted place in the global market. If we are going to have information technology in the classroom – and, of course, we will – then much depends on teachers' consciousness, on their ability to understand and challenge the rules of ed.com. The outlook is not encouraging.

Trade-offs

One might expect school librarians, as education's information experts, to be outspoken about the limitations of the Net. Surely they must be wondering why so many books have been idling on shelves all these years if everyone is so desperate for more information. Whatever some of them may be thinking privately, a glance through a typical school librarian's publication suggests that they are busy promoting the techno-enthusiasm that is, among other things, putting them out of work. *The Bookmark*, published by the British Columbia Teacher-Librarians' Association in the spring of 1997, includes "notes and news" of interest to their members:[23]

Item 1: Librarians are urged to attend a "national" (i.e., American) educational computing conference; this "great opportunity" features Bill Gates and "the largest national exhibition of educational technology products and services in the country."

Item 2: A Web site is promoted as an essential resource for professional dialogue: "Librarians need to create, foster, beg, borrow and steal digital skills . . . or risk becoming an anachronism in an increasingly on-line world."

Item 3: "Better students through technology": a study has concluded that students with on-line access can "become independent, critical thinkers . . . able to express new knowledge in compelling ways." (The study was, in fact, sponsored by Scholastic, which has expanded into the Netware business. Its findings were reported in a corporate press release.)

Item 4: A Manitoba correspondent worries that school libraries will soon be asking local travel agencies to sponsor their geography collection and pet stores to purchase books on animals, since general cuts to education budgets (and an additional 20 per cent in cuts targeted to libraries) have created a crisis. Only one quarter of the province's school libraries still have a teacher-librarian. Nonetheless, the Manitoba School Library Association announces that its new brochure promotes librarians as sources of "the instruction to integrate the new technologies into programs that promote the information age."

Item 5: The Library Council of the New Brunswick Teachers' Association (NBTA) announces that it is folding due to the decline in the number of school librarians. Libraries are now staffed by volunteers. A motion to NBTA's annual meeting will ask delegates to support a call for a new ratio of 1 teacher-librarian to 1,500 students; currently, the ratio stands at 1 to 2,400.[24]

Item 6: It is reported that Alberta teacher-librarians "have become a diminishing species." Nonetheless, their association will once again hold its annual meeting, on the theme "Information Skills: Keys to Future Success."

Therefore, librarians devoted to tools that allegedly encourage "independent, critical thinkers" (Item 3) publish brochures that "promote the information age" (Item 4). Perhaps the chat lines (Item 2) provide a space where downsized teacher-librarians (Items 4, 5, and 6) can express their ideas "in compelling ways" (Item 3).

What do we make of these teachers, these librarians, these administrators – the entire profession? Are teachers who unthinkingly promote the same goals as the techno-corps naïve, or are they negligent? Unconscious or unconscionable? On the one hand, teachers can point to Bill Gates or Apple Computers or other symbols of manufactured consent as the villains who have anaesthetized them against their will. But stories about SchoolNet propaganda or smut on the WWW or corporate-funded microcomputer miracles are not the product of sophisticated forensic research, just the ordinary application of consciousness. Anyone unaware of the overselling of technology is choosing not to know.

On the other hand, like others in the dichotomized, over-worked-or-unemployed labour force, teachers face what experts call "intensification" – working harder and longer. Teachers work under conditions that make already unattainable goals ("zero-defects," as one group of education reformers proposes) truly ludicrous. When policy mandates (stream! destream! apply common standards! individualize learning! compete! co-operate!) collide, consciousness can be crazy-making. Survival can seem to depend on pushing the escape key – bailing out into an unappreciative labour market or, literally and figuratively, closing the classroom door. "Just let me teach!" can be heard from one end of the country to the other.

If only it were that simple. Behind the classroom door, teachers sometimes find little relief. Their relationships with students once provided teachers with the emotional wherewithal to persist. Yet the education reforms of this decade have coincided with changes that make these relationships harder to build and sustain. Larger class sizes, increased workloads, mandated curricula, and external evaluation depersonalize the acts and decisions of teachers. Greater numbers of students turn up with needs so great that good relationships with teachers barely make a dent. As the student population becomes more diverse, the ageing, much-less-diverse teacher population confronts a cultural divide deepened by rapid social change and hastened by technology. Teachers may still reach out – and so may students – but the gap widens and opportunities for relationship disappear.

Many teachers have internalized the sweeping criticisms made of their students and their schools. Albertan Jean-Claude Couture writes that teachers are struggling in "a culture of insufficiency," in which being "behind" on the technology file – and let's face it, no matter where you are, you are still behind – has created just one more way for teachers to feel inadequate.[25] Teachers who feel indignant rather than inadequate are not necessarily better prepared to deal with their students or themselves. Policy decisions are beyond their reach, and politicians intend to keep it that way. When Jean Charest appears just before the late-night TV news to wildly misrepresent Canadian results on the Third International Math and Science Study, teachers in the audience have choices. They can look up the analysis of TIMSS (see Chapter 2) and enjoy righteous indignation. They can ignore Jean Charest and keep marking the stack of exams propped up beside them in bed. Or, choosing unconsciousness, they can roll over and go to sleep. None of these options will deter Mr. Charest in the slightest or correct the misinformation he has spread. Why choose consciousness when it just doesn't matter?

Smart techno-marketers are capitalizing on teacher unconsciousness and teacher stress by promising that only technology can "put their students at the head of the class" and restore their sense of professional pride. The marketers are aiming their pitches primarily at younger teachers, many of whom are (almost) products of the Nintendo generation themselves. Demographically speaking, younger teachers tend to be more comfortable with an entrepreneurial, individualistic approach to life and to teaching, and for good reason. Those fortunate enough to have been hired as new teachers during the 1990s know they can be replaced in a moment. Thousands of others, with equally good credentials, are prepared to work even harder given half the chance. New teachers trying to make their professional mark are quite aware that senior administration tends to prefer teachers who lead multimedia demonstrations over teachers who lead political ones.

Techno-Teachers

Good teachers, then, teach students with technology. Well, someone does something to somebody, anyway. The window on education's future roles opens a crack at events such as Technology in Education: Meeting the Challenges of the Information Age.[26] One session at this 1997 Toronto conference promised (along with the opportunity to "cultivate mutually beneficial partnerships with industry") to show "education professionals" how to prepare a "team of administrators, classroom instructors, librarians, learning designers [sic] and learners." One forty-five-minute session will deal with the "retraining of existing personnel and the

ACCORDING TO REPRESENTATIVES from twenty countries attending a 1997 teacher-educator's conference at Brock University, the first question the world's prospective teachers are being asked in job interviews is not why they want to teach, or what their qualifications prepare them for, but whether they are computer literate. An affirmative answer can mean almost anything. Theodore Roszak writes in *The New Internationalist*, "Computer literacy is a commercial fashion, not a specific skill, let alone a subject matter. If computer literacy does not include material on what computers can't do and shouldn't do, it is advertising, not education."

engagement of new staff; changing instructor competencies; a human resource model for the 'wired' educational institution, the library and other learner support services"; and even "serving the needs of the learner in the 'new' classroom." Catching our breath at the refreshment break (for which sponsorship opportunities were apparently still available), we may ask what has happened to the noun *teacher* and the verb *to teach*.

This conference is not the place where participants will discuss research with a solid empirical base. A landmark meta-analysis of recent research on the relationship between expenditures and student achievement has found that smaller schools, smaller classes, and better educated, more experienced teachers very strongly influence student achievement. The results were so "robust" and consistent that even the authors were surprised.[27] It's an inconvenient finding to share with people who insist that schools can achieve better results with less money and more computers.

What teachers are expected to know and do, and how they are valued, are becoming tightly linked to technology. Yet, as professional development budgets are slashed, the gap grows between the amount of money and attention spent on technology and the amount spent on teaching teachers how to use it – let alone use it wisely. Although they are fond of telling teachers how schools must operate more like businesses, edu-crats implement human resource development decisions that would be laughed out of business school. Few corporate managers would buy and install complex new technology, and then tell their employees to get up to speed by playing with their new software after work or on weekends. In its report delivered to the 1997 meeting of Commonwealth Ministers of Education, the CMEC says it intends to deal with "the teacher training problem" and the "anxiety" problem by downloading both of them: "Lending teachers a computer and software for use at home on weekends and holidays is a practical way of giving them the opportunity, motivation, and time to gain experience as well as developing a level of comfort with the technologies."

COMPLAINTS ABOUT TEACHERS' unmet professional development needs surfaced so forcefully at CMEC's 1996 national consultation that the ministers agreed to look into it. A task team representing teachers' organizations, school administrators, ministries, and deans of education was struck in early 1997 to "outline the principles of teacher education on the use and teaching of IT," and to examine "issues and barriers." Despite the millions of dollars spent on technology by the governments that CMEC speaks for, the project budget was set at only $25,000, which meant the meetings would be conducted by e-mail.

When the task team reacted with intense criticism to the CMEC's proposed questionnaire to be sent to ministries, boards, and universities, one face-to-face meeting took place that made considerable progress towards an expanded mandate for the project and new ways of collecting information. Even the technocrats were in favour of something more meaningful than a checklist of "technological competencies" that teachers should be able to demonstrate, even if they have had no opportunity to learn them. Then the CMEC put on the brakes. No new mandate, no more meetings – and no minutes from the one that was held. Consultation had concluded.

Without a conceptual framework to think or talk about curriculum or computers, without time or encouragement, teachers have little choice but to strive for technical proficiency and assume a dangerous level of enthusiasm. The CMEC wants teachers to know the *how*; it is silent on the need for teachers to explore the *when* and *why* of using technology in the classroom. But then, regimes of all kinds have found ways to prevent people from asking dangerous questions.

Equity Markets

Ed.com is built on a foundation of misrepresentations, manipulations, deceptions, and deceit. It is built on myths – half-conscious assumptions that prevent us from thinking clearly and acting wisely. But ed.com is also built on hope, on an appeal to the part of us that wants the world to be a better place, and wants our schools to help make that happen.

The ideal of public education is defensible only in a society committed to pursuing equity. Private schools for those who can pay for them and literacy training for the rest better serve a political system that is resigned to inequality or determined to perpetuate it. We can understand, then, why public education is under attack. It poses – or, at least, it threatens to pose – the most serious challenge to those with power. A poster shows a defiant young African-American holding up a T-shirt that reads, "Danger! Educated Black Man." We know to whom he could be dangerous. We can only imagine what would happen if his entire race and generation could make good on the same threat.

Giving all children the opportunity to enjoy an equal education, determined not by the wealth of their families but by the resources of their communities, is not only a danger to those with power, but a truly radical democratic ideal – and, of course, one that has never been fully realized. Public education is aligned with the pursuit of equity because a shared public commitment to achieving greater equity is the only reason for public schools to exist. Anything that undermines this goal will be opposed by those who care about schools; conversely, innovations that promise

"THE REASON THAT public education is under attack is that our young people have more talent and intelligence and ability than the corporate system can ever use, and higher dreams and aspirations than it can ever fulfill. To force young people to accept less fulfilling lives in a more unequal, less democratic society, the expectations and self-confidence of millions of them must be crushed. Their expectations must be downsized and their sense of themselves restructured to fit into the new corporate order, in which a relative few reap the rewards of corporate success defined in terms of huge salaries and incredible stock options and the many lead diminished lives of poverty and insecurity.

"If my analysis is correct, it means that you public educators, every person in this room, and all the staff and colleagues you have worked with these many years are under attack not because you have failed, which is what the media and the politicians like to tell you. You are under attack because you have succeeded in raising expectations which the corporate system cannot fulfill."

Source: David Stratman, national director of the American Parent-Teacher Association

to advance equity will attract support. As we lurch to the right and witness progressive public policies and ideas ridiculed or shut down one by one, it becomes easier to accept the promise of techno-equity than to live with no promise at all.

Cyber-merchants have come to understand that public education's attachment to equity is non-negotiable, and they have used this insight to their advantage. It took a while. At first, technocrats argued that the use of information technology in the classroom would reduce or even eliminate the gaps associated with race, class, and gender, but the evidence so strongly contradicted these assertions that the claim wasn't credible. Recycling computer closetware simply does not redistribute power in the classroom, the workplace, or the community. The failure of this argument led to Plan B, the redefinition of educational equity. No longer a function of race, gender, class, or hemisphere, equity has been redefined as equal access to technology.

What a clever bit of sophistry. One of the central projects of public education – to reduce the effects of inequity – superficially remains intact, but the problem, its causes, and its solutions are redefined. We are no longer to think of students as the haves and the have-nots, but as the information-rich and the information-poor.

Suddenly, everyone is the champion of equity (redefined), including those who previously had little use for rebalancing power through public education. It is no longer just squishy liberals who champion equity and social justice. The New Right no longer claims that welfare rips off hard-working taxpayers. Now, welfare is a scourge because it robs the poor of their self-respect and their right to be self-sufficient. Redefining equity is so much simpler than opposing it, and doing so attracts so many more voters. As the new champion of the disadvantaged, right-wing politicians push the same agenda that has marginalized millions, repackaged in equity-friendly terms.

Politicians and marketers understand this ploy only too well. Why argue with the goal of equity when you can win more support (and increase sales) by pretending to embrace it? Early techno-marketing campaigns tended to dismiss differences: an Apple Canada advertisement from 1993 features a pre-teen girl. The copy reads, "Everyone is created equal. Until someone gets a Macintosh."[28] But the evidence that girls continue to face disadvantages in schools and in life, whether created equal or not, was too strong to dismiss so easily. A new plan was hatched. Gender disadvantage would become a legitimate part of official knowledge, and thus become exploitable. Gender equity at the click of a mouse!

This strategy has been internalized so thoroughly that the stereotype of computer-phobic girls and women has supplanted blatant discrimination, sexual harassment, and low self-esteem as the cause célèbre of gender-equity activists as well as marketers – even though other kinds of gender gaps, such as the wage gap or

CLICK ON THE WEDDING cake icon and she appears. The Barbie Fashion Designer CD-ROM has sold half a million copies in six months. Like her plastic counterpart, virtual Barbie exists to be dressed and undressed; unlike the real Barbie, the virtual version performs a bump-and-grind as she moves down the virtual catwalk. Industry insiders say Barbie has single-handedly cracked open the market for girls' computer games. Although some women (described by virtual Barbie's creators as "feminist activists") find Barbie-type games and software offensive, most women are reluctant to reject "girlware" outright since the games promise to lure girls into the all-important world of technology. After all, says one women-in-engineering spokesperson, "anything that develops computer skills is good."

Source: Electronic School, June 1997

the part-time versus full-time employment gap, are much greater (and do more damage) than the technology gap.

While it is true that women are largely absent from IT design and decision-making, they are not lagging behind in computer use. In 1994, Statistics Canada reported that women between the ages of twenty-five and forty-four were more likely than men to say they were computer literate.[29] More men than women use the Internet, but given the information highway's time-sucking properties, this fact may say more about men's access to leisure than women's access to technology. One study found that women who use the Net tend to do so at the expense of sleep. After midnight, the Net is a woman's world, unless that woman happens to be poor.

The real techno-gap, like the real equity gap, is shifting away from race and gender and towards poverty – although, of course, race and gender are still excellent predictors of who will be poor. The best predictor of whether a child will be poor is poor parents – a self-evident observation that our sympathy for poor children frequently overlooks. More than half of Canadian families with an income over $70,000 own home computers, compared with just 11 per cent of those whose income falls below $15,000.[30] When this factoid is put alongside the recent finding that Canada's most advantaged children are two to three times as likely as poor children "to be rated by their teachers as being near the top of their class in reading, writing and mathematics,"[31] an argument of great political convenience is born. Kids aren't struggling at school because of family poverty, but because they are computer-deprived! Remember these words from the 1997 federal election campaign? "A Jean Charest government will assist all Canadian students in acquiring the computer equipment and knowledge they will need to succeed. . . . The problem is not a lack of money, but a lack of priorities and standards."[32] We could substitute the name of any politician, any province, any country.

Technology's link to equity works best if we divorce our new definition from the idea of special treatment. This distinction is sweeping North America, as governments are abandoning any program that can be associated with quotas and resurrecting the myth of impartial merit. Technology's claim to impartiality fits perfectly with this new standard of fairness: computers will promote equity by ignoring difference and treating every child the same. One school superintendent (quoted by IBM) promises that "the new technology will help overcome barriers that may [!] exist due to race or ethnicity. A child's skin colour becomes irrelevant in a technological environment."[33] This analysis situates difference as the problem and homogeneity as the solution. If only people could be more like computers – ignorant of diversity and hard to tell apart! Give the child with a disability access to a computer and access to buildings and jobs will surely follow. How much easier life becomes, inside and outside schools, when more computers will take care of our obligations to equity!

This equity-friendly reform rhetoric is not limited to promoting technology. It figures prominently in school-choice debates, where equity is suddenly in favour. Even Ralph Reed, executive director of the Christian Coalition – the political arm of the American religious Right – argues at length that "conservatives must be on the side of social justice."³⁴ The posturing of school-choice advocates as deeply concerned about disadvantaged students is nothing more than a cynical ploy, according to Alex Molnar, who has watched the Milwaukee school-choice movement gain ground:³⁵ "Neoconservative ideologues have learned to trot poor African Americans and Latino parents before the cameras to make the case for vouchers. By focusing on voucher programs that serve only low-income, mostly minority students, neoconservatives have very effectively blunted charges . . . that their real purpose is to construct a market-based system that will inevitably hurt poor families the most."

But championing educational equity does more than just rob the Left of its traditional arguments and its political constituency. It also makes good market sense. Installing thirty laptop computers is more lucrative than hooking up one per class. Techno-marketers cannot maximize profits by selling information technology only to wealthy schools, public or private, in wealthy districts. There are simply too many poor kids in poor schools in the richest nations on earth. Jonathan Kozol writes passionately about the "savage inequalities" of public education in the United States, where dependency on local taxes has created gaps of an unimaginable size between rich public schools that spend $16,000 per year on each student and rat-infested schools without running water or toilet paper.³⁶ The rich routinely defeat tax proposals that would better fund the schools of "other people's children." He says if rich parents do not want to let their children compete on an equal playing field, that's their right. However, he continues, "they ought to know what they're doing. They ought to recognize that they're protecting their children against democracy."³⁷

Redistributing wealth in the name of equity is not on the political agenda. Nonetheless, convincing equity-sympathizers that technology will make up for the difference is only half the battle. The other half is actually gaining access to whatever cash is available. Profits are not tallied up simply because people want computers and believe in them – someone must actually purchase the machines. Enter techno-marketing disguised as philanthropy.

"Apple works with schools to implement a 'required computer purchase' policy. By making computers a requirement, as textbooks are, students are eligible to purchase them through traditional financial aid programs."[38] What a great idea! Apple has found a way to help poorer schools find the money to buy its machines. The corporation's idea of disadvantaged schools is sometimes laughable, however. It proudly boasts that it gave $1 million in technology, cash, and technical support to a project "dedicated to bringing technology into Silicon Valley schools over the next three years."[39]

There are children in far greater need. If we give kids in Harlem laptops, we're told, they will transcend the violence of drugs and poverty. IBM boasts that once Harlem parents had anted-up for the lease of their children's laptops, they formed patrols to ensure their children weren't mugged as they lugged them home.[40] The kids may be forgiven for wondering why they had to go it alone until something of value was at stake. Their parents are no doubt grateful to the corporations that gave them discount prices on the hardware and the software, and even easy payment plans. They were probably almost as grateful when the Clinton/Gore administration

---

PHILANTHROPY IN THE global city: "Few companies have invested more in education technology than AT&T, which has pledged $150 million for the effort. Its Learning Network . . . provides 100 schools with five months of free unlimited Internet access via AT&T's World Net service. In addition, the schools receive three months of free voicemail service and two years of wireless phone service on school grounds. After the initial free period, the schools receive discounted service." AT&T also sponsors "learning points," in which customers can assign points earned when they pay their phone bill. Schools can put these points towards the purchase of "computer hardware and software, including many programs and resources offered by Scholastic, Inc."

Source: Learning Connection

announced Internet hook-up discounts for schools, promising that "our children will not be stranded in the high-rent districts of cyberspace."[41] But poor children are still stranded in the low-rent districts of the global city.

Are discount prices on laptops and long-distance rates evidence of good corporate citizenship? No, says Theodore Roszak. They're intended to hook users into what becomes an expensive habit once dependency is well established: "All freebies from the computer industry should be regarded as you would a free sample from your friendly neighbourhood crack dealer."[42]

Roszak has a point. The assertion that technology, unlike any other valuable educational, social, or economic resource, will be distributed freely and equally, or even applied to equal benefit, is either naïve or blatantly manipulative. If technology naturally sought to reduce inequality, then the telephone would likely be accessible to more than 20 per cent of the world's population, and the flush toilet would be used by more than just half.[43] Technology doesn't beget equity – it begets excuses to sell more technology, but only to those who can pay for it, one way or the other. Is equity what motivates AT&T and the World Bank to run fibre-optic cable around the whole of Africa, or is it the contract, which will extract millions of dollars from countries that already pay billions more in debt charges than they can spend on health and education?[44]

As the Luddites claimed, every technology has been used to the advantage of those who control it. The rest of us are left to redefine, retrain, rethink – but not resist. Ursula Franklin calls this "the culture of compliance." Once retrofitted by technology, we are left making functional decisions, not principled ones. As long as the haves believe they can both profit from and protect themselves from the have-nots, the course is set. Functionalist rationales will not favour equity because principled decisions can't be based on greed or compromise. They can't be leveraged by false claims of success or coerced by warnings of disastrous consequences. Franklin proposes a checklist for us to ponder in order to reach principled positions on public policy, especially policy related to technology:

"One should ask whether it (1) promotes justice; (2) restores reciprocity; (3) confers divisible or indivisible benefits; (4) favours people over machines; (5) maximizes gain or minimizes disaster; (6) conserves rather than wastes; and (7) promotes the reversible over the irreversible."[45]

Applied to questions about technocentric classrooms, Franklin's list exposes our headlong rush as unprincipled in every way. This list would make an excellent starting point for teachers pursuing their computer literacy qualifications, but for those who find seven questions too many, Theodore Roszak has an even simpler rule of thumb: "Find out what Bill Gates wants your school to do. Don't do that."[46]

Radio Redux?

Perhaps we critics are guilty of the same excesses as the techno-boosters, exaggerating the dangers of ed.com as egregiously as the marketers exaggerate its benefits. Perhaps techno-thrall is just a phase that will pass once we become less impressed with technology's dazzle.

After all, enthusiasm for untested education reforms, especially those related to technology, isn't new. In 1942, a tract called *Motion Pictures in the Schools* claimed, "Motion pictures have all the vital ability to influence and improve education that the printing press had five hundred years ago."[47] Then came the overhead projector: "There is no limit on imagination. Thus there is no limitation on how you can use transparencies and overhead projection to communicate effectively with your class. Just as science is opening new vistas for mankind, overhead projection is opening new doors for teaching."[48] Someone ought to post this 1965 paean on the door of every school storage room stuffed with dusty filmstrip projectors, 16 mm projectors without reels, and overheads with burnt-out bulbs.

Too bad there are no radios left in these storage rooms, or their shelf could have its own testimonial, issued by the University of Chicago in 1931:

. . . the radio can do its part; . . . it is a perfectly legitimate and satisfactory way for distribution, that it would carry more genius to the common child than he has ever had or ever possibly could have; that it is the greatest system for training teachers that we know; and all together I think it is justified even in a technical sense as a medium for instruction in public education.[49]

The radio and the filmstrip projector found their way from academe to classrooms to storage rooms without any documented harm to teachers or students, and perhaps many benefited from the novelty or even the information these tools made available. It is tempting to put our overenthusiasm for computer technology into the same benign category – but that would be wrong. There are some parallels, of course, but the differences are more significant.

School boards did not find the funding to acquire radios by eliminating teachers and increasing class sizes. Guidelines were not rewritten to ensure that "radio across the curriculum" became a benchmarked objective. Students were not expected to make a study of the impact of the radio, to plan their careers around the radio, or to use the radio to create virtual friendships. There was little or no political investment in the success or failure of the radio. The health of the stock exchange did not rest on its adoption. People hoped this new technology would make a difference, but radio served to support the existing goals of schooling, not to become its central purpose.

Nothing in public education was broken intentionally so that the radio could be introduced to fix it. No crisis was manufactured, no skills decried, no partnerships leveraged. What the radio and the computer have in common is that they were both welcomed by a world swept up in the worship of technology. What these technologies do not share is the same opportunity to be found limited or wanting.

When the radio proved to be trivial or distracting or less real than human beings, the teacher turned it off, and the classroom that had been there before was still intact. But once the plans for technology-driven education at any price are implemented, there will be no going back. If and when information technology is found to be less satisfying than its promoters claim, there will be little left to go back to.

In theory, we could start over, rebuild a grand project of public education around the principles of equity in a democratic society, write curriculum that recognizes the limitations of information in resolving human problems, replace instructional technicians with thoughtful teachers – but we won't.

In an ideological climate of Me, Inc., and an economic climate of reduced public spending, when the private sector thinks it will gain rather than lose if public education stumbles, then the outcome is obvious. If public education fails now – through political neglect, through its subjugation to technology markets, through public disinterest or professional exhaustion – it will be gone forever.

6

BIG BUSINESS TARGETS CHILDREN

The conference brochure promoting Kid Power: Creative Kid-Targeted Marketing Strategies promises that participants will learn how to tap into the market generated by 4.4 million Canadian kids who spend $20 billion every year.[1] We will find out how to ensure "gatekeepers" don't intercept messages intended for kids, and how to use "school-based programs" to support "kid-marketing activities." As word of the event gets around, a handful of teachers, labour leaders, and parents plans a little nostalgic resistance: a picket and a press conference.

News of the anticipated protest surfaces during registration. Candi Schwartz, conference organizer for the New Jersey–based International Quality and Productivity Centre, is bewildered. "Canada is so *conservative*," she tells arriving participants. "In the States we've been doing this for absolutely years, and no one ever complained." In fact, there's been a fair amount of complaining, especially from Ralph Nader, the Consumer's Union, and the Center for the Study of Commercialism, but to little effect. Curtailing the freedom of marketing in America is about as popular as curtailing democracy, and assumed by many to be the same thing.

Whatever peculiar Canadian sentiments are being expressed outside, inside it's business as usual. Keynote speaker James McNeal, marketing guru from Texas A&M University, says that "being a child consumer isn't an accident in our society, it's a requirement." McNeal even dedicated his book, *Kids as Consumers*, to his son Chad: "A marketer's prize/A father's treasure."[2]

McNeal introduces us to markets without borders and kids without cultures. He says that children not only control enviable amounts of their own money, approaching $100 billion (U.S.), but influence $1 trillion of their parents' spending on everything from breakfast cereal to cars. Better yet, children are consumers-in-training, imprinting constantly as they prepare to take their place as adult customers.

McNeal claims that children from different countries no longer possess any defining cultural characteristics. This globalization means American-style consumerism can be cultivated anywhere. True, American children organize their thinking around brand names by twenty-four months of age, a feat not matched by Chinese children until forty-eight months, but this developmental lag is apparently just a vestige of socialism. To illustrate his theory of cultural convergence, McNeal projects slides drawn from his ongoing market research. Beautifully drawn Chinese children's self-portraits, set in markets and shops, appear on the screen. He tells us that through their drawings, children offer us windows into their souls. "You see, they see themselves as customers! Isn't it wonderful that when you're so young you can say it so clearly?"

Yet sometimes kids have to repeat it. McNeal chuckles over "the pester factor." It seems North American children nag their parents to buy them something an average of fifteen times during each shopping trip, but Mom gives in only half the time. China's one-child policy and comparatively high disposable incomes mean that Chinese parents and grandparents are much more indulgent. European and Asian children also excel in shaping their parents' general spending. They successfully influence almost half their families' purchases, compared with American children, who can claim only one fifth.

We can blame this shortfall on North American corporate myopia. McNeal says unenlightened giants such as Kmart and Sears are in big trouble because they don't respect the potency of children, while Delta Airlines and AT&T have done it right, raising their future customers from childhood. Marketers squander opportunities when they fail to think globally and long-term. McNeal predicts the collapse of an unnamed major convenience-store chain that regards children as nothing more than today's customers for "cigarettes, beer, and girlie magazines."

"THERE ARE ONLY TWO sources of future consumers: Competition and kids."

Source: James McNeal, marketer

Free trade presents special opportunities. Why focus on the Canadian and U.S. markets when Mexican parents spend only one tenth as much on toys and treats? U.S. marketing savvy is miles ahead, since foreign retailers haven't caught on to exploiting the tactile needs of children, who must be able "to see and touch and yearn" if they are to be properly socialized into consumers. McNeal projects a final self-portrait of a child gazing at toys placed out of reach. "There he stands with his bag of books and his wishes. What a tragedy. If I could have one wish it would be to make it possible for all kids to be buyers."

Marketers who do it right will realize that "kids are more giving – they'll give you more profits," says McNeal, but first you must come to know your customer. Kids everywhere want imported (i.e., American) goods, bearing brand names imprinted through movies, TV, and advertising. This is a pre-sold market, but businesses must still tailor products to each setting. For example, North American marketers should be aware that, inexplicably, "learning, education, and schooling" are much more important in many other countries, where children are actually known to spend their own money on school supplies. General laughter ensues.

According to McNeal, this is because Chinese kids identify with achievement, while North American kids prefer play. It is up to marketers to fuse achievement with the ownership of brand-name products in the minds of children who haven't yet made the connection. Imprinting brand names should be the pre-eminent goal of marketers. "What a wonderful way to communicate with kids as consumers," McNeal says. "We are talking about the moulding of the mind."

Mind Games

The mind of a child is a wonderful thing. Two representatives of Youth Marketing Systems Consulting, the California team of Drs. Dan Acuff and Robert Reiher, take the podium and present a well-rehearsed précis of their one-day post-conference workshop, available to participants for an additional $379.85 (U.S.).

"It's all about essence – getting to the essence of essence." What is essence? "Essence is what can be *evoked* in the *consumer*," the consultants emphasize. We search for it as our workshop leaders take us on a glib trip through research (Harvard is cited in passing) on multiple forms of intelligence, followed by a fast-forward version of Maslow's hierarchy of needs, Kohlberg's stages of moral development, topped off with a little biological determinism. It seems that between the ages of four and fifteen, the right brain (affective, non-rational, emotive) predominates. Marketers pay too little attention to the opportunities presented by the brain stem dominance of two-year-olds, the pre-conventional moral sense of three- to seven-year-olds, and the sexual preoccupations of thirteen- to fifteen-year-olds. As cranial paraplegics living in our left rational brains, adults must learn how to find essence from the developmental perspectives of children and youth.

We practise by completing a worksheet that helps us analyse the essence of Madonna. Can we apply developmental psychology to expand her appeal to children? We are reminded that today's children are fast-forwarding through the stages of development. The soft cartoon characters of the Peanuts gang may appeal to the preschool set, but by age six or seven kids (especially boys) want attitude, even in their cereal box personalities. Clever Captain Crunch is sufficiently bland to fool parents, but he has enough edge to appeal to wanna-be teens. He's also a guy. Little girls can be wooed with soft characters for longer than boys, and will also identify easily with male characters. Boys, however, will never bond with anything feminine unless they are stuck in the pre-conventional stage. (Apparently, the conventional stage begins when bonding with Madonna comes naturally.)

Manipulating reality is the purpose of advertising, and deception is the common thread that runs through all truly ingenious marketing. Luckily, kids are still easier to fool than adults. When Nintendo was about to go under, the company saved its video-game empire through the innovative marketing of Donkey Kong Country. Nintendo mailed a 15-minute video infomercial promoting Donkey Kong to 170,000 kids, making them feel special and select. This clone insider's report may have been a dirty trick, but it was a stroke of genius that has become marketing lore: "Kids love to think they're getting the real goods."

It's a dog-kill-dog world: getting by in the highly competitive world of video games is tougher than just outsmarting kids. One of Nintendo's ongoing marketing problems is the high price of its products, which means the peculiar tastes of parents can't be ignored. "We have to be careful not to be completely offensive," says Kirsty Henderson, Nintendo of Canada's marketing manager. "We have to position ourselves to be seen to respect parents, but not lose kids."

Nintendo was concerned about the bad press Mortal Kombat had received. Mortal Kombat became famous for its gut-spilling death scenes, but what really attracted kids was the secret "blood code" that activates the final orgy in which the winner gets to rip out the loser's heart. Time for damage control. The parent-friendly ads for Nintendo's Donkey Kong Country placed in TV guides featured a gentle real gorilla, not the animated search-and-destroy version. Nintendo's ads designed for kids' magazines drop the pretence. The copy for another hot game, Kirby's Dreamland 2, reads: "Next one to call them 'cute' gets a fire ball in the butt. What's that smell? Oh, it's your butt. Sizzling, scorched and smoking. . . . Kneel before the hamster that coughs up white-hot spheres of justice. Cuddly? Hardly." Since Kirby's packaging features the kind of cute and cuddly pastel characters that would appeal to parents, Dreamland 2 is perfectly positioned to work both sides of the street.

Somewhat daunted by the size of Nintendo's $2 million Donkey Kong advertising budget, workshop participants are ready for something a little more modest. Phoneworks' Cybelle Snour moves to the podium to tell us that the secret of bargain-priced relationship marketing is to "create positive experiences" for kids, since their experiential memory is so powerful. "Let's think of your brands as the rides on the playground," she says.

The telephone can help marketers keep track of all those kids on all those swings. "Kids understand the telephone is key to dialoguing with Mom, Dad, and Grandma," Snour explains, although these conversations are generally between real people. Phoneworks is really promoting dialogues between real children and pre-recorded messages – virtual relationships on call. Apparently, virtual relationships are better than none at all: 4.5 million calls were logged in ninety minutes during a Halloween special, when YTV was "blast programming" four episodes of *Are You Afraid of the Dark?* The two pre-teen hosts assured each other that they weren't afraid, they could hack it, they were cool – call them and chat. Only the uncool resist this initiation into ghoul.

Ghoul is gold. Acuff's and Reiher's handouts on children's developmental stages highlight the appeal of the dark side among children as young as eight, peaking (with cultivation) by late adolescence. Another conference handout reports on *Fright Fiction Devoured by Kids.* "*Drip, drip, drip. Blood covered the floor. The body's face was purple, the eyes sunken. They ran for the door but it was locked. There was no way out. And the killer was still there.* Are you scared? If you're a young reader of horror, these are the feelings you want," the handout proclaimed. If you're a middle-aged marketer, this is the information you need.

Behaviour Modification

The promo for the next session is the one that has really irritated the protesters gathering outside. Carole Green Long, president of Children's Creative Marketing, tells a colleague that she has changed the examples in her presentation, a just-in-time adaptation to suit consumer opinion. This is disappointing, because the agenda promised that Long would explain how to use "school-based programs" to support "kid-marketing activities," and how to "incorporate your school-based program with new product launches, promotions, special events, direct mail, kids clubs, and advertising." We were anticipating private sector insights on "how new Canadian education developments will impact on marketing."

Long apologizes for having skipped out to give media interviews, where she was trying to dispel the misconception that marketers were somehow exploiting students. If that were the case, she said, people would have every right to be offended, but the parents and teachers outside just didn't understand. She was talking about "good" in-school programs, not the kind "with very little educational content." The programs she would be describing were "serious," endorsed enthusiastically by school boards and ministries of education.

Endorsed goes a bit far. On the whole, corporate curricula prosper in Canadian classrooms because officialdom ignores them. The United States seems more alert. A 1995 report called *Captive Kids*, published by Consumers Union Education Services, says that fourteen state departments of education have adopted strict guidelines, and that almost all national education organizations have taken cautious, if not hostile, positions on commercialism in schools.[3] Not that their resistance has made much difference: the report concludes that increasing commercialism "poses a significant and growing threat to the integrity of education in America."

According to *Business Week*, the classroom is starting to look more attractive to advertisers as kids migrate from television to computers. Marketers can no longer assume all kids are tuned into the same sitcom, but they're all in school, where overworked teachers are hungry for resources and short on time. Those inside the classroom can't call on a team of analysts and fact-checkers before they decide whether to use Nike's sneaker-making kit, which is alleged to impart "a lesson on environmentally responsible manufacturing."[4]

Captive Kids reports that some teachers are eager to trade a few principles for much-needed resources: "If it's free (and good) it's for me!" said one teacher. "Great, glossy, up-to-date, motivating materials . . . are a heck of a lot better than the 1966 textbooks that many teachers are refurbishing to pass out each September." Others fret the real problem is that schools are selling mind-shares too cheaply, or even giving them away for free. But according to *Business Week*, "Even the severest critics recognize that schools simply can't afford a blanket ban." Says Ed Winter, the co-founder of Channel One, a news-and-advertising gimmick, "Marketers have come to realize that all roads eventually lead to the schools."

The road doesn't detour when it hits our borders. No one seems surprised when Carole Green Long leads with an American product to promote the good, educational materials to which she has referred. A nutrition unit sponsored by the Dole Food Company goes beyond "eat your (Dole) fruits and vegetables"; the free CD-ROM–based program includes directions to Dole's World Wide Web site, a kids' cookbook, fridge magnets, and large characters for classroom display, including Barney Broccoli. Let's think cross-curricular integration! Lesson plans for use in social studies, language arts, and mathematics can all be printed from Dole's master disc, although grocery store tours are the most important component of the "5-Day Adventure." During 1994, 1.5 million American children embarked on the Dole adventure, and sales of fruits and vegetables increased. "It's a win-win situation," says Long.

Win-win is today's descriptor of choice. Lego and Spar Aerospace certainly won big when federal tax dollars underwrote the

THE MARKETING FIRM Cover Concepts distributes free book covers to 25 million American students. The covers advertise a variety of products, from Calvin Klein to the NBA. Corporate clients pay $129,000 for a semester's exposure, pleased that students' "unaided recall" of the logos and brand names on their covers approaches 80 per cent. Advertisers target their markets: Nike distributes to inner-city schools; Lego goes to middle-income areas. Gatorade has three covers: one for predominantly black schools, one for Hispanic students, and one for predominantly white schools.

Source: *Education Life*, January 5, 1997

"Red Rover Project," a Legoland simulation of a "prototype multinational settlement on Mars," intended to engender "a positive vision of the technological society of the 21st century." Closer to home, Long says, teachers "desperate for this kind of resource" are entering contests sponsored by the Arts and Entertainment Network, hoping to win a grant, a VCR for their classrooms, or copies of A&E programs. She says the goal of this project is to help teachers understand "how they can work with the cable industry in the era of convergence."

Some lower-tech activities deserve recognition too. Pizza Hut's "Book It" program has teachers handing out pizza reward certificates to children who read a specified number of books of any length, at any reading level. Pizza Hut reports increased restaurant traffic because few small readers turn up alone to order a single two-topping pizza. Long may have planned to mention Ziploc's national sandwich day contest, Armour All's curriculum on "maintaining your car's appearance," Hoover's curriculum on "clean living" (carpet care, not sex education), or Snickers' unit on "making the connection between food and fitness" – but time is running short. It's a shame. This group would have enjoyed hearing about "Count Your Chips," a math unit sponsored by the National Potato Board and the Snack Food Association, or

Scholastic's environmental issues package based on *Jetsons: The Movie*. Budget cuts have hit extra-curricular sports almost as hard as they've hit libraries, so team sports have become a natural market niche. School Properties is an American firm that brokers "arrangements" – otherwise known as exclusive contracts – with companies such as Nike and Reebok in return for uniforms, bags, shoes, backboards, and scoreboards, all carrying the sponsor's logo. A promotional video from the broker explains how easy it is to change a school's crest to more closely resemble its mentor's logo.[5]

MONEY IS TIGHT all over. Parents know that it is becoming harder to be original when it comes to fund-raising. Door-to-door chocolate bar sales just aren't going to fill the funding void, but how many parent groups can imitate ASBA? The Alberta School Boards Association organized a raffle to raise funds for three schools: the prize, a quarter-section of land and a few head of cattle, netted $234,000 for exhausted volunteers.

Source: Globe and Mail, March 27, 1997

Whose Shade of Green?

Selling to captive kids is the easy part. Sponsors who want to cultivate students' attitudes, not just pick their pockets, face a greater challenge. Some well-known success stories can be emulated. Georgia-Pacific distributes an activity kit called "The Tree Trunk" that defends clear-cutting, emphasizes the indispensable nature of paper products, and preaches environmental responsibility (to which Georgia-Pacific is deeply committed).[6] Procter and Gamble contributes to students' understanding of labour issues by recasting the labour unrest of the late 1800s as a problem of insufficient closeness between management and workers.[7] Students are asked to ponder how Procter and Gamble could have convinced workers "that their overall interests were truly inseparable from those of Procter and Gamble."

Take a cue from Mobil, which produced a pro-NAFTA curriculum, or the Ontario Farm Animal Council, which has a particular take on the hazards of vegetarianism and the extremism of animal rights activists. Those who order this resource from the Ontario Curriculum Clearing House will also receive a free set of posters, suitable for classroom display, featuring celebrities such as actor Patrick Swayze posing with their pets and promoting the continued use of animals in research.[8]

Marketing new attitudes to kids can be a hard sell. Children's attachment to environmental issues, despite adults' declining interest in these concerns, creates some marketing dilemmas. For the last decade, most manufacturers have tried to position themselves as so environmentally responsible that they can be trusted to regulate themselves. This challenge requires gaining public respect, and therefore products marketed to kids – the Teenage Mutant Ninja Turtles, for example – try to cash in on kids' pro-environmental sympathies. Pale green is good.

But dark green spells trouble. There are signs that environmental education may be succeeding all too well, as a generation of kids moves from celebrating Earth Day to having a crack at shaping public opinion and public policy. Corporations should be cautious, even though governments have demonstrated that only the most toothless monitoring of environmental standards will accompany trade agreements and transnational investment. Yet, as the Fraser Institute and the Business Council on National Issues claim, any environmental regulation is too much if it cuts into market share.

Environmental activists are tracking a new attack on schools' earth-friendly pedagogy, and the promotion of new corporate curriculum supplements to offset its effects. The oil and chemical industries and conservative coalitions are sponsoring seminars for American teachers to set the record straight: the science curricula taught in schools are biased towards environmentalism. The ultra-conservative Marshall Institute produced a 1997 report that says children "are being 'scared green' by textbooks and a mass media that serve up a steady diet of gloomy, politically-slanted messages about the planet's future."[9] A well-funded media tour made sure the report received lots of political attention.

The criticism is sticking. The anti-green backlash is so powerful, according to the *Washington Post*, that the federally sponsored environmental education program may have lost too much political support to be reauthorized.

The anti-green lobby pays particular attention to environmental education's alleged bias against technology: "These [text]books ignore the fact that if the people of the earth are to become healthier and live longer, they will do so through technology, not ideology," states Michael Sanera, author of a parents' guide to environmental fearmongering. He's pleased that teachers got the blame for brainwashing Grade 2 students in Arizona. The kids wrote letters to the editor – "people are too greedy" – when developers turned their school's backyard cactus desert into a subdivision. The *Post* says the controversy led to the cancellation of the state's mandated environmental education curriculum. Funds earmarked for it were turned over "to loggers' and cattlemen's associations," who could be trusted to be more objective than teachers.[10]

Teachers are apparently fighting back by staging a total retreat. Even the principal of the only American magnet school for environmental studies insists teachers follow a strict "no advocacy" policy: "Most of our kids have never heard of the Sierra Club – and they have no reason to."[11] If the timber industry that backs an Oregon bill gets its way, neither will anyone else. The bill proposes circumventing teachers by establishing an industry-controlled "clearing house" to vet and approve all classroom materials on the environment.

According to the Centre for Commercial-Free Public Education, these attacks are backed and funded by right-wing think-tanks and corporations with their own version of an environmental issues curriculum ready to go.[12] In Canada, the Fraser Institute is taking up the anti-green cause. Writing in the *Fraser Forum*, Laura Jones claims "Trash in Schools" has resulted in an appalling 63 per cent of school children "lobbying their parents to recycle," an example of how "advocacy is replacing literacy and propaganda is replacing reason."[13] She hints that environmental education could even be un-Christian, since students "are then taught their salvation lies in the religion of recycling." This has got to stop. The schools are out of control.

Opportunity Knocks

Back at the conference, we're on to another risky subject that has been edited with the protest in mind: how new Canadian education developments are presenting new marketing opportunities.

First on the list is the emergence of SchoolNet, education's on-ramp to the information highway. As it finds ways to become self-sufficient (i.e., private), SchoolNet is giftwrapping an unparalleled opportunity for corporations with on-line aspirations. Carole Green Long admits that although "the commercialization issue" has been contentious within SchoolNet's advisory board in the past, the climate is at last welcoming to responsible partners. (She was only too right. Tired of seeking consensus, Industry Canada simply disbanded the board in 1997.)

There are other hopeful developments. Increased standardized testing will make curriculum more central, says Long, and marketers can expect ministries of education to be receptive to corporate curriculum, since "people won't pay more taxes." Long also explains that "the number and power of school boards are diminishing"

SCHOLASTIC, PUBLISHERS AND distributors of educational materials, mailed out "Introducing Indonesia" to 77,000 teachers in 1997. Backed by the Lippo Bank, the Indonesian government, Mobil, Texaco, and other Suharto-friendly corporations, the guide explains that sneakers are manufactured in Indonesia not because labour is cheap, but because rubber is a natural resource. East Timor is portrayed as just another Indonesian province, joining the others in a united territory, governed by a "just and civilized humanity." The guide profusely thanks its many political and corporate partners for the opportunity "to increase understanding of a country . . . that offers a great number of opportunities for American business."

Source: The Progressive, May 24, 1997

as they are "replaced by parent councils." This is a stroke of luck because it means neophyte parent councils, not seasoned bureaucrats, will have the power to decide whether corporate-sponsored programs will be welcome in their schools. Parent councils are easier to tempt with promises of cash donations, free teacher materials, or free technology.

This window of opportunity opened when parents of students in Ontario's Peel and Lakeshore boards of education opted for computer screen savers that carry corporate advertising.[14] ScreenAd, the project's corporate partner, pitches the breakthrough that will allow corporations "to take advantage of the fact that schools have made it a priority to put more and more computers in the hands of students," a priority that must, of course, be paid for somehow. ScreenAd's Web site asks rhetorically, "Wouldn't you like to expose your brand identity to over 1.5 million students in Ontario classrooms every 15 minutes of the school day? Well, you can! We are pleased to introduce this exciting new and innovative way to capture the minds of the dynamic student market in Ontario!"[15]

According to parents, advertising on classroom computer monitors "wouldn't be their first choice," but in a time of "dramatic cutbacks" to funding, it's a compromise they say they can live with. Advertising is easier to swallow when the corporate logo comes complete with an inspirational message. A Pepsi ad that advised students to "develop a thirst for knowledge" was approved as sufficiently subtle, but the parent council rejected a fast food ad that displayed the phrase "Hungry? Get the taste now!" under a picture of a hamburger.[16] The rent-a-screen revenue, estimated at half a million dollars, goes to schools in direct proportion to the number of computer monitors in use. Although the revenue is not yet tied to the amount of time students are required to stare at the computer screen, this problem may take care of itself, if Channel One is any indication.

Channel One is the spawn of entrepreneur Chris Whittle, who has packaged nine minutes of "news" around three minutes of youth-targeted advertising. American schools signing on with Channel One receive a satellite disk and TV monitors for "dedicated" student viewing. Schools strapped for technology sign on; not surprisingly, the poorer the school and district, the more likely its students will be forced to tune in. Viewing is mandatory; learning is optional. Forty per cent of American students between Grades 6 and 12 – eight million students – watch every day.[17]

A study of students in Channel One schools found – one hopes, to no one's surprise – that exposure to rap-paced fifteen-second clips of items such as "arms negotiations in Vienna" did nothing to improve students' comprehension of current events, although many had perfect recall of the ads.[18] The more subtle and super-ficially pro-social, the more insidious the message, according to advertising's critics. Some students repeated and re-enacted their favourite ads whenever they had the chance, and the ads became the subject of lively free-time discussions. But their lasting impact came from their subterfuge: students were not sure whether a Pepsi-sponsored "stay in school" message was advertising or not. Most had no clue that sports celebrities were paid to endorse prod-ucts. Remarkably, some of their teachers weren't sure either.[19]

All truly great marketing ideas beget spinoffs. The Youth News Network (YNN), known for the ambitious (and often ambiguous) claims of its promoter, Ron McDonald, is once again pitching itself at Canadian schools. McDonald says an all-Canadian Channel One is not only in the works, but inevitable. McDonald's pro-posal was met with scepticism rather than hostility in most quar-ters, although his claim that he has backers (including IBM and Stentor) ready to invest $100 million in YNN over the next ten years sent shivers through the SchoolNet empire. Using some questionable arm-twisting tactics, with the help of school admin-istrators keen to get with the program, so to speak, YNN made a modest breakthrough in the fall of 1997, signing on two schools in Alberta, one in Quebec, and two in Ontario as part of a twenty-week pilot project. Minutes from the Calgary Board of Education meeting that approved the deal reveal that the two schools involved were persuaded by the promise of monitors, videotaping equipment, satellite dish, and fifteen computers that would be donated to each school in exchange for access to students. The board minutes note the equipment "would fit well with Phase 2 of the school's technology plan" in one case, and that "technology is a major school priority" in the second.[20] The superintendent's report to the board claimed that each school would be given $150,000 in technology – and that, after all, there was already advertising in schools. The report avoided mentioning YNN's unhappy prior history in Alberta. In 1992, parents vigorously and successfully opposed the whole scheme. Memories are short; the motion to approve the pilot was carried.

It may be only a matter of time before the rest of us sign on. It is not clear on what grounds Calgary or Peel or Lakehead parents – or any other group – would accept screen-saver ads and corporate-sponsored paper supplies (coming soon, according to the *Globe and Mail*), but reject YNN or even Channel One. The ethical lines are as fuzzy as the ads-cum-platitudes served up to students – as fuzzy as the lines between public and private interests, or between fact and fiction.

The Hoax Is on Us

It becomes increasingly difficult to spoof commercialism in schools. The rumour that the makers of Prozac were proselytizing in high schools (on behalf of mental health, of course) sounds fantastical, if not paranoid, but it turns out to be true.[21] What next?

Adbusters magazine has been publishing send-ups of advertising for a decade. An item called "Branding" in the Spring 1997 issue was illustrated with a photo of three girls baring their shoulders to show off tattoos of Nike, Pepsi, and Guess logos.[22] "With so many school districts strapped for cash, the monetary void is increasingly being filled by corporate sponsorships," wrote *Adbusters*. "The newest . . . has been the Tattoo You Too! program. In exchange for a fixed fee (based on the number of participants) students 'volunteer' to receive a tattoo of a famous corporate logo."

"It's a win-win situation," a participating school principal said. "Kids get a chance to look 'hip.' . . . It only takes four tattoos to purchase a new computer – we've been overwhelmed by its success." Says an enthusiastic student, "It makes it all worthwhile, somehow. . . . It's a permanent keepsake of my formative years." The companies were also pleased with the response, and happy to give tattooed students 20 per cent discounts on their "branded" products. The principal said the students were limited to three tattoos each: "The last thing we want is for students to become walking billboards."

The giveaway was in the small print at the bottom of the feature: "Reprinted with permission from the *New York Times*, December 12, 1999." Despite the anachronism, reporters looking for more information kept Adbusters' phone ringing. Adbusters' Allan MacDonald says in an e-mail to one of my colleagues:

> I for one thought it fascinating that "Branding" was within the realm of belief of so many media professionals (including not one, but two inquiries from the CBC). The general consensus seemed to be: "No, it can't be. The multinationals have gone too far. It has to be a hoax . . . but then again . . ." I am convinced that somewhere, hidden deeply within that "but then again," there lies a great story on modern culture.

Putting the Cool in School

Screen savers and tattoos were not on the agenda at the Kid Power conference, but there's always next year. Temporarily, at least, most marketers have to use standard print-based approaches such as kids' magazines. According to MIR Communications, *Kidsworld* magazine is distributed to more than 1,600 English-language elementary schools reaching 40 per cent of the target school population, where 70 per cent of classroom teachers use it as a teaching aid. The bright purple media kit handed out to conference participants says, "*Kidsworld*: Putting the Cool in School." Everything inside the folder is in hyper-colour, except for the plain white insert, for teachers, that soberly pitches literacy: "The product will entice children to make the voluntary decision to read."

The pitch to prospective advertisers, however, drops the pretence that this publication is about literacy:

Kids spend forty per cent of each day in the classroom where traditional advertising cannot reach them. *Kidsworld* magazine is in class, too, and can provide your brand with an opportunity to stand out! . . . Competition and clutter can kill the chances of great advertising creative being noticed by kids. *Kidsworld* magazine stands out from all the other kids' media because our publication is enjoyed in the non-cluttered, non-competitive and less commercial classroom environment.

An advertising *oasis*. Imagine a classroom of ten-year-olds using your brand creative in a class assignment. . . . Envision groups of children huddled over your ad trying to solve its puzzle. Can it get any BETTER than this?

Yes, it can, if the services of MIR Communications are engaged by marketers wishing "to maximize their in-school presence" through "product sampling, sponsored lesson plans, sponsored school/class activities, [and] individual and class contests." The advertising oasis falls open at a two-page spread placed by the Bank of Montreal. A young reader wants to complain about the unfairness of different PST levels in different provinces. According to the Bank of Montreal, it's because Alberta is "very wealthy" and "Newfoundland has a higher unemployment rate." A column called "bizwords" helps kids add important acronyms such as GST and RRSP to their vocabularies.

A few conference participants wander outside the hotel to take a surreptitious look at the press conference. Jim Turk from the Ontario Federation of Labour is trying to explain that when they're at school, his members' kids deserve protection from the commercialism that surrounds them every other waking moment. The Ontario Secondary School Teachers' Federation hands out leaflets that say the principles of Kid Power are inverted – the power isn't with the kids, but with the adults and their corporations. I ask one participant what she thinks about the protest. "I don't know and I don't really care," she says. "It's kind of pathetic."

Two Toronto teachers' federation members who have been attending the conference look on. One is drooping but the other is as animated as he's been all day, raising his hand to ask polite questions, keen to call back "Good morning" to each one of the parade of presenters. He tells me he's sceptical about some of it, but he has to admit that the space activity and the A&E project look pretty good. Later, at the YTV wine and cheese reception, he picks up another freebie – a YTV mouse pad. "But I *need* one," he pleads as he piles it on top of his handouts. He does not return for day two.

But day one is still not over. Sunni Boot, managing director of Optimedia Canada, is about to explain "The Changing Canadian Media Landscape." Using existing media to reach future consumers can only take a product so far, especially when Canadian children are watching almost 20 per cent less TV today than a decade ago. A positive TV culture is required; thankfully, the "new regulatory environment" is obliging. Boot says infomercials are terrific opportunities for astute marketers, since the CRTC's relaxation of rules means that infomercial hours can now coincide perfectly with kid hours.

Unfortunately, TV is so open to parents' scrutiny that the unexpected, no matter how off-base, can happen. Witness all the fuss over *Power Rangers*, Boot says: "If you're in the child business, if you have merchandising rights, then there's no such thing as too much *Power Rangers*." This detour into *Power Rangers* appears to set off a new train of thought, as Boot pays brief homage to "pro-social" action – a fitting subject for the past president of Concerned Children's Advertisers, an industry watchdog that guards itself from unidentified predators. Certainly the protesters outside, whom she dismisses as naïve and misinformed, pose no threat to her organization.

Coming back to her message, Boot urges participants not to overlook the marketing potential of edu-tainment, a win-win opportunity for "companies to assist where taxpayers no longer can." But the real money isn't in programs or advertising: it's in merchandising and licensing, both of which are "far more lucrative." It's wise to be a little subtle, she warns. Children's TV programs such as *Tiny Toons* can drive parents – who recognize them as thirty-minute commercials for spinoff products – to fly into an "apoplectic rage."

So, get in the loop, Boot tells us. There's another medium with a much higher parent-approval factor – computers! Interactivity – especially if it's established from an early age – gets children "to bond with your branded characters," not just at home, but in wired day-care centres and schools too. She sums up with a somewhat enigmatic statement: "In today's world, we all have to look for strange bedfellows." The future is about "relationship marketing," and while everyone "must exercise sensitivity, there's room for advertisers who can meet the interactive challenge." The future belongs to the marketer who gets the mix among relationships, sensitivity, children, and technology just right. Welcome to the future. Welcome to Tamagotchi.

Cheep Thrills

In the first months of 1997, a new craze swept Japan. Suddenly, thousands of kids had something millions of others wanted – a virtual pet named Tamagotchi. The object of Tamagotchi is to hatch and nurture an LCD image of a chick into adult chicken-hood, tend it by pushing little buttons, and then watch it die.

If caring for a doomed virtual chicken doesn't sound appealing, imagine becoming a slave to feed it, scoop its poop, give it medicine when it's sick, and monitor its vital signs. Its hold on its owners/ parents isn't well understood. Bandai, its manufacturer, claims that it "runs on the notion that humans have a motherly instinct." This theory may explain Tamagotchi's popularity among high school girls, but not the increase in arrests for violent robberies of Tamagotchis – custody battles, perhaps? The parental instinct hypothesis doesn't speak too well for future fathers, either, who have been known to race their friends to see who can kill their chick the fastest through extreme neglect. Mikey (U.S.A.), an unrepentant bereaved father, e-mailed his eulogy for "l'il goober" to the cyber-cemetery for virtual pets: "I'm sorry it had to end this way. . . . I'm sorry that I left you at work. But hey, now I don't have to take your shit anymore."

Despite the toy's annoying habit of beeping interminably to demand virtual food, clean-ups of digital droppings, and discipline, Tamagotchi has tapped into a worldwide yearning – although whether it is for pets, children, relationships, or responsibility isn't clear. Since the chicks are programmed with personalities that allegedly respond well to strict discipline and regular care, but "go bad" when neglected or overindulged, a chick that lives to the ripe age of twenty days reflects well on its master. Says Reiko Zanna, a Japanese essayist, Tamagotchi's secret is that it isn't alive, so it provides "satisfaction on a 'virtual' level, which has been instilled in young people today."[23]

Five million Tamagotchis were sold in Japan in less than six months at prices ranging from sixteen dollars to thirty times that amount on the black market – the virtual game was virtually always sold out. Thousands of Japanese camped out overnight waiting in front of toy stores rumoured to have received a new shipment. American toy stores were sold out instantly when the eggs arrived in June. Bandai, which also manufactures Power Rangers and Sailor Moon toys, says its profits will depend on its success in launching lawsuits against its imitators. It is also branching out, allegedly planning a sequel that will feature "a male and female creature breeding a new chick." Whether nature can compete with the thrill of organized crime is another question. A Hong Kong competitor is launching a Triad-friendly version, featuring a teenaged hero who must be fed cigarettes and alcohol to keep his place in the secret society.[24]

Teachers across Asia were reported to be "already facing periods of chaos and sometimes near hysteria from children with the Tamagotchi pets. Classes were frequently disrupted when little alarms warned that their virtual pets were facing a life-threatening need for cleaning or sustenance,"[25] according to the *Ottawa Citizen*. Some Asian schools banned virtual pets. Children worried that their mothers, although usually at home, might neglect their little charges.

North American teachers, knowing that the typical mom is not always available at the peck and call of a demanding chick, had to choose between possibly condemning their students' pets to an untimely death or facing constant classroom interruptions. Either way, they got involved in the most bizarre form of grief counselling, and wondered what kind of sadism could lead parents to buy a creature their children would love and then watch die in a few days. To marketers, each chicken's death was a bonanza. To Tamagotchi's attached parents/owners, it was a burial. In the virtual graveyard for expired chickens were posted eulogies from England, the United States, and Singapore. From Ng Serene in Singapore: "My beloved Agi, I am very sorry that you had to die so young because your mommy overslept. Rest in peace. Amen. Love." Perhaps children would find it less traumatizing to raise a virtual virtual pet, downloaded from Tamagotchi's home page, accessed via Channel One's home page. Gee, it's a small world after all.

Day Two

Candi Schwartz welcomes participants to what she hopes will be a quiet day after yesterday's media attention, "which everyone handled really, really well." Most of us had seen a one-minute clip of the protest on last night's news, followed by a defence of the conference by its organizers. The *Globe and Mail* ran a 250-word story. Hardly bold media scrutiny, but enough to discourage a couple of presenters who backed out of day two, including Gordon Cressy of The Learning Partnership, a Toronto-based consortium founded by "education and business leaders who believe education is everyone's business."

Today's first presenter is Linda Magnall, president of Imagination Youth Marketing, on proprietary kids magazines – "a reach on the rise." We discover a PKM is an extended advertisement in magazine format, published by corporations with marketing smarts and deep pockets. The number of PKMs has doubled in the last decade, as marketers discover that kids find magazines more "hands-on and personal" than books. Magnall explains that overexposure has made even the youngest TV viewers cynical, but luckily for PKMs (or their owners), kids still believe that if it's in print, it must be true.

Magnall claims that the most successful PKM ever is McDonald's *Fun Times*, honoured world-wide as an "overall company image-builder." *Fun Times* is a "pro-social effort to fight illiteracy," says Magnall, and it's even "endorsed by Frontier College and the Canadian Library Association." Originally, *Fun Times* was designed for "pre-literates" (more conventionally known as pre-schoolers), and its goal was "to build character recognition" of Ronald McDonald et al. But in the mid 1980s, Magnall tells us, McDonald's underwent "a radical change in its marketing objectives." Environmentalists – led mainly by youth – had made the connection between hamburger consumption and rain forest destruction. Ever-sensitive to customer opinion, the retrofitted *Fun Times* would drop Ronald in favour of rain forests with its savvy audience of eight- to twelve-year-olds. McDonald's would be repositioned as a friend of the environment. So-called facts about eco-friendly McDonald's are now dropped into articles throughout the magazine. The corporation's drawn-out but finally successful prosecution of British environmental activists has not yet been mentioned.

Success breeds imitation. Magnall speaks admiringly of a major financial services corporation that has established a PKM, even though few children require investment advice. The investment firm knows that it is possible to "develop a solid relationship that will stay with kids through their decision-making years." Magnall urges PKM hopefuls to respect children's "cognitive levels," a point she illustrates, peculiarly, by observing that "pre-literates still have their parents involved." Avoid misspelling and anything too complex, we're told; words such as *metamorphosis* are out. Subtlety is an issue, but with care your corporate message can be inserted in such a way that the company will receive "absolutely no negative feedback." Done right, a PKM doesn't just avoid criticism, but will attract public financing. What could be better than using tax dollars to get your corporate message to kids? Let's hear it for the Junior Jays!

The Junior Jays' success story is recounted by Eric Conroy, president of Community Programs Group. Conroy explains that he learned the philosophy he applies to the Junior Jays at teachers' college, but that he knew elementary school teaching wasn't for him when his first principal discouraged him from moonlighting. Teaching at the high school level better accommodated his ambitions, but in the end, teaching just couldn't compete with "alternative methods to reach young minds."

Conroy obviously relishes telling the convoluted history of the Junior Jays. We learn that this PKM began as the solution to a problem of political correctness. For a decade, police officers had been visiting classrooms across Canada, preaching bicycle safety with varying levels of enthusiasm and with indifferent results. The Canadian Association of Chiefs of Police wanted to spruce up the program by handing out comic books when officers visited schools. Naturally, just like real comics, the play-safe version would need lots of advertising. A partnership was born: Marvel Comics handed over Spiderman, and with McDonald's in the lead, "the conscience of corporate Canada opened." The police chiefs' association raised $10.5 million in no time flat. The Spiderman comic was an instant success with both kids and police officers.

"Then came the day the earth stood still," said Conroy. He met with officials from what was then Health and Welfare Canada. The feds were dealing with the perennial problem of how to get their messages to kids when education and health were both jealously guarded provincial turf. The government was interested in a vehicle, and Spiderman looked appealing.

Alas, Spiderman was about to succumb to the strange illness of political correctness. Spidey was "white, male, Anglo-Saxon, and middle class . . . just the kind of thing the people outside yesterday wouldn't appreciate," explains Conroy, with a smirk. What was worse, someone noticed that kids who didn't speak English or French – "immigrant kids" – were being ignored. "Now who'd think of that?" asked Conroy. Spiderman was banished; the Junior Jays were born. The group of pre-teen baseball fans portrays several races and includes one girl, one dog, and one boy in a wheelchair, led by an octogenarian coach, Dr. Jay.

Conroy boasts that more than one million copies of the spring issue of *Junior Jays Magazine* were handed out to children through elementary schools. The issue included full-page ads from Mighty Morphin Power Rangers, Cheesestrings, and National Trust. An assortment of more subliminal messages is buried in the illustrations: Dr. Jay's time machine is a Coke can, the kids eat at McDonald's, and they wear Warner Bros. T-shirts. The Junior Jays even seek adventure in the wetlands with Ducks Unlimited, another corporate sponsor.

The copy is unrelentingly pro-social: physical fitness, inclusiveness, tolerance, anti-bullying, fire-prevention awareness, environmentalism, and personal safety all find their place. Advertisers are obviously eager to associate themselves with such important causes. Presumably, Hubba Bubba, Nintendo, Eggo, and Esso are among those stalwart corporations toiling to support employment equity, fair corporate taxation, an end to child poverty, and more strict environmental legislation. Both Health Canada and Heritage Canada must think so too, since their logos appear throughout.

Social responsibility, post-modern style, is definitely on the agenda. Alan Ayward, a specialist in social marketing, warns us from the podium that he intends to "provoke and annoy" participants – a consumer advisory, repeated several times during the presentation, that proves to be unduly alarmist. Note-taking has ceased almost entirely. Perhaps it is Ayward's admission that he considers himself a SNAG – a "sensitive New Age guy." Obviously a high-disclosure type, he explains that he began his career working with children with physical disabilities, but he lost interest once his program became "bureaucratized."

Ayward's upbeat and fast-forward presentation seems to be about enabling corporations to act on their conscientious instincts. He proclaims that we now live in a consumer-driven society, and that anyone who doesn't accept this "will be annihilated." He claims to be "astounded" by the illiteracy of Canadians, and quotes wildly distorted literacy figures in passing. It's not that corporations don't care deeply about problems like illiteracy, says Ayward, it's just that there are "too many layers preventing corporations from confronting social problems."

Ayward moves quickly to his next proposition. Product-driven information is out; consumer-driven information is in, because "it empowers citizens to become better." While I'm still trying to figure this out, he provides a concrete example: "Molson's has the essence on community," he explains. I am not yet provoked and enraged, but I am certainly mystified. "There is no distance between the seller and buyer, between the corporation and the customer" in the new economy, because we have "a shared destiny." Marketing must have a "democratic ring to it. It must be driven by value-based, cus-tomer-controlled integration, and outside-in marketing that dis-tributes personal freedom and liberty. . . . Don't play deceitful games," he exhorts us. "Exercise shared-destiny values, premised upon virtual behaviour, inside and outside!"

Could he have meant *virtuous behaviour*? If he did, would his explanation make any more sense? Perhaps he is saying that, given half a chance, corporations will flock to cause-related mar-keting, and then any remaining distinctions between corporate values and citizens' (or rather customers') higher principles will disappear. It is not clear whether this merger will be subject to conflict-of-interest guidelines. I look around: participants register indifference rather than consternation. Ayward invites reaction and pauses dramatically, but no questions are forthcoming.

In Focus

I guess we're ready for something a little less New Age. Goody Gerner, conference chairperson and president of Generations Research Inc., is about to tell us how to talk to kids. Kid research through focus groups is a vital component of marketing, but there are "parameters," we are told – not the kind that safeguard kids, but the kind a smart researcher learns from experience.

First, Gerner explains, an effective focus group should be made up of kids no more than two or three years apart in age. The sub-jects must be same-sex, kept for no more than forty-five minutes, and never expected to participate in groups of more than ten or "it's just impossible to get anything done." I wait for an expression of admiration for teachers who routinely work with diverse groups of thirty or thirty-five students hour after hour, but none is forth-coming. "Don't assume kids know anything," she advises. "Just explain what you want and they'll play it back to you. . . . Be realistic: kids can't abstract; if you ask them to they won't know what you're talking about. And don't expect them to read. Even teenagers, who hopefully can read, won't."

Wise researchers recognize that kids have unique personalities. If you want them to work together, you have to learn how to control the dominators and encourage the ones who are reactors, not idea-generators. "Be sensitive: don't push them to the point of tears," she warns. "I've seen that happen." This comment leads to a discussion of gender differences and how they can be accommodated and exploited. Gerner maintains that most girls are stuck in "acquiescence" mode. "It's horrible!" she says. "But you have to get around it." One-way mirrors are a real problem since girls will waste most of the researcher's time looking at themselves. "You feel for them sometimes," she says.

Good researchers should apply a little creativity to work with the boys who show off and the girls who are too quiet. Gerner advises focusing on "the non-conscious level" by observing play, fantasy, children's drawings, and associations. She says she has encouraged twelve-year-old best friends to tell each other "the worst thing about getting your period" while they are being observed through a one-way glass. Someone asks for other exam-ples of fertile subjects for kid-group research. Gerner hesitates for a moment, and then apologizes: she's unable to come up with an example that doesn't invade corporate privacy. The irony passes unnoticed.

"Is it a good idea to do focus groups in schools?" a participant asks. Unfortunately not, says Gerner, although her clients keep suggesting it. First, you typically get "a really bad room" to work in, and the kids aren't all that interested. There's also too much bureaucracy. Apparently, getting approval to conduct first-hand research in classrooms on what kids think about bubble gum still takes time. Better venues, like malls, have fewer rules. If you're smart, however, you don't need to follow any rules at all. Spying in schoolyards is effective. So is watching children making consumer decisions in corner stores.

While these time-tested techniques still work, they aren't cutting edge. The Kid Power staff distributes flyers advertising the next conference: Techno-Kids: Reaching Today's 38 Million Kids with Technology. "Dear Executive," the promo reads. "Kids today are tuned in to high-tech as early as age 2. . . . [They] are becoming increasingly formidable consumers. . . ." Attend this conference to learn how school programs can be used to support marketing efforts, how to mix education with marketing to reach a broader audience, and how to develop brand and product relationships with kids. The secret is to get in early, "flanking competitors by developing young loyalists who move on to become adult buyers of a company's full range of products." It seems the kids are changing along with their technology. How can marketers mine the essence of relationship with these new customers? Attend Techno-Kids and discover "how psychology and anthropology merge to reveal kids' underlying and cultural connections to interactivity," and then turn this knowledge into money. Apply years of PhD expertise to your "child consumer" problems. Special price for two days: $1,195 (U.S.).

Techno-Kids

No wonder the organizers saved techno-marketing for another seminar and another set of registration cheques. These seminars are sell-outs. No one who wants to sell to kids can afford to ignore the horde of on-line two- to seventeen-year-olds, expected to be a force of twenty million by 2002. Site sponsors have been eager to get in early, getting first crack at the lucrative cybertot category. Once conditioned to regard the computer as a kid-friendly mall, they're hooked for good. The Internet's transformation into an electronic flyer is annoying to most adults, but at least they know when they're being pitched. Kids are more vulnerable. As they log on rather than tune in, they become engaged in a medium more private and more interactive than television. As Web technology matures, new levels of interactivity, real-time video technologies, and VRML (Virtual Reality Monitoring Language) will lure kids into an even more captivating environment.

The possibilities of marketing on-line to kids have been exploited so unscrupulously that publicity generated by American watchdog groups has made headlines. The fuss that prompted this response arose from a study called "Web of Deception: Threats to Children from On-line Marketing," published by the Centre for Media Education (CME) in 1996.[26] Unlike other high-profile critiques of the Net, "Web of Deception" doesn't focus on personal safety or pornography, topics that marketers would like to see get all the attention. Nor does CME deal with obscure, two-bit on-line hucksters – they take on Disney, Nintendo, Kellogg's, and Frito-Lay, corporations with stables of lawyers as well as marketers.

CME says advertising agencies such as Saatchi & Saatchi set up units to study children on-line and refine marketing strategies to target them. According to CME, cultural anthropologists have been hired to examine the nature of kids' culture, researchers have studied how children process information and respond to advertising, and psychologists have conducted one-on-one sessions with focus groups. These experts conclude that children, whose "learning skills are at their peak," can easily master the new media. According to child development experts, the on-line world corresponds to the four themes of childhood: attachment/separation, attainment of power, social interaction, and mastery/learning. Better yet, when children go on-line, they quickly enter the "flow state," that "highly pleasurable experience of total absorption in a challenging activity." According to CME, these factors combined make on-line media a perfect vehicle for advertising to children: "There is nothing else that exists like it for advertisers to build relationships with kids."

Meeting children's developmental needs through on-line advertising means convincing kids that products and/or technology are all-purpose problem-solvers that can substitute for human interaction. Marketers carefully cultivate this techno-illusion of

relationship by collecting data about individual kids, their prefer-
ences and habits. To make "microtargeting" work, they must
extract the information from kids themselves.

Once in a site, kids are asked (often in the guise of joining a
"club") about themselves and their families. ("Good citizens of
the Web," reads the Batman Forever site, "help Commissioner
Gordon with the Gotham Census.") The survey is often sweet-
ened with an incentive, such as a free screen saver or a mouse pad,
and both greedy and gullible kids cheerfully disclose personal and
consumer information on demand. Disclaimers such as "check
with your parents first" can't compete with opportunities to win
KidsCash, or with the thrill of receiving a personalized e-mail
from Mickey.

Technology offers marketers even more: an opportunity to track
where kids have been within a Web site, and a record of other sites
they have visited. This information is known as "clickstream data"
or "mouse droppings." According to CME, "a burgeoning industry
has developed to provide such online tracking services," led by
Netscape Communications Corp. Mouse droppings not only give
marketers feedback about how well users are interacting with their
advertising, but can also be used to trigger personal product messages to children, urging them to return to a certain site. More
sophisticated systems will soon permit marketers to individualize
advertising, "based on intimate knowledge of a child's interests,
behaviour, socioeconomic status . . . and unique vulnerabilities."
The compiled data can also be sold to other marketers without
breaching any law.

At least television has been subjected to regulatory safeguards,
based on kids' documented inability to distinguish between
advertising and content, and their vulnerability to the pitches
made by spokespersons – real or animated. The (U.S.) Federal
Communications Commission (FCC) requires "separators" between
children's programs and commercials, forbids the host from pitching products, and limits the amount of advertising on kids'
shows. The rapidly evolving world of cyberspace has no such
rules or traditions.

Marketing on-line has no natural boundaries. Unlike a TV ad that has a fixed duration, an advertising site can hold a child's attention indefinitely. To keep the user from moving on, the ad must be made as engaging as the content or, better yet, melded with the content for maximum effect. Banners and icons on kid sites turn out to be gateways to new advertising environments. Tooth fairies suddenly pitch toothpaste. You don't want to know where 101 Dalmations will take you, unless you have a yen for dappled wallpaper.

CME found dozens of sites that promote a "smoking is cool" culture, such as Smokey's Café, on the Smoker's Home Page. Against a backdrop of glamorous photos of famous celebrities lighting up, "smokers (and would-be-smokers) can chat with other smokers [and] read pro-smoking articles," one of which is entitled "Secondhand Smoke: The Big Lie."[27] Kids can drop into Molson's Berserk in Banff to play an interactive game, or visit Budbrew Budfrog, who "likes to hang out on the beach with a hot babe, a cold bud and a folio edition of the Kama Sutra."[28] Many sites encourage on-line purchasing. There is no way to check whether the buyer is of age.

As advertising is integrated with content, we can see the future unfolding. An investment firm boasts that "we are seeing the beginning of what will happen on interactive television: the info-mercialization of all programming."[29] As Saatchi & Saatchi says, the goal will be to interrupt "the flow state" as little as possible, seamlessly blending ads and content. When a children's television program was built around Frito-Lay's Chester Cheetah, a vigorous protest made the Fox network back down. But now Chester is quite at home on-line, playing host and sponsor, building brand loyalty with impunity. With techno-enhanced capabilities, a 3-D Chester in full-motion video will be able to solidify his relationship with children around the world.

The Centre for Media Education called for FCC regulations "to protect children from manipulative, invasive, and deceptive advertising on line." These regulations would prohibit the collection of children's personal data (including clickstream data) on-line and its sale. Advertising on children's sites would not be banned, but clearly labelled and separated from content. The content areas could not establish hotlinks to advertising sites. Product spokes-characters would not be allowed to interact with children, and the microtargeting of ads (including e-mail messages) would be prohibited. After the media dust settled, what the CME and children got were insipid self-regulatory industry standards. As a result, only the marketers' approach will be slightly curtailed, while their access to kids will actually increase.

According to NBC, "Rather than hinder marketing to kids online . . . the standards will encourage marketers who have held back from Web advertising because there hadn't been clear direction."[30] Wanna-be Web advertisers who were allegedly reluctant to jump on-line will be encouraged by the "responsible parameters" that leave lots of room for them to manoeuvre, according to the industry. The rules are simple: advertisers should "seek parental permission" before asking personal questions, children should "clearly understand when they are buying something," and "a strong line should be drawn between content and advertising."

This "strong line" means that playing a game with Tony the Tiger isn't advertising until Tony actually tells a child to buy something[31] – a convenient distinction that capitalizes on young children's inability to identify advertising under any circumstances, and our collective inability (à la screen savers) to identify limits, let alone set them. Despite its catalogue of marketing offences, CME insists that the Net medium itself is not the problem, just its lack of regulation; and the centre still enthusiastically supports policies "to ensure all children are connected to the Internet."[32] Nothing will deter the march of technology, because the future is at stake.

Marketing in the Global City

Technology is credited with hastening our convergence into one world. Techno-enthusiasts boast that because information technology homogenizes experience and information, it strengthens the common foundations and shared assumptions on which civilization rests. This conclusion mistakes cultural imperialism for cultural convergence: the McCulture of McWorld is distinctly American. It also mistakes consumer culture for civilization. As the whole world adopts a taste for name-brand consumption, it is easy to overlook a parallel trend in the global city – the fragmentation of interests, communities, and nations.

Horrendous ethnic, religious, and tribal conflicts have replaced wars between nation-states, but less violent "tribes" also thrive. In the global city, small groups of like-minded individuals pursue their special interests by disassociating themselves from others who differ by class, colour, religion, or ideology. As McCulture and obligatory globalization become more pervasive, this dissent is intensified. Shaking a tribal fist at an encroaching KFC franchise in India has much in common with choosing to create a charter school in Calgary. In both instances, groups are seeking to protect their own against the encroachment of McWorld and its fall-out. But tribalism isn't restricted to geography. Technology encourages groups to form around everything from UFO abductions to libertarianism – around common interests or common wealth, not just common physical circumstances.

Technology is the ultimate mercenary soldier, serving both convergence and tribalization at the same time. While these two forces are in conflict with each other, their real enemy is democracy. Tribalism needs adherents, not citizens. It has no use for the nation-state, in which democracy exists, or the values that support it. Democracy requires a level of compromise and accommodation that is intolerable to "true believers" devoted to self-interest or the entitlements of their own group.

The democratic nation-state is also the enemy of McWorld, since it represents the only potential barrier to unrestricted, unregulated commerce, and the only possible impediment to the utter triumph of markets. Democracy's most important attribute – an informed citizenry – is equally problematic. McWorld seeks customers, not citizens: free-floating consumers whose tastes can be manipulated and whose skills can be adapted to the interests of capital.

Not surprisingly, schools – those democratically governed creations of nation-states, churning out believers/citizens/consumers – are contested and prized terrain. It is one thing to capture a market; it is another to capture the mind of a whole generation.

Asia Connects

The Asia Connects project was sponsored by the Students Commission of Canada, the Asia Pacific Foundation, Foreign Affairs and International Trade Canada, Human Resources Development Canada, and Bell Learning Solutions.[33] According to its sponsors, Asia Connects was designed to help teachers and students get the "global team feeling" about APEC and celebrate 1997, Canada's Year of the Asia-Pacific. Teachers were promised that exciting on-line activities would "encourage personal interaction and connection at the relationship level as well as the cognitive." The pitch to students was more direct: Go on a free trip! Play with new technology! Find a friend! Schools in every province and territory signed up and logged on.

The project's home page provided details: the week started with a Web welcome to all participating classrooms, and moved quickly to site development of a home page. One day was spent looking at "Asian and Western Values," another at "Making Asia Part of Your Life." The week ended with a full day devoted to "Your Future in the Global Economy." Students who demonstrated a particular aptitude for the global team feeling were invited to a conference held in Winnipeg, all expenses paid, where the young participants generated recommendations to the leaders of the APEC economies.

The backers of the project were evidently concerned that students might be harbouring some misconceptions about the issues that APEC insists be ignored, such as human rights and labour standards. The Asia Connects organizers relied on adolescent self-interest to work in their favour: "Think of this simple example. Go to your closet and look at the tags on your clothes. . . . Many of them are from Asian countries like Thailand or Indonesia. What about your walkman, CD player and television?

How might your life be affected if Canada stopped trading with Thailand or Indonesia?"

These questions set up an all-important session called "Behind the Headlines: Environment, Trade and Human Rights." According to Asia Connects, students must understand that "there is a growing tendency in many societies to look only at headlines and news stories to make judgements." These news stories are apparently unreliable and fail to convey the complexity and context of the issues.

For example, Asia Connects tells students, "Many headline[s] about the horrors of child labour have graced the front pages of Canadian newspapers." Canadians leap to the conclusion that "such a practice is inhumane and should be stopped immediately." They fail to realize that when the choice is between prostitution and "working in industries that may be considered below standard in the Western perspective," often "becoming a child labourer is the better option."

Advocating trade sanctions is also the kind of superficial position that students might pick up from reading news stories about human rights issues. "It's easy to say [we should impose sanctions] . . . but so what if Canada alone does this? . . . Maybe Canada could keep on trading with such a country while pressuring for UN-imposed sanctions which is [sic] much more effective." Students can forget about pressuring leaders and governments; apparently, even in totalitarian states, "It's not usually the people at the top who have the power to change things, but the people at the bottom."

When the week ended, organizers asked participants to ponder the long-term, real-life applications of what they had learned: "Tomorrow morning when [you] wake up, what concrete actions can [you] take to carry on the legacy of Asia Connects?" Report via point-to-point videoconferencing. Thank the Canadian government for underwriting your learning experience.

E-mail copies to the global city.

7

SELLING EDUCATION

Robert Moses designed roads, parks, and bridges in the state of New York between 1920 and 1970. He planned more than two hundred parkway overpasses that allowed only nine feet of clearance, effectively preventing the twelve-foot-high buses carrying blacks and the poor from gaining access to the parkways. Moses believed that only the white middle class should be entitled to enjoy his smooth, modern highways. The supposedly neutral tool of construction technology masked his racism, perpetuating his parkways and his politics long after his death. Generations of civil rights activists have tried and failed to dismantle New York's segregated communities.

Philosopher Langdon Winner began asking, "Do artifacts have politics?" almost twenty years ago.[1] Winner tells the parkway story to illustrate how artifacts – things – can produce intended political effects. But Winner goes further: he concludes that things can have intrinsic political consequences, independent of the motives of the people behind them. He believes that it is not a society's dominant ideas, but its dominant technologies – its artifacts – that determine how each society hoards or distributes power. If Winner is right, then the power of our intentions declines as the power of our artifacts increases. Our objects shape us more than we shape them, so our intentions are somewhat irrelevant. To test this idea, Winner examines the effects of technologies that seem, superficially, to be value-free, or even progressive.

The development of the mechanical tomato-harvester was not a political statement, but its introduction dramatically shifted power relations nonetheless. Because the harvester decreased the need for field workers, Mexican labourers lost their jobs. The profits of Anglo farmers increased, but only until they too lost their livelihood to big agribusiness. While the inventors of the harvesting machine harboured none of the racist or mega-capitalist biases of Moses, their motives were irrelevant. Artifacts have their own politics.

The natural political drift of technology is towards the concentration of power. The owners, designers, and first merchants of any technology will determine how it is used, and by whom. These elite and self-serving interests will always benefit much more than any of technology's downstream users, who will gain access only when it suits those who control the technology. If we remain mindful of this reality and also suspicious of our artifacts' political tendencies, we may be able to offset these mutually reinforcing effects. Unfortunately, our determination to see information technologies as only a tool, albeit an inevitable, inescapable one, blinds us to the power shifts – the political consequences – imbedded within them. We convince ourselves that our intentions as users are all that matter. This mistake delivers the politics of technology into a very few hands.

When Winner said that our willingness to accommodate technology could trick us into tolerating otherwise unacceptable ideas, he was not speaking about information technology or the privatization of public education. After all, he was writing in 1980. But by 1996, Winner was warning that "thinly veiled corporate ideas, contexts and initiatives," justified by "technological necessity," were redefining education as just another commodity. The language of business – of customers and clients – was replacing the language of inquiry and community. Information technology was becoming the excuse to deform the meaning of education, and was gaining the power to make this disfiguration seem inevitable, even desirable. Power was shifting because a new set of artifacts was beginning to have its way with our public institutions.[2]

The marketplace language that Winner criticizes is more than the annoying encroachment of biz-speak. Our language and our thoughts shape each other. Once education is commodified, restricting its delivery to the not-for-profit, state-managed sector becomes indefensible. Automobiles are also commodities, but the idea that the state should govern and finance car dealerships died with the Soviet-style command economy. If students and parents are only customers and clients; if the curriculum is merely market-sensitive training; if the school is just the production facility/factory; then what is left of the rationale for public education? What logic excludes entrepreneurs from demanding access to education's customers, particularly if the existing public system, which we are told we can no longer afford, is failing to prepare students for the (etc. etc.) future?

"PUBLIC EDUCATION . . . HAS not outlived its usefulness to this country, but unless it embraces the emerging education marketplace, its power and significance will rapidly diminish. . . . It's time for education to roll up its sleeves and play hard-ball on capitalism's new frontier."

Source: Education Industry Report, March 1997

This is the laundered version of the argument for dismantling the state monopoly of public education. This argument is effective because, having bought the assumptions imbedded in its language, we are obliged to accept its conclusion. We have become so accustomed to the market metaphor that it no longer seems out of place, either in our language or as the model for our institutions and their reform. Both the metaphor and the argument perfectly suit the politics of technology. Technology becomes the mechanism and the excuse for education reform: the value-neutral rationale that can't be challenged. As a result, the real reason for bringing the market to education – giving corporate North America access to the profits to be skimmed from the $600 billion education industry – can remain buried. This motive tends to surface only when privatization's ideologues are seeking converts or investors are seeking capital.

The Education Industry Report

Occasionally, demographic trends and technologies converge to allow an industry to experience strong growth for several years. The education market appears to be positioned in exactly such a favourable environment. . . . We base this belief on the ongoing shift of our society to a knowledge-based or information economy.[3]

Subtitled "News and commentary on the growing education industry," the *Education Industry Report* (EIR) is published and edited by John M. McLaughlin. He is one of a burgeoning group of experts anxious to help investors profit from the privatization of public education, an "industry" that is about to be "blown up by technology and demographics."[4] Like most investment newsletters, EIR has editorial opinions beyond what's hot and what's not. McLaughlin compares the problems of public education to a malingering and annoying virus: "The cause of the common cold which affects our education system is not limited to the unions, television or welfare. It is not only special education expenditures, aging facilities, or an overindulgence in sports. It is not simply desegregation. . . . The cause of the malady is all of the above and a lot more."[5]

According to McLaughlin, the cause of the malady, from a market perspective, is that there is too little market and too much monopoly: "Since public schools are a monopoly, one would expect public schools to function less efficiently than private schools. . . . Most public schools lack the incentives necessary to cause them to pay closer attention to their clients' wishes."[6]

Speaking to a one-day seminar held in Toronto in 1997 – the Education Industry Summit – McLaughlin claimed Canada could actually move faster than the United States towards deregulated education markets because Canada has "less political baggage about the whole privatization thing." We need not worry; McLaughlin's bio, reproduced in the summit's program, says that he is "an advocate of the power of individuals and the free enterprise system to enrich lives and improve society through education."[7]

Some investors no doubt agree that the cure for education's supposed ailments is privatization. Others may be sceptical of privatization as a cure-all, but they can sense the political winds, which are assuredly blowing towards the privatization of public services. What began with health care in the United States is spreading to education. Once privatization takes off, the suppliers, managers, customers, and services of the education industry will constitute an enormous, largely unexploited market with unlimited investment potential.

The number of publicly traded education-related corporations has grown so quickly that EIR divides the for-profit education sector into several categories. EMOs are education management organizations, ESOs are education service organizations. Post-Secondary Schools has its own investment index, as do Training and Development, At-Risk Youth, and Education Products. Other education industry analysts, such as the Lehman Brothers, add pre-EMOs – child-care businesses – to their spectrum of goods and services ripe for investment.

According to an assortment of Wall Street analysts, the education industry is in the early stages of a significant growth cycle. People with money have figured out that education is an "investable" sector. Two decades ago, American hospitals that had depended on government money experienced serious financial problems as expenses outpaced revenues, according to Kian Ghazi, a Lehman Brothers' investment analyst. This funding crisis opened the doors to for-profit health maintenance organizations (HMOs), which grew until they could derail any government's plan to reassert the public interest. Ghazi says the parallels with education are obvious: "The concept of making a buck off the dying and sick was outlandish twenty years ago. Making money off kids – that's the same kind of thing. So change is possible."[8]

The change that matters most is changing the way we think about education. One of the marketers featured in the *Education Industry Report* has put his finger on the problem: "I am overwhelmed by the fact that . . . in education, profit is a filthy word. . . . To battle this prevalent bias, companies must not apologize for turning a profit. . . . The more we use the word, the less sting it has."[9] Once we think differently and become used to the education-profit connection, confusion is easily resolved. The investment firm KPMG Peat Marwick says it is this confusion that bogs down public education. The "Why are we here?" question tends to elicit dozens of different answers from faculty, but for-profit institutions don't face these existential dilemmas. "They'll say, 'We're here for profit! There is a focus! It's really neat!'"[10]

Neat Niche

In the name of efficiency and/or ideology, governments around the world are moving towards the full or partial privatization of services that have been traditionally public, from prisons to welfare. In education, privatization possibilities include everything from the operation of entire school systems, at the most ambitious, to niche opportunities such as janitorial services, transportation, catering, and other non-classroom functions.

These niche ventures are less risky from a political standpoint because their privatization can be sold to the public relatively easily. If it saves money for the classroom, surely privatizing certain services must be a good idea? A 1997 Vector poll found 49 per cent of respondents across Canada thought private employees would provide more reliable non-classroom services than public employees, while 38 per cent disagreed. Sixty-one per cent thought private employees would be cheaper than public ones; 29 per cent disagreed.[11] More than 60 per cent of the public said they didn't care one way or the other whether these jobs were privatized.

IF PRIVATIZATION IS the solution, what is the problem? According to the General Accounting Office of the U.S. government, where private contractors have been hired to take care of cafeteria services, the number of low-income students who are entitled to a free lunch has mysteriously declined. Yet districts contracting out have spent, on average, 21 per cent more than districts that provided their own food services. A majority of contractors were found to have ignored federal standards such as following federal nutrition guidelines and carrying out food quality inspection.

Source: "Privatization Alert," American Federation of Teachers

With public opinion on privatization so soft, it isn't surprising that school board decisions to contract out plant operations and maintenance have met limited resistance. Companies such as ServiceMaster Canada have done well in this area. This subsidiary of an American parent company, which positions "service to God" as its primary reason for being in business, has found religion a powerful sales and management technique. In exchange for lower wages and loss of job security, employees are promised "dignity and income through productivity." ServiceMaster's annual report quotes Proverbs: "In all labour there is profit, but mere talk leads only to poverty."[12] Although allegedly the company has cut corners on services and maintenance standards while chalking up a notoriously poor health and safety record,[13] investors' advisories single out ServiceMaster for doing "a wonderful job" in a niche with great potential.

The bread and butter of the educational services market – school maintenance, food services, and transportation – may soon be outpaced by the growth of other specialized services. These spill over into what were formerly the non-profit responsibilities of school boards. The Lehman Brothers remind investors that 83 per cent of education spending is service-driven, an even greater service-to-products ratio than found in health care. Specialized for-profit opportunities include "child reform services" (defined as residential juvenile justice programs), juku services (tutoring businesses named after Japanese-style cram schools), and employee leasing (temp-type placement services that help school districts "offload personnel costs").[14]

Even though analysts warn that some education market segments are complex and risky, they say other niche markets are every investor's dream, especially those that target students at risk. "It's a no-brainer," exults Michael Moe of Montgomery Securities. "The at-risk market for K–12 is doing very well, with great opportunities looking forward." EIR's education investment index confirms bullish prospects for companies carving profit out of the neediest kids in America, whose numbers, happily for investors, keep increasing.

BOASTING THAT HIS new business Score@Kaplan is exceeding all expectations for growth and productivity, Seppy Basil describes his new niche as providing parents with "outside opinions on their children's academic performance." The greatest growth comes from "the special education market," which demands tests and more tests. Basil is enthusiastic: "I call it the commodification of education!"

Source: Education Industry Report, May 1997

Any enterprise that emphasizes technology for kids is in the right business at the right time, but information-age angst may also explain an increasing demand for other specialized services. These include child study teams – psychologists, social workers, and learning disability consultants – who work with disturbed children but "add value because they don't require benefits that drive up the cost" (according to the Lehman Brothers), and home instruction for parents who like home schooling for their children but don't actually stay home themselves. These contracts can be monitored by employees recruited through administrative/supervisory services: agencies that supply "master [retired] administrators for temporary assignments, additional supervisory services and project work," who are available despite "a low daily rate and lack of benefits."

New thinking means new opportunities. Investment gurus insist this is only the beginning: reforms that promote charter schools, vouchers, outsourcing, corporate sponsorship, and tuition fees will soon replace public funding for K–12 education. Beyond being good news for investors, these reforms "share a common trait: they promote the notion that schools will benefit from a more competitive market place," according to EIR. Whether schools or only investors will benefit remains debatable.

THE FELLOW WHO WON the contract to start an alternative school for emotionally disturbed teenagers in Washington, D.C., had no building, no staff, no money, no experience in education, and no degree. He submitted invoices for fifty students, but fewer than twenty turned up. "Robinson never supplied students with books, frequently failed to provide lunch and allowed students to run wild," according to one former staffer. The contract was finally cancelled. The FBI is now investigating what happened to $407,900 in district funds.

Source: "Privatization Alert," American Federation of Teachers

---

In business terms, the public education system is uncompetitive because it's so slow to adopt high technology. This is a deficiency that private providers can exploit by doing business with the education products sector, which is on a tear. According to Smith Barney's investment advisors, the instructional media industry is heating up because the multimedia CD-ROM is every educator's (and busy parent's) dream. Software companies are ideally positioned to exploit increased sales of multimedia computers to schools and to upper-income families purchasing their second or third PC.[15] Privatization, or even the threat of privatization, will drive up sales because "competitive" schools will acquire more computers to show how up-to-date they are. Technology attracts customers in the marketplace of education.

Schools that at one time may have boasted about the superior quality of their caring and committed staff must rethink what really matters to customers. The most avid boosters of edu-tech actually refer to teachers as the vertical (i.e., standing) workforce. These vertical educators are inevitably imperfect. Fortunately, however, "unlike their human colleagues [!] computers are never too harried, never too distracted to notice a student is puzzled," says *Technos* magazine.[16] "The best computerized tutors can capture and hold a child's attention for hours. . . . In many ways, computers are the ideal teacher."

The threat of privatization means that this perception, no matter how off-base, cannot be ignored. Public schools that want to keep the for-profit mongers at bay will try to ensure their technology is as current as the kind the private competition is promising. This is a high-stakes contest. Bad decisions can be costly, or even disastrous. The for-profit sector is ready to provide expert advice to both sides. Corporations such as ServiceMaster have branched into technology outsourcing, which promises school systems the flexibility to get the technology they want "without breaking contracts or fighting with unions. . . . Outsourcing is the only way to ride the technology wave safely."[17]

It isn't difficult to understand why a school system would welcome this kind of help. Once a technology contract is signed, busy teachers and beleaguered superintendents can sigh with relief because taking care of technology has become someone else's problem. Investors watch their fortunes rise. The Lehman Brothers boast that, for "socio-political" reasons, there will be an "explosive demand for visionary companies" that understand information technology. Both the friends and opponents of privatization will maintain this demand: if those who favour privatization are touting technology, those who oppose it must push technology in self-defence. As Paul Starr writes in the progressive magazine *The American Prospect*, "Conservatives would like nothing better than to use the technological limitations of schools as a rationale for privatizing them or substituting a kind of high-tech home schooling. Inevitably, choices about technology become entangled in larger choices about politics."[18] The artifacts are at it again.

EMG

Towards the end of 1996, an American corporation known as EMG – the Education Management Group – made overtures to the Canadian market. Former directors of education of large Canadian school districts, now on EMG's payroll, pitched EMG's multimedia "curriculum on demand" to their former colleagues. EMG was footing the bill for interested senior board officials to visit their Scottsdale, Arizona, headquarters. There, prospective clients could discover just what EMG's owners – the telecommunications and entertainment giants Simon and Schuster, Paramount, and Viacom – have in mind for Canada's schools.

EMG sells an on-call library of multimedia instructional materials that are transmitted by satellite to its client schools. It has ambitions to become a one-stop provider of all curriculum content. Ideally, the teacher who is about to teach asexual reproduction, for example, could place her order with EMG; stock footage, perhaps augmented by interactive experts, would be ready to roll. What EMG doesn't have on hand, it will make overnight. EMG provides (on contract) the hardware as well as the software, and teacher training for both. In addition to on-line resources, EMG promises other services: to deliver pre-packaged or customized lesson plans that integrate appropriate Internet sites; to identify which curriculum standards are associated with the content; and to provide student assignments to match the content, and even "evaluation rubrics" for grading students. This is as close to paint-by-numbers as education gets. As EMG boasts, "real Internet, real curriculum, really easy."[19]

Several superintendents have taken EMG up on its offer to visit the group's American headquarters. Others want nothing to do with it. A few of the travellers have spread the word that EMG tells prospective clients that the way to finance the prorated $50,000 to $200,000 cost per school per year is to get rid of teachers. Officially, EMG says nothing of the kind in its promotional materials, which are full of references to "pedagogy" and "exemplary practice."[20] They also feature a growing number of references to Canada, where the "Pan-Canadian Group" of "school boards/districts, universities and corporations" supports "Canada's leadership in the emerging global economy."[21] York University is named as the site of EMG's Canadian studio.[22] Advisors from Memorial and Simon Fraser universities, and a handful of Atlantic, Ontario, and British Columbia boards, are also said to have been consulted. Together, they plan to Canadianize EMG content to be delivered to teachers and students "on demand." No doubt EMG materials will meet rigorous standards of excellence and, yes, prepare students for "the emerging global economy."

According to an enthusiastic article in *Scottsdale Magazine*, interactive education à la EMG is built on the idea that old-fashioned classrooms and textbooks just won't cut it anymore.[23] EMG knows that today's kids are more "visual," so having Ted Danson explain *Gulliver's Travels* was a great way for kids to study literature, and they learned a lot more when talk-show host Rosie O'Donnell "graced EMG's airwaves to inform and inspire [their] young minds."

EMG claims that 3,500 schools in forty-two states have signed on. The company is now gearing up for expansion into Mexico and Canada, adding new production capabilities to what it calls its war-room. According to EMG, once its interactive offerings have expanded, the company will be ready to set up an "Electronic High School," a home computer–delivered curriculum through which students can enjoy everything that high school offers – except real people.

Most high school students probably wouldn't be too thrilled with this proposition, but we can understand the appeal of EMG and its imitators to school boards. One-stop shopping for curriculum, technology, teacher training, and evaluation can sound appealing at almost any price, given rising expectations in all of these areas. Many teachers who are short on equipment, resources, and planning time, but overwhelmed by ever-changing curricula and increasing numbers of kids, might be willing to give EMG a try. EMG can even make up for the casualties of educational restructuring: "We know the importance of the arts and humanities, but with declining budgets, these 'special' teachers are frequently overextended or nonexistent."[24]

This kind of logic convinced West Vancouver's Rockridge Middle School to sign up with EMG in the fall of 1996. According to Kit Kreiger, now president of the B.C. Teachers' Federation, the technical problems that plagued the opening-day demonstration – and delayed start-up for three months – were an ominous sign of the gap between the shiny promises and what EMG actually delivered.[25] Once the system was running, despite what Kreiger calls "considerable pressure," most teachers found little use for what EMG had to offer. In short, says Kreiger, "teachers found the material dumbed-down and Americanized." They soon learned to order materials geared to American Grade 11 kids for their own Grade 7 and 8 students.

The pre-existing resource library that EMG offered turned out to have a lot of gaps, and the produced-on-demand materials tended to be limited to talking heads. True to its word, EMG did Canadianize some of its content – most memorably by dressing an Arizona-accented presenter in a Toronto Maple Leafs hockey sweater, an effort that probably didn't go over too well with the Vancouver Canucks fans in Rockridge. Before long, even the enthusiasts on Rockridge staff became disillusioned, particularly when they realized the money flowing south to Scottsdale could have bought a lot of teacher time and locally available Canadian materials.

The board has rejected requests by the West Vancouver Teachers' Association to evaluate EMG, on the grounds that it is "too early" to assess the program fairly. Teachers say they are concerned that if and when an evaluation takes place, it will be influenced by people too closely tied to the American group. According to Kreiger, any fair evaluation is unlikely to show that EMG has "transformed teaching and learning" at Rockridge, but the EMG-supplied TV monitors do serve at least one useful purpose: "Teachers no longer endure disruptive announcements reminding students to pick up their lunch in the office – the kids' names come up on the monitor."

Given this inauspicious debut, could EMG become a serious contender in the Canadian education market? Some say no. Anyone who thinks multimedia-on-demand, with or without Rosie O'Donnell, can substitute for what really takes place in a classroom hasn't been in one lately. Others aren't so sure. It may well have occurred to a few ministries (whose representatives have also visited Scottsdale) that if the teaching machine could be perfected, seamlessly linked with a standardized curriculum and evaluated by standardized tests, then technicians or instructional aides monitored by a few supervisors could probably take care of classrooms. As long as human beings account for the largest portion of education budgets, ways to use fewer people, pay them less, and control them more closely will always have some appeal. EMG's other advantage is technology. Do enough decision makers believe that anything electronic is by definition superior to anything that is not? Do enough believe that EMG (or its clones) constitute the wave of the future, like it or not?

At a July 1997 meeting of the SchoolNet advisory board, Industry Canada signalled where it thinks all this should lead.[26] SchoolNet's first five-year mandate was to connect every school in the country to the Internet, and three and a half years later, progress on connectivity was ahead of schedule. What next? Doug Hull, SchoolNet's director, raised the spectre of EMG in an attempt to convince SchoolNet's multi-sector board members that their fealty to home-grown not-for-profit "product" was touching but impractical. Now that SchoolNet's advisory board has been disbanded in favour of what Hull calls info-tech "players," SchoolNet II is positioned to finance and promote a Canadian version of EMG, serving up sophisticated virtual product for export purposes. However, unless Canadian schools buy into it too, the product will be tough to market internationally. Time for some strategy. A consortium of school boards, universities, and technology companies has already convened to work on "the vision thing," which will lead quickly to "the profit thing." Industry Canada will have a new plum to offer the high-tech sector. To the savvy entrepreneur, EMG isn't a problem after all: it is an opportunity.

Manufacturing Criticism

> The classic investment opportunity involves a company that has a systematic solution to a problem. . . . There is no question that there is a 'problem' in education. . . . The timing for entry into the market has never been better. . . . Businesses complain that they cannot employ the product coming out of our schools because graduates cannot read and write. . . .[27]
>
> – Lehman Brothers

Public sentiment is the only real barrier to privatization. Teachers and their unions can be de-legislated or disempowered; school boards can be eliminated; kids have no political voice; parents are disorganized; friends of the public good can be distracted and demoralized. But public opinion, if not the public itself, still matters.

Despite government and media claims that parents and the public are increasingly disaffected – if not disgusted – by public schools, public opinion remains stubbornly behind the education

---

TELECOMMUNICATIONS GIANT NORTHERN Telecom is donating between ten and fifteen surplus computers to students at an elementary school in a poor district of Washington, D.C., after reading about its woes in the newspaper. Aline Chrétien and Hillary Rodham Clinton visited Washington's Burrville Elementary school as their husbands met at the White House. The first ladies watched students take part in an Internet session with Ottawa's St. Elizabeth Elementary School. Problem was, it was a bit of a high-tech sham. The computers on the Washington end were carted away soon after the show.

Source: Ottawa Citizen, April 10, 1997

system. Canadians like their schools, not because they see them as perfect, but because they believe schools are doing pretty well, under the circumstances. Two-thirds of Canadian parents give their children's schools an A or a B.[28] Sixty-nine per cent of Ontario's students (a two-decade high) and 58 per cent of their parents (a fifteen-year high) claim to be satisfied with their schools.[29] While these percentages may not rate an A on report cards, a 1997 Gallup poll found more "respect and confidence" among Canadians for public education than for any other institution – including the Supreme Court and the Church. Therefore, any crisis of public confidence in schools seems to be manufactured.[30]

PRIVATIZATION AT THE post-secondary level will take care of itself, according to the Lehman Brothers, who advise investors on the education market. But, they emphasize, "Change in K through 12 education must come from a broad-based voter perspective that the current system does not beget value at the existing price points [taxes!]."

Source: Lehman Brothers, "Investment Opportunity in the Education Industry"

Although education restructuring – through privatization or other means – is obviously not a grass-roots priority, in one respect public opinion is soft. A 1997 Vector poll found that Canadians were almost equally divided on the value of charter and voucher schools, although these concepts were unfamiliar to more than 90 per cent of respondents.[31] As the Vector analysts astutely pointed out, people don't need to have accurate information to form opinions; they have opinions just the same. Canadians want good schools, period. Either they are indifferent to whether their schools are privately or publicly managed, or they have not made the distinction between the two systems. This is not entirely surprising. When the language of customer satisfaction and competition is applied to both types of schools, the concepts of private and public begin to merge. Perhaps this is why the phrase *private health care* has an alarming ring to it that *charter schools* does not.

Let a Thousand Flowers Bloom

Let a thousand flowers bloom is the motto of the charter schools movement. If the phrase sounds familiar, you may remember that it was adopted as the motto of the thousands of Chinese students who protested in favour of democracy in Tiananmen Square. Ironically, their cry for democracy has been warped into a pitch for educational capitalism. This time, it is not citizens in the street demanding change, but the political and religious Right. True democracy seems far away for the Chinese; charter schools are much closer for Canadians.

The "thousand flowers" connection is obscure; perhaps it is lost even on the insiders who want us to think free markets and democracy are interchangeable. Unfortunately, as the 1997 Vector poll indicated, the Canadian debate over charter schools seems to be an insiders' discussion. Most people don't know what they are. When the pollsters defined them as "schools run by a private group with a charter or permit to receive full public funding but without being subject to many of the rules and regulations that apply to public schools," just over 40 per cent thought charter schools sounded like a good idea.[32]

Perhaps it isn't surprising. Charter schools have attached themselves to the market-friendly language of choice, and what consumer/citizen is opposed to choice? In the consumerist state, we cherish choice, not because we associate it with freedom of thought and expression, but because it offers the illusion of variety – democracy as a buyer's buffet. We can choose from an uncounted array of shampoos (although they may be chemically interchangeable). With deregulation, we can choose which corporation will profit from our long-distance telephone calls – although, ironically, our choice may well be the offspring of the same parent corporation. Advertisements – for products and political parties – lure consumers with the promise of greater choice. Education reform in a consumer culture takes a predictable turn: American arch-conservatives John Chubb and Terry Moe sum it up when they title their paper on education reform "Choice IS a Panacea."[33]

Charter schools have become the dominant vehicle of the school choice movement, operating in twenty-five American states and eagerly anticipated in the rest. Under other names, charter schools have swept New Zealand and Great Britain. Eleven have been chartered in Alberta. They vary so much that a succinct description is difficult, but definitional difficulties can be turned to political advantage. Any politician who claims to favour charter schools in general leaves constituents free to assume the speaker is referring to their favoured type.

Despite important variations, nearly all charter schools adhere to some common ground rules. Those who want to set up a charter school follow an applications procedure, usually directed to a school district, state, or province. The applicants describe their vision for the school, set out their business plan, promise to abide by whatever conditions the legislation requires, and agree to report on their results after a specified period. This document constitutes the charter. Chartered schools receive funding based on a formula tied to enrolment, so the more students enrolled, the greater the school's budget.

> "THE TROUBLE WITH public schools is they have to take in everyone who walks in the door."[34]
> Source: John Chubb, charter school promoter

Through a variety of means, from instructional methods to expulsion criteria, charter schools exclude the students who don't suit the dominant ideology (or level of ability, or class, or religion, or race) of those seeking the charter. Their purpose is to filter out students who don't fit. Claiming that debates over philosophy and methodology have gridlocked public schools, charter schools seek unanimity: a community of parents, teachers, and students who are of one mind about everything, whether it is the place of creation science in the curriculum or how to teach students to read.

Although charter schools march under the banner of choice, uniformity and exclusivity – not diversity – mark these schools.

Their evangelists like to refer to weak and strong charter schools. Their notion of weakness and strength is based on how thoroughly the schools have been deregulated, how many can be opened, and how easy it is to make money from them. States providing only for weak charters, such as Kansas, write legislation that spins off existing schools, giving them relative independence in budgeting and self-governance, but keeping regulatory control in areas such as the use of certificated teachers and state-approved curriculum.

Strong charter schools legislation, such as Arizona's, encourages both non-profit and for-profit ventures to finance and manage schools as they see fit. The legislation gives them, for example, the right to pay teachers (or uncertificated "educators") whatever they will work for, to experiment with the curriculum, and to serve whatever student niche they find most rewarding. Strong charter states are the equivalent of educational free trade zones. Under strong charter legislation, permission to ignore state and local regulations is guaranteed, including (in many cases) any obligation to serve students with special needs. An ideological battle has already been lost when the word *strong* gets associated with a concept that is intrinsically inequitable.[35]

Marketing Chartering

The charter schools movement itself was once considered a weak alternative to voucher schools, the reform that dominated the American education debate of the latter part of the 1980s. The idea of voucher schools is attributed to Milton Friedman, an American economist who proposed in the mid-1950s a plan to give each family a voucher in an amount equivalent to the annual per-student public expenditure.[36] Families could then redeem this voucher at any public or private school, although private schools would want the voucher topped up with tuition fees, of course.

Couched in the language of liberty and markets, the voucher idea was at first popular only among the extreme Right, but it took

"VOUCHER PROPONENTS APPEAR to have lost ground to the more mainstream charter school movement. . . . The strength of charter legislation and the potential for profitable business activity varies significantly state to state. However, we believe charter schools will provide fertile ground for companies wanting to penetrate the K–12 education market."

Source: Education Industry Report, June 1997

hold once certain other groups realized vouchers could be used for explicitly racist purposes. In 1956, Virginia was the first of several Southern states to adopt a version of a voucher system that had the effect of maintaining segregation and evading the Supreme Court's 1954 decision on school integration. In 1983, 1985, and 1986, the Reagan administration tried to move voucher legislation through Congress. Opponents argued successfully that the transparently elitist, sectarian, and possibly racist voucher proposition was un-American, and that to use public dollars to finance the private education of wealthy children or to support religious purposes was wrong. The voucher movement faded, but not the enthusiasm for choice. Gradually, the language and arguments of the choice movement changed, although its ideology did not. Charter schools replaced voucher schools as the brand name for Schools of Choice, Inc.

Voucher hard-liners, including the religious Right, had to be soothed and reminded that all things come to those who wait. Voucher activist Roxanne Premont told the American Christian Coalition that "Christians can enjoy the control they exercise in charter schools even as they push for vouchers."[37] The political Right softened its rhetoric. Voucher school advocates learned from their tactical errors, which included overt references to religion-based schools. They were determined not to make the same mistakes twice.

Instead, they would pitch charter schools as secular and egalitarian, the antithesis of elitism. They would sell the concept as the key to empowering the poor, who were trapped in America's moribund schools, ignored by complacent teachers who had never had their feet held to the fire of competition. Quality would improve because charter schools, like voucher schools, would be forced to compete for students, and competition would work its magic. The individual voucher would be gone; instead, school systems would simply write one mega-voucher cheque to cover the number of students who registered in each school. Whether the charter school chose to spend this money on computers, teachers, or advertising campaigns would be left in the hands of the management board, which would be dominated by parents. Schools that wanted extras could make arrangements with interested private sector partners.

To make these proposals more palatable to the public, early charter school advocates pushed a relatively weak version of regulatory independence. Alarmed by a more radical voucher school movement that refused to rest in peace, American teachers' unions gave their qualified support to limited experimentation with charter schools. The kind they had in mind would be prohibited from maintaining any religious or denominational affiliation.

THE FINE PRINT that describes the kind of charter schools supported by American teachers' unions is routinely dropped when Canadian charter proponents claim that American teachers are on board – a favourite assertion of Canadian charter-marketers, including Joe Freedman. Dr. Freedman does not often quote Bob Chase, president of the National Education Association, the largest American teachers' union. Chase writes that "permissive charter laws are a strategic masterstroke. After all, why go through the grief of trying to pass tuition-voucher bills – which fare poorly in opinion polls and have been consistently rejected by voters and the courts – when you can get back-door public funding for schools that remain effectively private by relabelling them as 'charters'?"

Source: Education Week, December 4, 1996

They wanted no charter granted to a for-profit group, and no capital or other start-up grants provided. And groups of teachers and universities would be encouraged to apply for charters. All charter school teachers would have to be certificated, although local contract provisions (including salary and tenure) would not apply to them. Most important, support from American teachers' unions depended on equity: no student "for whom the program was intended" could be disqualified, nor could the school charge tuition fees. Failure to meet these terms or to show acceptable evidence of success should result in the charter's being revoked.[38]

All the Right Reasons

By and large, these were the terms written up in Alberta's 1994 legislation, under which eleven charter schools have since been established. Alberta was a likely site for Canada's first official charter schools, and not only because of the province's penchant for rightist populism and its historical role as a conduit of American ideas. Joe Freedman, a radiologist and Canada's most tireless advocate for charter schools, operates his one-man Society for the Advancement of Educational Research from Red Deer. However, with financing from the Royal Bank, the Bank of Montreal, Syncrude Corp., and the right-wing Donner and Marigold foundations, Dr. Freedman has made the case for charter schools across Canada.[39]

Charter schools are for and about incrementalism: the gradual transfer of economic and political responsibility for education from the public at large to private interests. Quite predictably, once Alberta's charter school legislation had been approved, Dr. Freedman and other like-minded supporters began complaining that Alberta's version was "too weak." They have told Ontario and Atlantic Canada not to capitulate or compromise when charter school legislation is drafted in their provinces, and have warned them against teachers' unions, school boards, and other critics who "intentionally mislead" the public by associating charter schools with privatization.[40] They remind supporters not to get dragged into debates about public funding of religious schools; the time for this discussion will be after charters have been secured.

There is no significant Canadian ground swell in favour of charter schools – yet. However, supporters believe the question is no longer *if*, but *when*, and they may well be right. Charter school advocates are determined, and their determination is well funded. The image of charter schools is gentle, even benevolent: it bears "the smiling face of disinvestment," in the words of Alex Molnar.[41] Charter schools are wrapped in the rhetoric of equity and empowerment for students, teachers, and parents – indeed, for everyone except bureaucrats and other friends of the status quo. American politicians of both parties and every stripe at federal and state levels champion charter schools. They have become President Clinton's personal project for school reform. They receive constant encouragement from right-wing think-tanks and research institutes. More important, "Their ace in the hole is the erosion of education funding," says journalist Murray Dobbin. "The deeper the cuts, the better their chances. There's nothing like a crisis to foster change."[42]

Whether we like them or not, therefore, Canadians may get charter schools. The history of Canadian education fails to turn up a single example of a significant American education trend, from new math to open-area classrooms, that Canadian schools successfully avoided. The future seems to be unfolding.

We can only change that future by turning what has been a limited educational-policy debate into a passionate and informed public debate about the future of our children. Charter schools transform the social contract between public education and citizens by putting decision-making in the hands of a self-appointed few. The accountability chain between those who are elected to make decisions and those who pay for and benefit from public education is broken. Once the public discovers that it no longer has any meaningful role in determining what schools are for, it will quickly begin to wonder why it should be taxed to underwrite the cost of educating other people's children. Charter schools not only short-circuit our collective right to have a say in what schools should try to accomplish, but reinforce privatization's assumption that pleasing today's customers is the same as serving society's long-term interests.

The flawed assumptions and the political drift of schools of choice must be exposed. The Canadian public is not so desperate for remedies for its supposedly failed school system that any solution is worth trying. We do not need charter schools to give parents and students appropriate amounts of choice. Seventy-two per cent of parents told Vector pollsters that they were satisfied with the amount of choice they could exercise in schools,[43] and even more were satisfied with the amount of choice they had in selecting the program of study their children could follow. In Canada, education choices are usually limited by practical problems of demographics or transportation, rather than by some kind of stultifying, state-mandated conformity. With parallel, publicly funded regular and Catholic systems, systems that operate in both official languages, specialized schools and specialized programs within schools, open boundaries, distance education, a variety of immersion programs, public alternative schools, storefront schools, and, in many provinces, publicly subsidized private schools, it could more easily be argued that our system's problems stem from too much diversity rather than from too little.

Who Chooses, Who Loses

If choice were the solution, Canadian schools would have few problems, but the dogma of the marketplace is that more choice is always better. We are told choice gives us wisdom we would otherwise not enjoy. Even inside a market metaphor, these statements are foolish. As customers, we appreciate having some choice, but when we set out to buy a new refrigerator, our choice is made neither infinite nor wise by the number of models on the sales floor. Our decision may be informed, ill-informed, foolish, or swayed by the ice-maker that we will never use. Our purchase is limited by the amount of money we have to spend. Most of us would never select a model only on the basis of a sales pitch – or so we like to think. However, at least in the department store, each sale

generates a similar sales commission. In the marketplace, every customer's dollar is of equal value. Proponents of schools of choice
pretend the system would work this way with students: "We must
seek to honour every child so that when she walks through the
school door she is worth $4,000," says the *Education Industry
Report*.[44] This idea is not only horrible, but inaccurate.

> "CHARTER SCHOOLS, LIKE private school vouchers and for-
> profit schools, are built on the market-inspired illusion that
> our society can be held together solely by the selfish pursuit of
> our individual purposes. The charter schools movement rep-
> resents a radical rejection not only of the possibility of the
> common school but also of common purposes outside the
> school."
>
> Source: Alex Molnar, *Giving Kids the Business*

Reduced to a cost-benefit ratio, some students will be worth
more than the $4,000 that follows them, because they will be well-
behaved, co-operative high-achievers who demand little in the
way of the school's most valuable resources – teacher time and
attention. These students will raise the school's average on the
marketing tool of standardized test scores, and look appealing on
promotional billboards. They will attract more of the "right" kind
of student. But some kids will be considered more trouble than they
are worth. What charter school will want to enrol the child who is
not "value-added," or who requires the (salaried) help of a special
education teacher, or who doesn't speak the classroom's language,
or who acts out in ways that get discussed around other families'
dinner tables? These children don't represent $4,000 when they
walk through the school's door – they represent a business loss. No
charter school that is competing for students in an open market
can afford to teach many students who become, in marketers'
terms, drags on productivity and profitability.

There are only two solutions to this problem. The first is to
demand that each school enrol a specified number of these so-

called losing propositions, thus sharing the pain. This solution would not only require some unacceptable system of classifying students – their abilities, backgrounds, behaviours, and other relevant characteristics – but would also require a zealous bureaucracy to ensure compliance. Obviously, this regulatory approach would conflict with the escape from bureaucracy that charter school/free market enthusiasts promise and promote.

The second solution is to maintain the façade of charter schools as open to every student for whom the program is designed, but to use the nature of that program to subtly exclude the kinds of customers the school would like to avoid. Designing a school around a "traditional, values-based curriculum, emphasizing rigorous standards, leading to an international baccalaureate" would tend to discourage applications from many low-ability, unconventional, work force-bound (or unemployment-bound) students. Locating a charter school in a wealthy suburb would tend to discourage inner-city children from enrolling, especially if transportation isn't provided.

The loophole of voluntary fees – which charter schools (such as those in Alberta) may charge, even though tuition is technically banned – provides another constraint on choice. A technology-focused charter school might well decide that a laptop computer is essential to its program, and find it necessary to charge a steep fee for supplies. Schools can achieve more covert filtering by demanding that parents sign contracts guaranteeing their involvement in the school (which translates into volunteer work in the classroom). This stipulation tends to discourage parents who are unavailable, or uncomfortable with the language or expectations of the classroom. Particularly when they are used in concert, these mechanisms achieve the true goal of charter school activists: ensuring their children get a good education while other people's children become other people's problems.

Equity's New Friends

It is not surprising that three of Alberta's first eleven charter schools were designed to serve gifted children – including the not-so-subtly named ABC School, which stands for All the Best Children. But other charter schools in Alberta, and many American ones, have been targeted to serve at-risk students. Enthusiasts argue that this "diversity" positions charter schools as an equity-friendly reform.

In an *Ottawa Citizen* editorial, Dan Gardner wrote that opponents who charge that charter schools are racist, elitist, and classist are "absolutely wrong."[45] As evidence, he cited Minnesota research that determined 25 per cent of the students in that state's charter schools had disabilities, 10 per cent had limited English skills, and 45 per cent were non-white. Gardner went on to claim that it was too soon to expect definitive answers to whether student achievement in charter schools had improved, although parents were allegedly satisfied and waiting lists were growing.[46] (Gardner's argument reflects charter school orthodoxy in every way. It is always too soon to measure student achievement, and often nearly impossible. These reformers who argue that schools should be results-driven are notoriously relaxed when it comes to evaluating their own schools. The same critics who condemn the public system for failing to measure and publish comparative student achievement data prefer to use "customer satisfaction" as an appropriate, market-sensitive barometer of quality. However, if popularity equates with excellence, then *Married with Children* is great television. For the record, the limited evaluation that has been carried out consistently finds that choice does not improve student achievement.)[47]

A promptly answered request for information from the University of Minnesota shed some light on Gardner's numbers.[48] It seems that Minnesota school boards were very selective in the awarding of charters. They gave priority to applicants who were prepared to take responsibility for the students who put the greatest "burden" on the existing system. As a result, schools set up to serve only deaf students, only students at risk, only inner-city students, and so forth were granted charters. These schools didn't receive anything like the resources they needed to teach these hard-to-serve students, so the schools relied on community volunteers, charitable donations, and teachers and social workers who in some cases worked for free. Aggregated, Minnesota's numbers look fine. Broken out, they uncover a resegregated school system that has put public funds to work for the children who already have the most of everything. Charter schools have put the welfare of children who need public education the most in the hands of charity.

Equity advocates can rightly argue that the schools we have now fall far short of providing equality of educational benefit. Some students and their parents, including some of those who are concerned about the education of deaf students and students with learning disabilities, argue that having their own schools and their own teachers would serve them better than the fragmented, over-stretched classrooms that now try to cope with exceptional needs. They see charter schools as an opportunity to benefit from the charity and commitment of teachers and volunteers. Most of these parents couldn't care less about the much-touted role of market forces, but ignoring the market will not make it go away.

Enthusiasm is no substitute for stability, and charity is no sub-stitute for justice. The market has no virtues – it has characteris-tics. On its own, the education market will not be interested in deaf students or students with disabilities unless their parents can make teaching them profitable. The values of the public space, not those of private interests, deserve the credit for the progress made towards integration in schools, workplaces, and communities, slow and imperfect though it may be. More than any other group, those with the least power in society have benefited from the bureau-cracy and regulation that charter schools try to slough off.

For, in the absence of regulation and accountability, charter schools are off the hook, free to direct children with special needs back to what is left of the public system. One Arizona charter school principal admits, "We tell parents that the public schools provide the special education. We can't be set up for everything."[49] Another from New Jersey advises charter-starter hopefuls to rely on reality therapy and/or luck. If approached by a special needs "situation," he says, "what you do is sit down with the parents, discuss reality and hope they don't sue you."

Market Math

Students who are unattractive from a business/education point of view may seem to be an unfortunate but small minority, a group whose needs can be met by prohibiting and punishing overt discrimination. This logic is false. If we assume that half of every group is below average, the education market will clearly disfavour half of any randomly selected group. As long as parents choose the schools, this little piece of arithmetic doesn't matter too much; but once the school is allowed to select the child, all the rules change. This is the cruel irony of these so-called schools of choice: inside a market metaphor, vendors are obliged neither to sell you something just because you want it, nor to sell anything at a loss. If landlords can protect their interests by asking prospective renters whether they are on welfare or how much they earn, why could deregulated schools not ask the equivalent of prospective students?

This is exactly what has happened in countries where charter schools are well established. In New Zealand, charter schools (and the reforms that made them possible) have set up a rapidly developing two-tier system of education based on social class.[50] Fees imposed as soon as school boards were dissolved kept good schools secure for the middle class and kept other kids out. The marketing of schools has contributed to parents' identifying less with their neighbourhoods and communities, and more with their social class. This shift has been characterized by white flight: white students have been fleeing mixed-race schools to attend exclusively white middle-class schools.[51]

Canadians who only read the odd editorial praising charter schools have no reason to be familiar with their history in New Zealand. In addition to creating a growing gap between rich and poor and good and bad schools, charter schools have driven New Zealand teachers out of the profession in droves, sent schools begging for parents to serve on mandatory parent councils, and plunged the majority of schools into long-term debt.[52] Murray Dobbin says breakdowns, suicides, and resignations have left 20 per cent of school principalships vacant, and sent recruiters overseas in search of a thousand teachers each year.[53] Charter proponents in Canada are unlikely to advertise either this information or the growing literature that tracks "who chooses and who loses."

Manufacturing Consent

Canada's shift to more neo-conservative and neo-liberal policies has been nurtured, if not driven, by smartly crafted campaigns to create a more welcoming climate for certain political ideas. Education reform is political reform. The Fraser Institute has targeted education for a lead role in its new five-year plan, with particular emphasis to be placed on charter schools.[54] It plans to spend $250,000 annually to establish international links with other groups devoted to the privatization of education, to work with the (Joe) Freedman Foundation, and to establish an "index of school effectiveness."

The institute intends to continue to use its "fax broadcasting system" to maintain its influence on talk radio. Since call-in shows discussing "what's wrong at school" invariably keep the lines lit up, radio stations look forward to receiving the think-tank's self-proclaimed education information. The Fraser Institute also proposes to redouble its efforts to penetrate the national media and "other secondhand dealers in ideas." The modest project it calls "Economic Freedom of the World" will include an index of "freedom of commercial speech, freedom of choice in education, and freedom in the labour market" – a telling juxtaposition. The institute says this index will be financed by no fewer than twenty-five multinational corporations.

The Fraser Institute will find support among other political allies. The National Citizens Coalition (NCC), fresh from lobbying for anti-union right-to-work legislation and staging an assortment of anti-government media campaigns, has shown sudden interest in public education.[55] The NCC believes that its thesis – public sector problems will be resolved best through private sector solutions – applies as readily to education as to health care. In one of its publications, the NCC describes OISE professor Mark Holmes's book *Canada's Education Crisis* as a "must read," and finds Alberta's experiment with charter schools evidence of true education reform.[56] Disappointed by California's resounding defeat of a voucher system, the NCC blamed the California Teachers' Association, but it predicts that the voucher issue will be voted on "again and again until it wins."

Within the growing right-wing think-tank industry, the Atlantic Institute for Market Studies (AIMS) is a comparative upstart. AIMS is funded by the Donner Canadian Foundation,[57] with whose help it publishes the rhetoric of the Right, repackaged for Atlantic Canada. It promotes the works of Sir Roger Douglas (New Zealand's restructuring guru) and Michael Walker of the Fraser Institute. This institute's mail-order library features unambiguous titles such as *Debtor's Prison: Public Sector Debt and What It Means to You*; *Towards Sustainable Development in Atlantic Canada: A Case for U.I. Reform*; and *Pensioning Off the CPP*.

The Spring 1997 issue of *The Beacon*, the magazine published by AIMS, includes an article on the desirability of port privatization, a summary of conservative poster-child Ezra Levant's speech to an AIMS student conference ("Canada's social safety net has turned into a hammock"), and a commentary entitled "More Spending, More Dependence" that trashes the report of the Royal Commission on Aboriginal Peoples.[58] But the cover story is reserved for the theme of the institute's 1997 conference, "Choosing Better Schools in Atlantic Canada."

The conference was held in Fredericton. Americans Chester Finn and Howard Fuller provided predictable keynote answers to the rhetorical question, "Does School Choice Improve Standards, Performance and Accountability?" The speakers' enthusiasm for charter schools was carefully framed in the language of equity and school quality. Between keynotes, workshop participants heard how charter schools would improve services to racial minorities and students with special needs. School quality was objectively examined in a session that asked whether "the needs of parents and students are being served by the current public monopoly." Helen Raham, previously director of another Donner-funded group known as Teachers for Excellence in Education, walked participants through this question: "Does choice free up more resources for the classroom rather than administration?"

Every Canadian conference on school choice includes Joe Freedman. Dr. Freedman dispensed with the pretext of questions and spoke to the answers found in his AIMS-published booklet, *Charter Schools in Atlantic Canada – An Idea Whose Time Has Come*. The Time is marked by an Atlantic education system that allegedly lags behind the rest of Canada, while (not because) provincial governments are cutting expenditures. Freedman writes,

> Chartering has a great deal to offer change-oriented governments. Since deficit reduction is the order of the day . . . the charter school idea makes perfect sense. . . . Many observers feel that despite their good points, teachers' unions have become too large and powerful, and that school boards are not working well. . . . The region's governments are well aware of and actively discussing the charter school idea behind closed doors.[59]

Freedman deserves credit for laying out at least part of the real charter schools agenda, but he continues to deny that charter schools are the precursors of privatization and the full funding of all religious schools. The religious Right is passionate about charter schools, but clever enough to choose when and to whom it exposes its full agenda. In 1995, I was asked to contribute to a publication with the not-so-subtle title *Busting Bureaucracy to Reclaim Our Schools*, published by the Montreal-based Institute for Research on Public Policy.[60] The essay that became the book's title was written by Stephen B. Lawton, a professor of education at the Ontario Institute for Studies in Education. (Lawton is perhaps best known for his close association with the people and politics of the Mike Harris government. When the OISE/University of Toronto education faculty voted unanimously to oppose Bill 160, the edu-chat lines wondered whether even Lawton had undergone a change of heart. Not so. Apparently, he was "absent on personal business" when the vote was taken.)

In *Busting Bureaucracy*, Lawton argued that charter schools are merely – but powerfully – the rational economic solution to the "inevitable" problems that plague a monopoly, namely waste, inefficiency, and inflated labour costs. In my chapter, I disputed his assumptions, and then suggested that some charter school supporters – but not necessarily Dr. Lawton – had a tendency to hide their real motives behind economic arguments. When the book was published, I discovered to my surprise that Lawton had rebutted my rebuttal. Evidently, I had touched a nerve. Dr. Lawton wrote that "left-liberals" practise "faithism" – discrimination against sincere believers. Then he cited Genesis, chapter 1, verses 1, 20, 26, 28, and 30, and chapter 2, verses 18, 22, and 24, and concluded with a stern lecture:

> Creation science, the exploitation of nature including both animals and plants, a subordinate role of women to men, the sanctity of heterosexual marriage – all on four pages! No wonder the scientific, environmentalist, animal rights, family planning, feminist and homosexual interest groups on the liberal left fear this book. . . . Robertson has done a service by broaching a topic I was too timid to raise.

Teacher, Inc.

Such timidity does not afflict the Fraser Institute, however, which (like Lawton) sees charter schools as the back door to any number of market-friendly reforms. Key among these is the right to determine what constitutes a teacher, and what teachers will be paid. "Flexibility in district contracts is the nub of labour relations issues surrounding charter schools," writes Helen Raham for the *Fraser Forum*.[61] "The flexibility to set working conditions gives charters their competitive advantage. Those conditions may include class sizes, longer school days or year, differentiated staffing, professional development, and teacher licensing and performance reviews."

Raham praises a Los Angeles charter school that has received well-orchestrated attention: the school's principal "is free to hire and fire her teachers and to lengthen their school day and year." (*Education Week* reports that the allegations of test-score fixing at this school that made headlines in Los Angeles press have not been substantiated. An "internal review" that explored how so many wrong answers were erased and replaced by an unexplained number of right answers found no grounds for "serious concern.")[62] Edmonton's Suzuki charter school apparently has no difficulty attracting teachers, even though it doesn't pay the local salary scale. Money still has to come from somewhere, however. Minnesota's New County charter school was determined "to bring in the type of equipment that will allow students to develop their employment and academic skills." It made a choice: "There is a computer for every two students – a luxury made possible because there are no administrators."[63]

American conservative critics Chester Finn and Dianne Ravitch, writing for the Hudson Institute, have fingered spending choices that lean in the other direction. They claim that school privatization schemes have failed because money was spent on "politically attractive purposes (salaries, mainly) rather than technology."[64] They believe charter schools will never be fully competitive as long as they "must pay union wages" and "hire only certified teachers."

The on-line newsletter *Enterprising Educators* says charter schools provide "a dazzling opportunity for the entrepreneurial educator," who can take "total control of the program, staffing and budget."[65] The investment houses agree. Montgomery Securities says privatizing the K–12 market is where the real money will be, and that private operators will be perfectly positioned to exploit political reforms, "such as school vouchers and charter schools."[66] Investors beware, however. Gerald Odening, a vice-president of Smith Barney, says that trying to privatize the potential bonanza of K–12 education can unleash "a snake-pit of local politics." He told participants at the Education Industry Summit that these

A PARTICIPANT AT the Education Industry Summit asks Gerald Odening of Smith Barney to comment on the parallels between the American and Canadian situations from the point of view of investment. Wherever government resources are stretched to the limit, Odening says, things look up for education (although he probably means investors). Job shortages fuel demand. Surveys allegedly prove 80 per cent of students enrol in university for career-related reasons. "Not that there aren't other reasons to go to the kind of universities you all went to," he acknowledges. "There are other reasons people go to elite universities . . . like sports."

schools are fiercely defended by vigilante squads of middle-aged women: "I call them the bitchilanties."[67]

Changing public policy to eliminate such impediments is important, but reforms will proceed more smoothly if educators can be persuaded that a deregulated marketplace is in their best interests. This is the goal of *Teacher, Inc.*, published by the Reason Foundation, "a nonpartisan, nonprofit [American] public policy research and educational organization dedicated to advancing the principles of a free society."[68] On the side, the Reason Foundation offers a privatization hotline for those in a hurry to find out how to "streamline government" or "enhance economic and personal liberty."

According to *Teacher, Inc.*, contracting out provides entrepreneurial opportunities for "private practice educators" who wish to enjoy "elevated professional status" by negotiating their own contracts. Employers can exploit this equally cheap alternative to hiring uncertified teachers – rather like getting a free upgrade with their low-end computers. Case studies testify to the "empowerment" enjoyed by private practice teachers, who are linked "by their enthusiasm for teaching, learning, and helping children." What sets them apart from other teachers, *Teacher Inc.* asserts, is "their willingness to assume risk, their desire for independence, and their ability to meet the demands of the education marketplace."

A sceptic might point out that their talent for pleasing the marketplace leads to stretching the facts a little. An anonymous survey of Arizona's three hundred private practice charter school teachers – 39 per cent of whom had no previous teaching experience, and 31 per cent no teaching certificate – provides some interesting data.[69] Despite (or because of) the primacy of intense parental involvement and teachers' accountability for results, just 8 per cent of the teachers privately judged the majority of their students to be performing above grade level, while 49 per cent said at grade level and 43 per cent below grade level. Somehow, the opposite message had been sent to parents, whose approval determines which teachers' contracts will be renewed. Among these parents, 31 per cent believed the majority of students to be above grade level, 52 per cent chose at grade level, and just 17 per cent below grade level. According to the results of standardized tests, the teachers were right: as a group the charter school students scored between 5 per cent and 12 per cent lower than the state's average. These findings put a slight dent in an otherwise upbeat charter school report published by the Barry Goldwater Institute, whose name says it all.

Creative accounting is yet another skill of the private practice teacher, one that extends to stretching personal finances. Says Susan Reno, one of the private practice subjects of the *Teacher, Inc.* case studies: "In the public schools, given the economic climate of the times, it's difficult . . . to get equipment, such as computers and programs. Even though it's coming out of my own pocket, I know I need the equipment to survive. It's what makes me able to serve teachers and kids" – and pick up contracts.

Meanwhile, administrators benefit from just-in-time teachers who can be hired and fired at will. The Reason Foundation recommends pegging teachers' salaries to an hourly amount, so the school doesn't get stuck paying for "down time" such as preparation periods or lunch breaks. Although the growth of charter schools does open the door to private practice teachers, the foundation still complains that legislation limiting teacher certification to those who have completed a teacher education program is a barrier to "many talented adults interested in teaching." Eliminating these requirements would not only reduce wasted time and money spent studying, but would usher in "the true test of teacher competence – performance."

Performing On-Line

Only a few incidental references to information technology appear in these policy platforms. But technology only *seems* to be divorced from debate over the skills of teachers and how to pay less for them. This artificial separation serves at least two purposes. First, the friends and funders of conservative think-tanks are more likely to prefer the idealized notion of traditional schools over the techno-schools that President Clinton favours. In fact, the Hudson Institute has invented the word *instructivist* to describe the ideal classroom. Second, by avoiding the issue, charter school advocates maintain technology's disguise as an apolitical tool, above the suspicions and below the radar of unions and other foes of privatization.

Why fight when you can reposition instead? Charter schools that please the profiteers can easily be described in ways that increase their appeal to a wider audience. People with no particular political agenda, and a genuine concern for their children's welfare, can easily be persuaded that charter schools are a harmless innovation that merely aligns education with the modern age of competition. These supporters give the charter school movement its air of respectability, and they are tenderly cultivated by the investors and zealots who have appropriated the language of equity and child-centredness for the purpose.[70] But these parents and education-minded charter enthusiasts are not writing the legislation or driving the movement. These tasks are left to those who see charter schools not as an educational reform, but as a political reform that brings schools one step closer to privatization, when the commodity of education will finally be available in different qualities and quantities for different customers.

Stephen Beatty of KPMG Peat Marwick says that "the value of

an education is what somebody is willing to pay for it."[71] Unfortunately, he adds, "the public sector has been giving it away for free," which is why customers have trouble getting their heads around paying profit-boosting tuition fees. Still, on the subject of value – realizing it, not appreciating it – Beatty explains that a name-brand education (i.e., a Harvard MBA) is more valuable than the no-name variety, because it opens doors and attracts customers. Once education's customers ante up, the edu-corp can realize value by raising tuition fees, processing students faster, and reducing staff salaries. The great thing about the education market, says Smith Barney's Odening, is that it's "countercyclical": the worse things get in the economy, the better they get for corporations that promise to train people for jobs that don't exist.[72]

JAMES MCKEEN OF Queen's University explains how the university's new privatized MBA program offers a fast-forward, intensive twelve-month route to an MBA. The residential requirement is key: "We want to own you, your heart, your mind, your soul, your life." The professors/instructors/managers shy away from using words such as *teaching*; instead, the whole person becomes part of "a learning environment." In addition to academic development, the school offers professional development, which McKeen describes as instructing the neophyte business elite in the finer points of squash, golf, and how to "wine, dine and look fine."

Source: Canadian Education Industry Summit, September 24, 1997

So the religious Right is onside, the investors are onside, the political Right and American politicians are (almost) unanimously onside – who is left to be convinced? The parents and public of the Vector survey, who don't know much about charter schools but who like the idea anyway, will be the next target. Canadian politicians who have wrung the available mileage out of school-bashing can start ruminating about charter schools and real reform, and see what happens. They can write new legislation

– like Ontario's Bill 160 – that makes charter schools possible, but not inevitable. They have already established the framework of parent councils and thwarted the ambitions of school boards; in many provinces, they have decreed school-based budgeting, turned principals into "management," and declared "open attendance boundaries." Most changes needed to introduce charter schools are therefore already in place. If support for charter schools grows, governments will be ready to respond to customer opinion. Teachers will object, but their concerns can be written off as the lazy self-interest of those who see education as a paying profession, rather than as charitable service or entrepreneurship.

The real agenda of charter school supporters turns out to be irrelevant. The consequences of charter schools will flow from how they function, not how people might want them to function. Whether they are the educational equivalent of the malevolent low overpass or the benign tomato-harvester, they will shift power and benefits not because of intent, but because of their internalized political drift. Charter schools are explicitly attached to the rules of the market. The role of the market is to sort the winners from the losers through the mechanism of competition. When poor refrigerators find no customers and no vendor is willing to keep them in stock, few people are harmed. But applied to children, the market's preference for some goods over others will have disastrous consequences, for both those who are chosen and those who are discarded.

Market competition is a package deal. The power of our intentions is too weak for us to select some of its features and discard others. The artifacts of the market have their own politics.

EAI – A Cautionary Tale

All of these indications point towards the fact that the education industry may replace health care as *the* focus industry, and if health care is a good indicator, private companies will benefit strongly from a climate that stresses change.[73]
– Lehman Brothers

Each industry has a legendary corporation that achieves fame by breaking new ground (and often a few rules) en route to notoriety. Education Alternatives, Inc. (EAI) is education's most tracked and talked-about privatization experiment. EAI was founded in 1986 by a Xerox salesman, John Golle, who envisioned a network of computer-intensive for-profit schools that would use a proprietary curriculum known as Tesseract. EAI would manage schools under contract with school districts, using public dollars to tuck away tidy private profits. Golle and his backers were convinced that they could pare away the waste and inefficiency that would surely plague any public monopoly, and pocket the savings. Staff cuts – in numbers and in salary – would create further profits, and technology would ensure student success. Golle believed the greatest opportunities would be found among the most desperate school districts serving the poorest children in America.

THE WALT DISNEY empire is building a school for Celebration, its model town. The town is a "neo-traditional American village reminiscent of Norman Rockwell images," according to a Disney brochure. The "state-of-the-art" school will be owned (and funded) by the school district, but Disney will build and own an adjacent teaching academy that will offer professional development for teachers. Michael D. Eisner, Disney's CEO, says the company "is seeking not only to entertain children with cartoons, movies and theme parks, but to educate them as well."

Source: Education Week, June 22, 1994

Parts of the edu-political establishment were enthralled by EAI's bold approach to school reform. John Golle enjoyed the support of friends well placed in business and government, including George Bush's secretary of education, Lamar Alexander, who praised EAI as his idea of how to fix what was wrong with America's schools.[74] Despite this kind of encouragement, it took

274 NO MORE TEACHERS, NO MORE BOOKS

until 1992 and almost $9 million before EAI managed to close its first substantial contract. Baltimore's school district, which enrols some of the poorest children in the United States, engaged EAI to run its most difficult schools.

Privatization's cheerleaders were thrilled. John McLaughlin's *Education Industry Report* called EAI "a trailblazing success story."[75] John Walton (of the Wal-Mart Waltons), a major EAI shareholder, arranged a visit and photo-op with Hillary Clinton, who dropped into an EAI school to extend her best wishes.[76]

Not everyone was so sure that EAI could deliver on its promises, however. According to research conducted by the Baltimore school system and the University of Maryland, the sceptics were right: virtually every student, teacher, and taxpayer paid an exorbitant price to keep Golle's privatization pyramid going.[77] This research found that test scores in Baltimore's EAI schools declined, while students in non-EAI schools showed modest gains, despite signs that EAI schools were preoccupied with testing and spent a lot of time "practising."[78] These poor results weren't immediately apparent because EAI "accidentally" dropped the lowest-scoring students from the data it presented to the Baltimore board. There were other "mistakes" along the accountability trail. Although EAI claimed student attendance had increased during the first year, in fact it had declined. An EAI press release boasting attendance gains of 22.2 per cent at one school was excused as a "clerical error" when the media discovered the real figure was 2.2 per cent.

Golle had promised that bottom line improvement would be achieved through EAI-funded technology, but many of the computers that turned up in EAI schools were financed by misappropriating federal funds intended for severely disadvantaged students.[79] The students who followed EAI's computerized reading program did not demonstrate improved reading skills, even though teachers routinely removed kids from regular classes to clock time on computers. The Baltimore community and media that had at first welcomed EAI began to ask embarrassing questions. What was happening to the promise of privatization?

Stung by increasing public criticism, EAI blamed teachers, whose numbers had already been cut by 20 per cent. Eventually, two-thirds of the disillusioned teaching staff left EAI schools. To replace them, EAI hand-picked cheaper teachers who had far less experience. To further trim costs, EAI dismantled the special education program in its schools, and eliminated half of the special education teachers – moves that violated federal regulations. The money carved out of the special education budget made up one-third of EAI's 1993–94 net revenue – $1.2 million – but Golle wanted more. EAI raised the teacher-to-student ratio from 1:18 to 1:25. By cutting teachers and replacing teacher aides with lower-paid, untrained "interns," EAI reduced its spending on instructional services from 65 to 48 per cent of its budget.

There was still not enough money. EAI had promised to revitalize Baltimore's struggling schools by bringing in new money through corporate investment, but the poor, not the rich, had to fund Golle's dream. Federal funds earmarked for poor students were redirected to pay operating expenses. EAI continued to bill the Baltimore system for "enhancement expenditures" that exceeded the original budget. Money intended for classrooms was being diverted to EAI facilities, administrative overhead, lawyers, accountants, corporate travel, and profits.[80] The Baltimore board had to slash the budgets of its other schools to pay EAI's invoices, which meant that non-EAI students were now directly subsidizing Golle's corporation.

Despite this additional revenue, EAI profits on the Baltimore operation were at best marginal. Although corporate year-end reports claimed profits in the range of $1 million to $2.5 million, some EAI-trackers, like Alex Molnar, believe that three of EAI's first four years ran at a net loss, even though per-pupil funding for these schools was well above the average for Baltimore's non-EAI students. Obviously, the public system had much less bloat than EAI had assumed. An accurate assessment of real expenditures and profits is hard to determine, however, since EAI's convoluted accounting contract with KPMG Peat Marwick is still under conflict-of-interest investigation.[81]

All the while, Golle and his friends kept their eyes on the rise and fall of EAI stocks. There are claims that insider trading netted Golle a clear $5 million. The volatility of EAI stock seemed excessive.[82] Neither corporate profits nor prospects could explain the jump of a share from small change to 48¾ in late 1993, only to drop again by half. Some think EAI itself was the source of rumours alleging financial problems, giving Golle and other investors a chance to sell short. When the crash came, speculators who had guessed right capitalized not just on EAI's troubles, but on the misfortune of thousands of students. The *Washington Post* commented, "While state-sponsored education may have its problems, one of them is not a group of speculators who stand to make a profit if the program is a flop."[83] Throughout EAI's ups and downs, Golle lived like a man accustomed to success. While people might have tolerated his two lavish houses and the palatial corporate headquarters, the stable of nine cars was a bit ostentatious. The Baltimore public was becoming outraged, investors were filing lawsuits, and by October 1994, the school board was looking for a way out.[84]

News must travel slowly. Despite the mess in Baltimore, that same October EAI signed a contract to run all the schools in Hartford, a city so poor that the right-wing Hudson Institute called it a near-perfect setting for an experiment in privatization.[85] After a rerun of alleged mismanagement and outrageous perks, Hartford also cancelled its contract with EAI. The soured deal had all the features of an acrimonious divorce, complete with custody battles. EAI threatened to repossess the equipment it had set up in its schools; the city solicitor said forget it. EAI then said that if it had to leave the computers behind, it would disable them. Fed up with what he called the politics of urban communities, Golle said that, in the future, EAI would only do business in more hospitable suburban systems.[86] EAI's very public collapse in Hartford pushed its stock down: by late 1995, shares were available at 4³⁄₈.

Despite these uninspiring performances in schools and in the market, the education investment gurus still rate EAI a buy. EIR's John McLaughlin blames the woes of Education Alternatives,

Inc., and other for-profit school management companies, on an unfair system that is about to change:

> From inception, EMO [education management organization] contractors have had enormous difficulty finding level playing fields. . . . Teacher unions and local school boards have forced EMO contractors to sign watered-down agreements that limit their freedom to make key management decisions such as hiring [but] K–12 EMO contractors will overcome social and political barriers.[87]

According to McLaughlin, health management organizations struggled with similar problems in the early 1970s, but HMOs took off when the federal government gave them the political nod in 1973. EMOs are about to celebrate a similar "symbol of substanti-ation," in McLaughlin's words. President Clinton's second-term promise to double federal funding for charter schools is the sub-stantiation that privatizers have been waiting for. John Golle says that, from an investor's angle, it is not charter schools per se that matter, but the doors that will open once the public gets accus-tomed to them. "We view [charter schools] as an interim stage," says Golle – the thin edge of the wedge that will acclimatize the public to "contract management."[88] Sure enough, when Arizona passed free-wheeling choice legislation in early 1997, John Golle and EAI were quick off the mark, picking up twelve charter schools in one contract.

Investors are happy. Politicians are happy. But what about the students and the public?

On one hand, students are unlikely to argue in favour of priva-tization, since none of the experiments have been able to sustain improved student achievement – a goal that is clearly more difficult than some reformers appreciate. On the other hand, since privatization is about politics and profits, not education, student performance will never be a primary concern. Public opinion is another matter. Left on its own, public opinion is unlikely to support school privatization. Canadians may not be too concerned

> "WE BELIEVE THAT A movement toward broader and more stringent national standards will create a strong investment opportunity for for-profit education companies."
>
> *Source:* Montgomery Securities, *Education Industry Report,* June 1997

about contracting out technology or school maintenance, especially if outsourcing is said to save money, but they are unlikely to jump spontaneously from ServiceMaster sweeping the halls to edu-corp running the schools – unless privatization can happen incrementally.

The privateers have shown they can learn from experience and exploit a changing political climate. We shouldn't underestimate these skills, especially when the public may be vulnerable. Worried by the alleged failure of schools, convinced dollars are being sucked out of the classroom by bloated bureaucracies, shamed by interprovincial and international comparisons, threatened by the imperatives of global (etc., etc.) competition, and convinced that only the high-tech schools they can't afford can save their kids, the public may be convinced to buy into privatization – especially if it is called something else, and if it can be done gradually, in a "win-win" way.

Partnerships

It's time to stop pretending that education and commerce exist on different planets. . . . Our education system is expecting too little of its graduates, teaching coursework unrelated to the requirements of employers, and failing to cultivate the personal qualities and habits of mind demanded in today's workplace.
– National Association of Business

Partnership is a higher type of relationship.
– Conference Board of Canada

The *Education Industry Report* has no partnership index, although one may be under consideration. As a way to achieve the inter-planetary merger that the National Association of Business demands, partnerships between corporations and individual schools or entire systems can be far superior to endless education summits and ponderous reports.

Business-education partnerships are reportedly "in explosion mode." Mary Anne McLaughlin, director of the National Business and Education Centre for the Conference Board of Canada, esti-mates that twenty thousand of them are in place across the country. They are proliferating in the absence of ministry policy. As of mid-1997, not one province had even adopted a policy on corporate involvement in education. McLaughlin thinks the most "beneficial" (and least controversial) partnerships have moved away from the donation of equipment, which was apparently suspect, to corporate influence on "learning objectives," a func-tion she claims is less likely to be criticized.[89]

If the Conference Board's numbers are correct, most Canadian schools now have a corporate partner. North American education partnerships, unlike those of other OECD countries, are almost exclusively forged with business. In continental Europe, commu-nity partnerships involve large and small businesses, parents, unions, and non-profit community groups. Some Canadian schools

---

PHIL DILLON, IBM's EduQuest account manager for Alberta, says the company's real and in-kind donations to Alberta schools, including teacher in-service, amount to $300,000. Dillon says every partnership is different, although the ratio-nale is always the same. IBM hopes to capture top market share in the province by developing and demonstrating the advan-tages of computer-assisted learning, says Dillon. He looks for every school "to contribute something back to IBM" that will help the company test or show off new products.

Source: Godfrey Huybregts, *Spectrum*, 1996

have non-business partnerships, but these take a secondary role, and at least some governments like it that way. When John Snobelen was Ontario's minister of education and training, he called for "the cultivation of innovative partnership between schools and their communities. . . . When I use that term 'community partners,' I'm speaking of business."[90]

Snobelen's encouragement was somewhat redundant. The *Financial Post* reported back in 1994 that the barriers between business and the educational establishment were breaking down.[91] Their survey found that 99 per cent of corporate respondents thought business could play a major role in improving the quality of education; 98 per cent of school boards agreed. The *Post* praised this new co-operative spirit, and contrasted it with the "perpetual state of confrontation" that had marred the past, when schools were anxious to resist the "taint of any commercial influence."

The *Post*'s survey suggested that this corporate activity in schools was taking place in a policy vacuum marked by crossed purposes. Corporations said they got involved in education mainly for the PR value. School boards, in contrast, believed partnerships were all about community ties and gaining access to materials and resources, especially those related to technology, mathematics, and science. School boards said 33 per cent of their partnership budget was earmarked for programs designed for students with special needs. Corporations, however, stated that just 1 per cent of their money would be directed to this area.

Since Webster's dictionary defines a partnership as "a relationship that pursues a joint interest," these differences suggest the word is being misused. So are some schools, and so are some students. Tensions created by patently corrupt arrangements nudged the Conference Board of Canada – voice of corporate Canada and enthusiastic supporter of business-education partnerships – to establish what it called ethical guidelines. Although these guidelines are notably vague and mild, the Conference Board reassures partners that they will still be "free to express their individuality" and to "agree on what the guidelines mean to them." Gentle ethics and flexible rules, indeed, despite the Conference

Board's somewhat pompous assertion that partnerships "have an explicit ethical dimension that needs to be discussed briefly. There are four important philosophical doctrines [to consider] . . . Ethical Egoism . . . Utility Ethics or Utilitarianism . . . Deontological Ethics . . . [and] Virtue Ethics."[92]

One doctrine or another will no doubt cover whatever a partner has in mind. When David McCamus – formerly CEO of Xerox Canada and an early enthusiast – talks about partnerships, it is hard to conceive of anything problematic coming up:

A successful partnership is a two-way relationship. Business can give students experience on sophisticated, high-tech equipment, which is beyond the scope of the school. The schools can help business by enabling students to develop their entrepreneurial skills, and their sense of enterprise, as well as by developing skills and attitudes necessary for success in the world of work.[93]

Note that, to McCamus, this two-way relationship is actually a one-way street. Everything from "exposing students to technology" to developing business-friendly "skills and attitudes" is framed as helping business. If business is helping education, it is helping education to serve business better. The merger of private and public interests, like the merger of education and training, is not a synergistic, value-added collaboration. It is a capitulation.

For Richer, For Poorer

> Technology in schools is a partnership magnet.[94]
> – Godfrey Huybregts

Bird's Hill School, located in rural Manitoba, has set out to prove that partnerships can work anywhere. In 1996, it boasted a roster that the Conference Board and SchoolNet praised for providing the country with "an exemplary model of an entrepreneurial approach to school improvement."[95]

According to the school's partnerships co-ordinator, Norm Lee, schools that want to imitate Bird's Hill must first learn to imitate their prospective partners. Lee warns that when education values are too different from business values, working together becomes difficult. If differences surface, Lee says, smart teachers and school administrators do all the accommodating, even if this means distancing themselves from their professional roots:

> In our dealings, we have never represented ourselves as part of the educational establishment. We have represented ourselves as being independent-minded and entrepreneurial. The terms we use are business terms. We describe ourselves as educational entrepreneurs staking our limited resources on finding solutions to the needs in the educational marketplace.

Lee claims that American business-education partnerships have taken a "precipitous plunge," declining by 25 per cent in just one year. He says many companies are leaving partnerships because they just don't work. Schools naïvely assumed the corporate sector would make up for reduced public spending and expect nothing in return. Bird's Hill didn't make this mistake. Teachers picked up hints from Northern Telecom (one of their forty partners), wrote mission statements, learned "how to pursue excellence through total quality management," and never forgot to emphasize the role

---

IN RECOGNITION OF its "leadership role in integrating technology into the learning process," Halifax's LeMarchant–St. Thomas school has been selected as an Apple Distinguished School. Only twelve Canadian schools received this award in 1997. Schools are appointed for a two-year period, during which teachers "will work closely with Apple and its software developer community to provide feedback on . . . new products." Teachers will also be expected to speak at conferences and host school-site visits for other educators. In return, the school will be entitled to display a plaque from Apple Computer, Inc.

Source: Nova Scotia Teachers Union, *NSTU Newsletter*

of science and technology in preparing the future work force. Lee says Bird's Hill has been successful because it has internalized the values of its partners, especially "a commitment to optimize the importance of technology."

Schools trying to look and sound more like their prospective consorts still face stiff competition as they try to snag a particularly desirable corporate partner. A technology partnership broker, who refers to such arrangements as marriages, tells schools to be prepared to give up some decision-making autonomy and to allow business "to access students and teachers." He says even if companies are denied on-site advertising, they will still expect their contributions to pay dividends in increased sales.[96] A software spokesperson explains: "Schools are basically ignorant of business. . . . They need to develop a culture that emphasizes a certain amount of hard work on the part of a business should bring a reward."[97]

One of Canada's most enthusiastic partnership boosters, Etobicoke's Ian Barrett, manages 555 deals for his district. He says the Etobicoke board has had its choice of partnerships because his schools always make sure they have "something to offer to potential corporate partners."[98] Barrett says the key is to show how the school can actively help the business find ways to improve its bottom line. This means Etobicoke students are made available when the Campbell Soup Company wants to taste-test new flavours on its target market, or when the publisher Harcourt Brace wants feedback on its new CD-ROM. Arrangements such as these have netted his system $1.5 million in donations, claims Barrett, an amount that perhaps receives more attention than the three-hundred-page handbook devoted to "subjective and objective measures of the partnership's relative success." No one can blame teachers and parents for happily accepting so much money flowing from what many of them consider to be small trade-offs.

One-way accommodation in the name of partnership should not come as a surprise. After all, the corporate sector would be among the first to agree that there is no such thing as a free lunch. But are there free breakfasts? When Kellogg's sponsors school breakfast programs and Kraft Dinner becomes the official sponsor of a food bank – yes, these are real examples – are we witnessing genuine corporate philanthropy, or shrewd and cynical marketing?

Pleasing the Partners

Few trends could so thoroughly undermine the very foundations of our free society as the acceptance by corporate officials of a social responsibility other than to make as much money for their shareholders as possible.[99]
– Milton Friedman

What we do isn't really philanthropy, which is about giving something away. This is about making an investment. . . . If we don't make those kind of investments, we're going to go out of business.[100]
– Intel executive

Not all corporate leaders share Friedman's opinions on the folly of business taking on responsibilities beyond the pursuit of profit. Some believe that social responsibility is good in and of itself. Others believe that it is good for business.

Many of the people who make key corporate decisions are without doubt community-minded and well intentioned. Nor does a corporation need to be huge to be philanthropic. Small companies willingly donate time and resources to worthy causes, and deserve recognition for their work. Yet despite the intentions of their managers and employees, over time these corporations can only succeed if they plan their good works strategically. It may make sense to do good, but it makes better sense to do good selectively. The school that agrees to promote Kellogg's at every opportunity is simply a better site to hand out free breakfasts than one that declines.

The political drift of partnerships elevates one group, one set of interests, and one point of view above all others. When we invite corporations to determine which good causes or which kinds of students deserve investment – or which "habits of mind" students should cultivate – we place our children's future in the wrong hands. We risk turning our schools into a farm system for corporations, one that churns out students who have been trained to be hired and unsurprised when they are fired.

It is also absurd of us to ask the same organizations that have clamoured for lower taxes and less public spending to rescue the schools that these policies are damaging. Corporations may add value in the short term, but we are naïve if we believe their appropriate role is to add values. When we encourage corporations to determine which desperate schools deserve to be partnered, and under what conditions, the outcomes are predictable. The problem is not just what some corporate partnerships demand of schools, but how tempting it is for schools to accommodate these demands even before they are made. The administrators, teachers, and students mimic and make compromises for their benefactors, becoming clones of their mentors. The corporate partners then claim that

---

AMERICAN EXPRESS HAS negotiated a special travel and tourism course to be integrated into the academic program at an Ottawa high school. The approach is based on "infusion," according to the teachers involved. This means that while the rest of the Grade 11 class is exploring the underlying tensions and historical context of *The Merchant of Venice*, lucky AMEX students will be musing over the best overseas routes, digging up seat-sale prices, and booking virtual hotel rooms in virtual Venice. The proud AMEX teachers tell CBC radio that their school had snagged their partner through a competitive bidding process, the ante being "volunteer teacher time and reassigned school resources." The interviewer encourages the teachers and students to reflect on what might be sacrificed by devoting one-third of their academic program to the travel industry. The teachers say nothing is lost – it's another win-win partnership. The students say the program is worth it if it means a job someday.

Source: CBC Radio, May 21, 1996

their educational philanthropy gives them the right to speak authoritatively on education policy.

Sometimes a corporation's influence is blatant; sometimes it is more subtle. Recently I was interviewed by a local high school student who wanted my opinion on partnerships. Towards the end of our conversation, I asked the student why he had chosen this topic for his research paper. He told me about the day he had walked to his buddies' usual hangout in the foyer of the school. Where there had once been a student gathering place, furnished with imitation park benches, there was now nothing but empty space. He asked his principal about the benches.

"They're gone," she explained, "because it's not very businesslike to have students sitting around on benches, hanging out and talking to each other. Our partner is [high-tech transnational corporation] Corel. Do you think Corel wants its employees to be just sitting around when they should be on the job?" When the student asked her whether Corel was influencing the curriculum, the principal smiled and replied, "In a subtle way, perhaps, but only when it comes to technology."[101]

Fifteen Minutes of Fame

One business-education partnership received an unusual amount of attention when it was highlighted in the Spring 1997 *Technology Quarterly*, published by *Canadian Business* magazine.[102] "See Johnny Surf," by George Emerson, took a rather critical look at Mississauga's Gordon Graydon Memorial School. Although the school is accustomed to media attention, Graydon's principal took exception to Emerson's story, which (in a letter to the editor) he called a "nasty and unfair" piece of journalism "that maligned students, staff and the community."[103]

The article describes a school that business built – or, to put a finer point on it, the one-third of a school that technology partnerships built. Graydon's International Business and Technology (IBT) program boasts almost one partnership for every five students, adding up to a stunning total of 78 partnerships for 440 students. The partnerships are only part of what sets Graydon apart; Emerson calls IBT the entrepreneurial equivalent of a French immersion program, with students eating, breathing, and eventually thinking like "the junior business set." The school has attracted a lot of interest. Partners including Bell Advanced Communications, Nesbitt Burns, the University of Toronto, and (the ubiquitous) Apple Canada share the credit when visitors pay a $25 fee for the full school/corporate tour.

George Emerson was taken aback when he had to pay a fee for a school tour. So was reporter Ann Kerr, who wrote about Graydon for the *Globe and Mail* one year earlier.[104] Kerr reported that the students were "infused with entrepreneurial zeal," courtesy of the donations of corporate time and products, and ready to "step right into well paid jobs." This prediction may or may not turn out to be as fatuous as the claim by IBT's director that his school is operating in the twenty-first century. Even with $1.3 million start-up money from the Ontario government, Graydon's students, like the rest of us, can persuade neither the calendar nor the jobs market to do their bidding.

Details, details. The big picture is more important: Canon's $80,000 worth of donated copiers and Cryovac's $100,000 printing press are the kinds of investments students understand. A tax write-off here, a steady stream of entry-level workers there. Graydon's IBT students benefit from learning real-world skills like videoconferencing, although speaking audibly and facing the camera do not sound particularly skill-intensive. Using computer-taught language programs, the students are introduced to Mandarin, Japanese, Spanish, and German, not because these are the languages of their heritage, but because they are "the languages of economic growth areas." Those who visit Graydon's Web site might conclude that these students and/or teachers could do with a more intensive introduction to English grammar and spelling. Perhaps correct language has been overlooked in fávour of more pressing matters. According to Kerr, Graydon adheres to provincial curriculum requirements, but "it always keeps the bottom line in mind." Principal Ray Beyer says that "when we do something in Shakespeare, we explain why it is relevant today, then how it applies to a business venue." He does not elaborate on precisely how this approach works.

The IBT students apparently catch on quickly, learning not only how to use the seventy Internet connections, but how to apply their knowledge and sell it before it gets stale. According to Emerson, teachers encourage them to find useful applications for the technology skills they are learning. Students not busy Web-chatting are taught "to evaluate what a customer wants, solicit the customer, negotiate prices and terms, then follow through and deliver the product or service." This entrepreneurial spirit can find a silver lining in every cloud. One of the students Emerson met was busy planning a multimedia kiosk to dispense health information to students, the perfect substitute for the disappearing school nurse. "Public health is cutting back," said the young designer. "How can we take advantage of that?"

Graydon has special permission to recruit students from across the region. Only 250 Grade 9 applicants were selected from a pool of 600 hopefuls, each of whom paid a $10 application fee. Some families pay up to $1000 for transportation each year. Student selection is always tough; however, IBT's partners help to determine not only "which business and technology skills students should be learning," but which students should get a chance to learn them. Graydon's corporate partners sit on the student selection committee.

IBT instructor Grant Wardlaw says any criticism of corporate involvement in education "really frustrates" him, and that his corporate partners, if anything, are too hesitant to get involved with matters such as curriculum. On the other hand, teachers can be a real problem. "You have to hand-pick staff," Wardlaw admits. "Teachers must be motivated and willing to change. Some teachers like it safe." However staff are selected, none seem to question the cornerstones of IBT: "It takes business to make our education system viable for the twenty-first century," says the principal. "Business has to be our true partner," says the program director.

It is not clear whether the two-thirds of Graydon's students who are not part of the IBT program share these sentiments. Half of these students are expecting to go directly into the work force, and not the high-tech part of it. They are not competing with IBT students for a chance to check stock market quotes over the Internet, or worrying much about HTML language. Given the global city's appetite for lower-skilled workers, they may be learning something with a longer shelf life than new Windows applications, but who is to know? Do these students have a true partner looking out for their best interests?

Within traditional philosophies of public education, we are all supposed to be the true partners of these students. By and large, we live up to this responsibility admirably when we understand the dangers of elitism and the consequences of turning public responsibility into a private concern. When given the opportunity, the public has far more often rejected than endorsed the privatization of education in any of its forms. In fact, it is precisely the public's distaste for privatized public education that has led voucher advocates to become charter advocates, in order to try to achieve their goals through the back door. Charter schools still have many Canadian opponents: is it possible that they too are being retrofitted as citizen- and democracy-friendly partnerships?

Consider Graydon. It selects students to suit not only the intellectual requirements of its program, but also the program's premise that the purpose of education is to teach students whatever their future employers want them to know. IBT selects its teachers to blend harmoniously into the school's entrepreneurial philosophy. Graydon operates with public funds under the blessing of the school board, but it enjoys exceptions to the board's regulations with respect to attendance, transportation fees, and curriculum. It is internally governed, and free to raise money independently. By any other name, isn't Graydon's IBT program a charter school?

Ontario's Ministry of Education and Training calls Graydon "the model that we're building towards," and why not? Why would any astute government endure the political fall-out from proclaiming charter schools when it can enjoy the benefits of creeping privatization without enduring the controversy? Partnerships, especially those involving technology, have such cachet that opposing them has become the political equivalent of endorsing the flat earth society. No teachers' union or other watchdog has done more than call for guidelines to govern them. Since they operate school-by-school, partnerships are usually below the radar of those who track sweeping systemic changes. Ministries of education look the other way. Meanwhile, the Conference Board of Canada churns out awards, encouragement, and "tool kits" that explain partnership ethics in reassuring terms. Corporations continue to write cheques – for the right schools, with the right students, and under the right circumstances.

If the brash arrogance of John Golle's EAI is America's template for privatization, Graydon's incremental absorption of corporate practices and values is its Canadian counterpart. We are allowed to think we are different, following a different, more ethical path, leading to a different destination.

We think our artifacts have no politics – until we bump up against a low bridge.

8

INFO-CULT@ED.COM

TALES FROM THE GLOBAL CITY

The global city has its own holy trinity: markets, technology, and information. Although we ascribe an omnipotence well beyond human control to markets and technology, we worship our third god, information, by honouring its management. Try as we might to limit, categorize, apply, forward, or massage it, information manages us better than we manage it. The worship of information has not just cluttered our minds, recycling bins, and desks, it has brought us to a standstill. We are rooted not so much in place as in time, for those who worship information are afflicted by *tempocentrism* – a fixation on the present. By definition, dated information is stale and therefore useless, and the future sends out no information packages. We are left with the present, and our struggle to manage the endless new supply of what we worship. The deities of markets and technology should be eternally grateful. Rendered uninterested in the past or the future, swamped by the present, we mortals leave the gods to their own amusements.

Information overload robs us of the ability to make connections, and thus undermines our ability to think. We may have learned to merge files, but we have shown only a limited ability (and sometimes less inclination) to merge meaning, to make the connections across past, present, and future that we so desperately need. The present distracts us from pondering the future, not just because info-worship keeps us stuck in time, but because thinking hard about the present casts a dark shadow over events to come.

The millennialists may have little cause for celebration. The details of the future may not be knowable, but the accelerating trends of the present, unless they are interrupted, will trigger predictable consequences. Because every indicator suggests that the political and economic distance between rich and poor, within and among countries, will intensify, the defining characteristic of the near future will likely be the struggle over resources and who is entitled to them. Ordinary people will lose ground on every front.

Although they may still ameliorate this shakedown and make it appear less intense and less intentional, the governments of developed nations will be less active in redistributing wealth, either through foreign aid or through domestic social programs. As politicians continue to sell off public wealth, represented in part by public institutions, we can expect further growth and consolidation of private wealth. Public debt may decrease, but private debt will increase as user fees replace and outpace taxes.

As transnational corporations formalize their power over nation-states – negotiating agreements that arrange economies to assure their continued profits – the transnationals' business affairs, especially investment and currency speculation, will become the overriding form of economic activity. But fortunes built on paper are vulnerable, and many expect the market to exact revenge, forcing mergers until perhaps no more than a few dozen mega-transnationals remain. These mighty world powers will bless a small global elite, while leaving the rest of the world's citizens to sort themselves out. Some people will end up among "the top third," those who will live well and with some security. The other two-thirds will not.

Especially among the bottom two-thirds, a ruthless, finger-pointing search for the culprits will ensue. Increasing tribalism rooted in culture, class, religion, and other social distinctions will be complicated by competing interests based on age. Canadians older than fifty-five now outnumber those younger than fifteen. More than any other demographic group, older Canadians fall at different ends of the economic spectrum. However, the ageing baby boom's decision makers are at the top end, and many are less dependent on publicly provided services. They may well have more concern with the quick availability of health care than with its public or private delivery. They can be expected to show more interest in pensions and health care than in public education. As a demographic group that enjoys relative wealth, older Canadians have a particular interest in maintaining the value of private capital, which requires coddling the stock market and preserving the conditions necessary for low inflation, including high rates of unemployment.

The children of the boomers appear to be more conservative (or resigned) than their elders, and less inclined to feel responsible for others, at least through the mechanism of government. Thanks in part (ironically) to public education, many of these younger Canadians are confident enough to believe that their children will be unlikely to need or benefit from the same public services they did themselves.

While this belief explains, in part, our growing approval of minimalist government, it is not the cause of reduced government any more than the deficit was. The pullback of government that has characterized this era was at first justified by deficit reduction, but it has been motivated by an ideology of less government – or, to put a finer point on it, less democracy. The corporate state cannot afford democracy, because democracy makes demands. With deficits under control, a new argument for less government must be found. It will be called tax relief.

Since less government provides poorer and less effective services, dissatisfied customers will begin to criticize governments, and the public's willingness to pay taxes will suffer a genuine decline. Governments will continue to pursue self-limitation, either by necessity or design. As citizens become more aware of how little governing takes place on their behalf and how much takes place on behalf of commerce, they will become even more cynical about the possibility of good government, and join the call for less of it.

Of necessity, we will turn to our own resources and our employability. The timeline for retrofitting workers' expectations is short, since many more young workers are about to come on-line to replace retirees. Governments and business leaders will continue to use the spectre of good jobs/bad jobs/no jobs to ensure an oversupply of highly skilled workers, which will in turn drive down the cost of labour and expectations for job security. Unpaid work, including unpaid overtime and volunteering, will effectively squeeze out new jobs.

"Good jobs" will continue to be exported or to disappear in favour of low-skilled service jobs, most of which are insecure and part-time. Fewer people will find satisfaction in their work. Those who hold the type of jobs that could be satisfying will work so hard and so long that they will not be content either. The pullback of government and deregulation will either remove restrictions on the exploitation of labour or make them irrelevant. Women will be hit particularly hard, since their advances towards equity in the workplace have largely been government-driven, and since they bear the brunt of declining government services in health care, child care, and other social services.

Techno-corporatism will exacerbate all these trends, and continue to act as the means and the excuse for many of them. Technological sophistication will be used to justify rising corporate profits, the "decoupling" of individuals from employers, and the growing gap between rich and poor nations and individuals. Corporations will proclaim advances in technology, while those pondering technologically induced problems will let technology off the hook. Experts will point instead to institutional failure, particularly any institution associated with government. The consolidation and shakedown of technology industries, which depend on a pyramid of economic and techno-positive illusions, will result in the emergence of a very few transnationals. These world powers will control all forms of communication and entertainment, the distinctions between which will rapidly disappear. Busy being info-tained, many of us may neither notice nor care.

The rapid increase in the status and amount of information will glut all but the most nimble and/or selective minds. Expertise will become, by definition, the mastery of an increasingly narrow band of information. Bewildered by information overload, people will increase their demand for more synthetic representations of news: it will be much easier to follow the peccadillos of celebrities than events in the Middle East. Once those with political as well as profit-driven agendas take over the filtering of all information, via the media or education, alternative information will be limited. Cautionary tales about desperate people who break laws and inspiring tales of entrepreneurs who break through will be popular: every oppressed group needs its folklore. The Internet, which some thought might have allowed unofficial knowledge to flourish, will be further developed as a commercial venue. This info-mall will still sell ideas and products (which will merge), but alternative retailers will have to charge, while the anchors will provide their information for free.

The Internet will become an important vehicle for the export of McCulture and its deities. Deceived by the promises of globalization and fuelled by communication and trade, citizens of developing countries will demand living conditions that more closely match those found in developed countries. This demand will drive the export of jobs, but also of environmentally toxic policies and practices. The deteriorating quality of the global environment is already spurring a demand for technological fixes, and perhaps the environment will become the most important focus of citizens' groups, which will abandon their current causes in favour of this overriding concern.

Since pollution in all its forms is a by-product of the acquisition and control of wealth, the battle over the environment will become the proxy for the real battle between citizens' interests and those of commerce – it is no coincidence that the Fraser Institute and the Business Council on National Issues have taken on the environmentalists. Although governments may at first be capable of determining whose interests will prevail, by the time an undeniable ecological crisis is at hand, they will have lost so many powers to transnational corporations through agreements such as the MAI that they will be as powerless to act as the world's citizens.

Any similar lists of trends and forecasts taken from almost any source of information will do. The question is not whether we are on the brink of a political, social, economic, or environmental abyss, but whether we will recognize when we have stepped (or been pushed) over the edge. There is more evidence of crisis than of public awareness of its immediacy and severity. How can this be when the world's population is more literate and better-informed than ever before? A much higher proportion of citizens of every nation is now capable of understanding the causes and consequences of the crisis – or, for that matter, of challenging this assertion – than at any other time. Yet the crisis deepens.

If we consider where info-abundance has taken us so far, devoting ourselves to the acquisition of yet more information is not just unwise, but pathological. We cannot afford to educate a generation to believe that the management of information holds the magic solution to human problems. We cannot afford to assume that the interests of profit and the interests of people are synonymous. While the education of our children could be civilization's most important ally in asserting this difference, there are no guarantees. Schooling could as easily – no, *more* easily – condemn our well-informed children to the outskirts of the global city.

What is worth knowing? Who decides? These remain the fundamental questions every society must answer about its schools. Every generation of adults must ask these questions anew, just as the welfare of every generation of children depends on the answers. We may believe that these questions have never before been debated in a context similar to today's, but we would be wrong. We are not the first to contemplate how to balance the interests that compete for education's favours. Perhaps we can shake off the present long enough to revisit the past – the better to think about the future.

The Commissioners' Lament

In 1910, Labour Minister (later prime minister) Mackenzie King established the Dominion of Canada Royal Commission on Industrial Training and Technical Education.[1] Education reform had become a matter of some urgency, for it was feared that Canada's schools were adjusting inadequately to the new economy. The charge to the commissioners warned that "industrial efficiency is all-important to the development of the Dominion and to the promotion of the home and foreign trade of Canada in competition with other nations." If Canada was to compete successfully, it would have to adopt "the most advanced systems and methods of Industrial Training and Technical Education."

In 1913, the commissioners tabled recommendations of astonishing familiarity. They described chronic international dissatisfaction with education systems. They found it curious that each country assumed in turn that other countries were modernizing education much more successfully. Foreshadowing today's debates, the commissioners despaired over the crowded curriculum, the artificial separation of knowledge into subjects, and even the tyranny of high-stakes examinations. Expectations were rising: the commissioners noted that "the demand is everywhere insistent that the schools shall meet the larger duties which are now thrown upon them by the changed social and industrial conditions." Times were changing, but even in 1913, people believed that schools were not.

When the commissioners put forth their recommendations, it became evident that these gentlemen had minds of their own. They concluded that students should be exposed to "career awareness," and that efforts to keep students in school should be redoubled. But they looked beyond schools, not just within them, and spoke to the deteriorating social and economic conditions that were preventing students from benefiting from their education.

Then the commissioners broke ranks with prevailing opinions about how schools should be realigned with changing times and changing workplace technology. They insisted it would be pointless and cruel to use the appetites of the workplace as an excuse to train students to command advanced industrial skills that few of them would ever need. As their position was contrary to an international movement that was advancing a narrow, vocational approach to the education of labour, their report caused some commotion. However, the Dominion's commissioners steadfastly insisted that cultivating character and citizenship was more important to Canada's future than training.

The commissioners saw industrialization as a poor excuse for limiting students' breadth of knowledge. They were not seduced by the positivism of their times, nor did they gloss over what the workplace had in store for students once they left school. The commissioners called the "factory methods" employed by industry "outrageous." Many factory workers were accorded a status "hardly higher relatively than that of slaves when civilization permitted that form of ownership of life." However, the commissioners' job was to reform schools, not factories. Since employment was more likely to deliver misery than satisfaction, the commissioners argued that schools must therefore provide every student with the means to counterbalance the dehumanizing effects of the workplace.

Industry had asserted a claim on how public education should evolve, but the commissioners wanted nothing to do with it. They looked at education from the point of view of students and the nation, not industry. If the working lives of students were destined to be menial and repetitive, then their preparation for citizenship was even more imperative: "The safety of the state and considerations for the welfare of the race demand that they should receive education suitable to their needs as individuals in the long chain of life, in order that it might not be debased or weakened in their hands."

The commissioners warned that the kind of education required "for the long chain of life" was threatened by industrialists who were concerned only with their own interests. They put their position quite bluntly, given the language of their times:

In the earlier stages of civilization industry was the servant of humanity, and was always employed to meet some need of service by individuals or communities. The question thrusts itself forward now, as to whether modern organized industry is to continue as the servant of humanity, or whether it is becoming an instrument in the hands of a comparatively few individuals, whereby they seek to obtain control of wealth and of the means of producing more wealth, including the control of human labour. When the main object of industry ceases to be products for service, and turns to profits for the employers and undue returns on capital, the conditions and situation are full of danger.

These dangers could be moderated only if the interests of organized industry ran a distant third to those of the individual and the state. The commissioners rejected the idea that employers or the economy had a prior claim on the purposes of education. They argued that even though individuals valued education for "pecuniary" reasons, they also valued it as a means to achieving personal happiness and maturity as citizens. The purpose of education, then, was to help each generation develop the inclination to see "beyond self-interest" to "the whole of which his individual life is but a part."

Thus it was not just the state's responsibility, but in the state's interest, to ensure citizens were able to enjoy an education that enriched them. The state would gain indirectly when well-educated citizens turned naturally to improving their communities and their country. A fine system of public education would serve the complementary goals of both individuals and the state: "What is true of the material gain which may result from improved education is true also of the moral gain. The temper, the outlook, the recreations, the ideals of a nation may be so refined and raised by the right kind of training as to secure for the mass of the people a more choiceworthy life."

The similarities between the commissioners' 1913 analysis of education and today's circumstances are remarkable. Secondary school reform (predicated on an economic and industrial revolution), the need for competitiveness, a compromised system overwhelmed by new responsibilities and challenged by a deteriorating societal context – these issues sound as familiar as last week's press release issued by any ministry of education. Yet what has changed over time is more important than what has stayed the same.

The Dominion's commissioners took two things for granted that no commissioners today could safely assume. First, they felt no need to argue that education must be more than acquiring information or learning how to manage it. Second, they assumed that Canadians viewed the role and interests of government as quite separate from those of industry. The ideological merger of government and commerce had not yet taken place. To the commissioners, the state's obvious responsibility was to limit industry's influence on education, not to promote it. Clearly, they believed, the government should entertain industry's education agenda only when it supported goals that first served individuals and "the ideals of the nation." The commissioners would have been appalled to see today's governments competing to become the brokers of industry's aspirations, in education or in any other sphere.

As this century turns, we seem to have given up on governments as our allies in the power struggle between corporate greed and citizens' interests. True, few governments in memory have done more than act as the local hosting committees for the interests of commerce. Most have been willing to sacrifice any social or environmental good to this purpose, and people have caught on. Yet, in abandoning hope that governments can make a pertinent and positive contribution to our struggle, we have abandoned our best and most powerful collective force. By refusing to see the potential of governments to act for our interests, we guarantee that they will not. When it sets up self-fulfilling prophecies, our cynicism does us no favour.

What has changed most profoundly since the commissioners' 1913 report is not the definition of an educated person, nor the rationale for public education, nor the imperatives for education reform. What has changed is the role of government, and assumptions about whom governments should serve. One by one, governments have shed any responsibility to act as the breakwater that protects society from the tide of industry. It is hard to imagine any royal commission today winning the government's ear by criticizing the role of industry in education or any other aspect of public life. Today's governments have become the champions of capital, the friends and apologists for the very sector that poses the dangers the commissioners foresaw.

The royal commissioners of 1910–13 made the connections. They pulled together the most important elements of the present and the past, made some assumptions about where trends of their present might lead, and recommended a course of action. However, the Great War made rather fast work of finding suitable employment for young men, and the Dominion government soon had political matters more pressing than school reform with which to contend. No doubt the commissioners anticipated that their recommendations would be shelved in the face of a national emergency. What they could not predict was how the triumvirate of individual, collective, and capital interests that they envisioned would be reduced, decades later, to a stool with two legs. They would be even more surprised to learn that we thought we could fix things by going it alone.

The commissioners had confidence that, together, citizens and their governments were strong enough to outwit industry simply by refusing to accept its claim that not only should it have a voice in education policy, but its voice should be the loudest. After all, the commissioners' lament was not a song of self-pity, but an assertion that when it comes to what is worth knowing, the public interest comes first. Will we be able to say the same about the schools of the future?

A Tale of Two Schools

Microworld High is located on the edge of inner-city Urbania, where it is surrounded by high-density, low-quality housing. Most of its students are drawn from the local community, but a few come from across the city, attracted to the showcase technology-training centre the kids call "Gates's Ghetto." The majority of the school's instructional supervisors commute to work, although the assortment of learning technicians, aides, classroom assistants, and technical support personnel lives nearby.

The school is part of the network that belongs to the Microworld family of schools. Microworld branched into franchised education in 2004, where it quickly proved to be a successful competitor in the education business. According to industry analysts, Microworld is an industry leader because it has been able to adapt quickly to client needs and to simplify the many choices available to parents. Building on the nomenclature that worked so well for its other virtual products, Microworld has given its high schools a versioning system. Since Grade 10.4 is a more advanced version than 10.3, tuition fees are scaled accordingly.

The introduction of student tuition fees turned out to be less contentious than critics had predicted. Once people realized that, when schools received only public funding, the very students who most needed a good education were the most severely hurt by cutbacks, then the equity arguments of the anti-tuition forces lost steam. When surveys of poor parents found that they would be willing to make financial sacrifices for their children, the plan went ahead. Wealthier parents were already accustomed to paying fees, of course, since many of them had opted for private schools once charter school legislation allowed these institutions to enjoy full public funding. These wealthier parents told pollsters they might consider giving the new public system a second chance, but only if the schools could demonstrate they were preparing students to take advantage of the future, and only if the public system could guarantee that their own children's contact with weaker or otherwise undesirable children would be minimal.

Realizing that public education would collapse for good without the political support of these influential parents, decision makers agreed. The most tangible outcome of this compromise was the racial and class characteristics of the different versions. The class of 11.1 stayed together, followed its own curriculum, and looked very different from 11.5. In the interests of building the school community, schools allotted each version its own instructional staff and its own section of the school building. The students in Gates's Ghetto, for all the official talk of intensive remediation and enrichment for the .1 versions, still worked and lived in the school's basement, although for some time there had been talk of building a new wing.

This new wing would probably not be built in the foreseeable future. Now that school construction had become exclusively a for-profit venture, any improvement to Microworld High was a losing proposition compared with ventures in suburbia. Developers discovered that building state-of-the-art schools, usually in partnership with technology providers and one of the franchising companies, provided a healthy boost to real estate sales. Investors quickly realized that the same security provisions that made their housing developments attractive – private security guards and technology-based screening systems that weeded out undesirables – could be applied just as successfully to schools.

Once the better prospects had fled the city's core, and immigration and poverty had overrun the older parts of suburbia, investors moved quickly to pick up a piece of the action. Still, it came down to people. The key to financial success was attracting the right CEO to a school, someone prepared to make tough decisions on behalf of the management board. Maintaining a popular staff became much easier once the dysfunctional protections of teachers' unions had been eradicated. Without school boards, the better schools such as Socrates Secondary merely had to keep local parents content, which they did by maintaining a school-wide focus on customer service.

They called it parental involvement, but it was really parental persuasion. Parents with the right contacts turned out to be very useful when it came to fund-raising to pay coaches for the school teams, and to finance the annual trip to the European Economic Union. Others were more than willing to expend a little cash to see their children jump the waiting list. Pleased to be among the fortunate third who had made it, and anxious to hold onto their good fortune in having their children accepted at Socrates, parents were more likely to boast than raise any questions. Around the neighbourhood, Socrates Secondary was even called "One-Third High," a name that said it all. The one-third/two-thirds shorthand to describe socio-economic status had caught on quickly because the metaphor was so useful and so apt. It was slightly less offensive than referring to the haves and the have-nots, and the old language of class really wasn't used anymore.

The top third was doing quite nicely, their parents having survived the restructuring of the economy (well, of everything, really) of the 1990s. They had survived through a combination of initiative and good fortune, but they would never again be complacent. They had learned that the enemy could wear a friendly face and that the world was full of excuses. They would never let themselves be vulnerable again. Their insecurity and their arrogance made them turn inwards, made them focus on protecting the advantages of their families first – only then would they consider the welfare of other members of their community. Perhaps this behaviour was only natural.

The students at Microworld High came from the other two-thirds. They were not yet a monolithic group, although some of their differences were blending. Parents who belonged to what had once been called the middle class still had hopes and sometimes pretensions that they could break through to the top third – or, if they couldn't, that their children, given the right skills, would have a chance to beat the odds. This more ambitious group alternated between feeling sympathy for parents who had no such hopes, and anger when the others couldn't or wouldn't take advantage of the few opportunities they were offered. These formerly middle-class parents were the ones who turned out for the monthly parent council meetings at Microworld High, where the school's CEO, George McLeod, tended to keep them occupied with fund-raising. Raising money made these parents feel as if they were working for everyone's benefit (on their sympathetic/guilty days) or investing in the future of their own children (on their more ambitious days).

Of course, funding was a never-ending problem. People mistakenly thought that just because Microworld High carried an impressive brand name, all the school had to do was tap its partner on the shoulder if it needed something. This assumption turned out to be far from true. Once education became a for-profit enterprise – even if those profits came largely from public dollars – the bottom line always came first. Sure, to the public and the students, George still talked about the value of education and the importance of learning marketable skills, but as CEO his main job was to figure out how to deliver the goods and produce a return on investment. The profit benchmarks – and the tuition fees – went up every year.

From time to time, George thought of moving to one of the new suburban schools, like Socrates Secondary, where things would surely be a lot easier and the enrolment of Version .5s much healthier. He became particularly bitter when the week of the quarterly exams neared. George and some of his colleagues had lost the battle to have different exams set for the different versions. They had argued that it was unfair to apply the same standard to students who came to school with very different abilities and motivations. At first it looked as if the government testing agency would go along with their argument in favour of differentiated exams for differentiated programs, but then the Opposition resurrected the old critiques of streaming that came up in the versions debate. If the tests were the same, the government could more easily boast that it was upholding its commitment to standards that "every child would achieve no matter what." The government enshrined this guarantee in Bill 960, the Equality for Every Student Act.

His teachers (as George still thought of them; he had worked in education for a long time) may have had personal or professional opinions about testing or other matters of policy, but they kept their views to themselves. His staff knew that the market for teachers was vastly oversupplied, now that the government had waived the need for certification. This measure had been introduced for a trial period as a short-term solution to the teacher shortage that had ensued when nearly all the baby boom teachers took early retirement at the same time. However, the trial period had now lasted years. The government had erroneously assumed that teacher-training programs would continue to churn out lots of fresh young teachers, but declining salaries and soaring tuition fees seemed to dry up the supply. Apparently, prospective teachers rarely came from the top third, and the troops of bright young women who had always taken up teaching were flocking towards other less troublesome vocations.

Turning teacher training over to private vocational schools had probably been a good idea, but the technology-based curricula must somehow have failed to prepare graduates for the kind of insight and maturity they needed to deal with real students. At any rate, when this group of edu-trained instructional supervisors bombed, the provinces decided to deregulate the whole system for a while. Given the rapid turnover and lack of experience in Microworld's staff, George was glad that the government had redefined the teacher-student ratio (one of its key input standards) as the adult-student ratio. This change gave him the flexibility he needed to get enough warm adult bodies into his classrooms and, not unimportantly, to cut payroll costs.

George had tasked his vice-CEO of business affairs to handle staff negotiations and terminations. After all, George couldn't help still thinking of himself as the principal teacher and the instructional leader of his staff, not their employer. He had even tried to convene staff meetings about something other than the versions getting in each other's hair. Unfortunately, these meetings about curriculum and instruction, the areas in which George had earned his master's degree (of which he was still proud, even though his M.Ed. didn't have the cachet of his colleagues' MBAs), fell flat. After two or three attempts, George gave up. What was there, really, to discuss? The Council of Ministers of Education set the national curriculum framework (harmonized with the OECD and APEC education indicators). The provinces established hundreds of outcomes to match the framework, agreed on measurable standards for each one, and then let go until it was time for the damn tests. Based on its budget, each school purchased courseware from an educational products corporation (although there were really only two or three to choose from in each price/version range), and then it was just a matter of booting up, as they used to say.

George had his reservations about what he still thought of as computerized curriculum, but he didn't discuss them. His teachers were already so frustrated with the inadequacies of the system that he didn't want to give them any more encouragement to whine. Just the other day the guidance counsellor (now known as the career and personal adjustment worker) had complained that the new interactive software for the sexual-abuse self-help group carried an implicit sexist bias. George had handled that one by asking the adjustment worker whether she would prefer to see all these students individually – and that was the last he'd heard about bias. Not that all his staff were critical of the technology. The young ones, especially the ones George suspected of busily grooming their résumés for a real job in high-tech, seemed to have been programmed for enthusiasm.

On the days he needed reassurance, George would head down to one of these classrooms, and in a few minutes he could see why they loved it, the simulations and the virtual reality stuff and even the chat groups, which his English teacher still insisted on calling "discourse groups." Surely all this activity was better than what George remembered from his own uneven experiences as a student, and probably even superior to the way he himself had once taught.

If he was honest with himself, George could not imagine how the Version .1s and .2s, especially, could possibly be controlled and kept amused without all the technology. These kids were wired, all right, and not just to their computers. It was worth the extra he was paying to keep a couple of his most experienced teachers in Gates's Ghetto – the type who knew how to keep a lid on things. He had lost some of his best teachers to suburbia, of course, and a couple more had left in protest when the parent council ratified its three-strikes-and-you're-out policy on low-achieving and/or misbehaving students. As far as he knew, every inner-city school had established this policy internally, according to the ministry's offer (Bill 1160, the Enabling Personal Responsibility Act, set it all out). Despite himself, George had to admire a government that found a way to download all politically dangerous decisions onto parents and schools.

George remembered that particular parent-council meeting well. The few die-hard liberals in the community who thought every child deserved to be in school were no match for the management board, who used progressive edu-jargon to talk about personal responsibility and consequences. One corporate type started to pontificate about how, in his business, anyone who didn't perform was out, but he was nudged into silence by one of the other suits, who knew better than to be quite so obvious. Despite his misgivings, George discovered that writing up the minutes of this meeting wasn't too difficult: something like, *In the interests of the majority of our students who are hard-working and responsible . . . blah blah.* Maybe the three-strikes policy was the right decision, after all. If these kids couldn't make it in Version 9.1, they weren't going to make it anywhere. Why lie to them?

And there were undeniable benefits. The departure of thirty of his 250 Version .1 and .2 students had made George's quarterly report look a little better. And since he had decided to spend the last of the school's budget on the ministry's new coaching software, *Better Tests: Better Students*, he hoped that his upgraded student population would deliver an improved outcomes profile. Not that Microworld High was likely to challenge Socrates Secondary for its top-ten provincial ranking, of course. Still, if he could just make sure his teachers were using that damned software he had paid so much for, and were getting across to those careless students how important these tests were, the school could do better. It would need to, if what George had read between the lines of the partnership committee minutes was any indication. The committee members had been polite, but the message was quite clear. The partners' annual contribution (even though most of it was more computers than Microworld High could ever use) was still 20 per cent of his budget, and if the partners wanted to see a better return on investment, as they had not so delicately put it, George would have to deliver.

George winced when he remembered stories he had heard about some cheap shots the retiring teacher who served on the partnership committee had made at the last meeting – something about capitalist vultures. He hoped the partners had excused this outburst as the crazy ranting of a dinosaur, but he knew this kind of foolish talk was on an alarming increase at what used to be polite celebrations and retirement teas. George made a note to mend some corporate fences, to look for a more compliant teacher volunteer, and to alert the fund-raising committee to the urgency of either finding more partners or losing one of the school's computer technicians. That should do it.

Not for the first time, George balefully considered his prospects for moving to a school like Socrates. At this thought, however, he suddenly remembered that he needed to get moving if he was to be in time for the parents' meeting at that very place – his daughters' school.

George nodded to his neighbours as he made his way into Socrates' newly renovated auditorium. The room was already in semi-darkness in preparation for yet another PowerPoint presentation. George wondered what Socrates' principal, Peter Molloy, had in store for the parents this evening. There would be the obligatory announcements of the students' most noteworthy achievements over the last few months, the introduction of the new staff, some printouts of upgrades for the Version .4 and .5 curricula, no doubt, and results from the last quarterly tests, reported by grade, version, and teacher. Even with all the graphics, the presentation could get a bit tedious, unless a sharp tongue posed an embarrassing question about the fitness of someone or other to teach, given a decline in quarterly results, etc., etc.

Peter Molloy wasn't appointed to be Socrates' CEO by accident, however. He knew when to chuckle indulgently and when to look tough. Molloy never failed to convey the message that he ran a tight ship, and that customer satisfaction was not only the school's motto and mission statement, but his personal and professional vision. George winced involuntarily: he realized that this kind of cynicism was exactly what kept him stuck at Microworld High. It was a sure sign to everyone that in some ways he was not with the program, as they used to say.

George told himself that he should be taking pointers. Peter Molloy was in fine form, saying all the right things about the school as a family, recognizing the school's corporate partners as full participants in the life of Socrates Secondary, thanking the volunteers for their time and contribution, praising the dedication and wisdom of the parent committee, and applauding the very successful fund-raising drive.

Everything was going as planned when, having invited questions and comments from the floor, Molloy pleasantly recognized the woman in the third row. As she stood, she said sarcastically that she wasn't part of the Socrates "family." Her children went to Microworld High, she said, and she had some questions for everyone in the room. Molloy fixed his face with a polite smile, welcomed the school's guest, and encouraged her to ask whatever she liked.

She said she was from the other two-thirds, the two-thirds whose quality of life and quality of education depended on the other third, the third who held the power and the money and decided how (or whether) they would be shared. She asked how many of Socrates' parents had been in her children's school, or walked through her children's neighbourhood. She asked whether they knew that Microworld High had metal detectors at the door, that the school had sold its roof and walls for advertising space, that janitorial services had been cut back to once a week, that the versions were really just tribes fighting over the few spoils the school had to offer. She asked the whole audience where they thought Microworld's thirty "strike-outs" were now, and what they were doing. She asked whether any members of the Socrates family had taken part in the downtowners' protest demanding more funding for education. She asked whether Socrates parents had ever thought of themselves as being in partnership with a food bank.

Finally, she asked, "Ten years from now, where do you think you will be once you have done this to us, and to our children? Do you think your children and ours will live in different worlds? Will there be two futures, one for your third and one for the rest of us? How long do you think we will take this? How long do you think we will sell our kids' souls and their futures so that your children can have it all?" Looking around the room, her gesture including the perfect community beyond, she asked, "How long do you think we will let you keep this?"

Molloy listened first with embarrassment, and then with growing panic. Her questions were legitimate, even important, but surely this meeting was neither the time nor the place. It was uncanny, really. The CEOs had had a similar discussion at their retreat just last month when, in an unguarded moment, one of the guys had said that educating the one-third was, after all, a snap. The real problem for the future would be what kind of education to give the other two-thirds. Too little, and they might become an even greater drag on the top third. Too much, especially too much of the right kind, and they might rebel. But surely

the CEOs had been speculating about the distant future, somewhere else – not the present, not here.

As Molloy tried to think of a suitably soothing and yet firm
response, his eyes fell upon George, who looked shaken and
guilty. Perfect. Molloy could buy some time while appearing to
graciously cede George the opportunity to defend Microworld
High – and, he hoped, the whole system – before this angry
parent and all the parents of the Socrates family, whose eyes
were now turned expectantly towards him. Surely, he and
George were in this together.

Anticipating Molloy's strategy, George struggled to collect
his thoughts, and to find the facile explanations he had used
so many times before. Separate but equal. The demands of the
future. The information age and the global economy. The failed
efforts of the education reforms of the past. The promises of
technology to eliminate differences and make everyone equal.
But what came to George instead was a line from the sci-fi
novel he had just confiscated from one of the Version .1s: *The
future has arrived, it's just not evenly distributed.*[2]

George turned to his community, to his tribe, and began to
speak. . . .

Consider George's situation. Whatever he decides to say will
probably not turn the tide of public policy on education. Nor is
he likely to change the minds of Socrates' parents about what is
right or inevitable. Surely we can forgive George if he chooses to
feel helpless, a pawn in a system he didn't design and over which
he has little control. He has his children to consider, after all.
His superiors need little encouragement to write him off for good
as the tail end of a dying breed of educators who couldn't adapt
to change.

And so, most plausibly, this scenario ends with George reliev-
ing Peter and everyone else in the audience of any personal
responsibility for what has happened to public education. There
is an outside chance that he will be seized by courage, that he will

recover some sense of the teacher and the person he wanted to be. Yet whether George chooses to soothe or condemn himself and his peers will be less important than how his message is received in that auditorium. Will they hear the question, or will they hear the answer?

Those of us who prefer a future that rejects ed.com and those of us who identify with George's dilemma may still not know what to do. We might look on-line for inspiration, to another leader just as fictional as George: Ned Ludd.

Lessons from Luddites

As Kirkpatrick Sale observes in *Rebels Against the Future*, the history of the Luddite movement was written by its enemies.[3] Ned Ludd became the personification of foolish and futile resistance to change, especially change associated with technology, and "Luddite" became synonymous with opposition to progress. But, as a vigorous opponent of technolust, Sale wears the neo-Luddite label proudly. He finds no shame in following the traditions of these first workers to oppose the technologies that ushered in the Industrial Revolution. When they raised the "machinery question," as it came to be known, in the early nineteenth century, the Luddites were onto something. Within a few decades, a third of England's population would be destitute, 57 per cent of the country's children would die before the age of five, and the life expectancy of the average factory worker would be reduced to eighteen years.[4]

According to Sale, today's neo-Luddites are rebelling against a technology-dominated future that is comparably bleak. In 1812, the Luddites were seen as a serious force; the same cannot be said, at present, of their modern counterparts. Toying with the Luddites and their pretenders is pursued as a sport by some technophiles, who occasionally amuse themselves by making a foray into neo-Luddite territory. The techno-hip magazine *Wired* even published a debate between Kirkpatrick Sale and *Wired*'s Kevin Kelly over whether Luddites "won" or "lost."[5]

Kelly begins by asking Sale what the Luddites accomplished apart from a certain amount of vandalism. Sale replies that the Luddite rebellion would forever be associated with the machinery question. Yet, the conflict in England's Midlands region, where much of the Luddite rebellion took place, was less about whether all technology was to be used freely by industrialists in their pursuit of greater profit, whatever the consequences, than about whether those whose lives were affected by the new technologies were entitled to a say in how they would be used. This legacy of resistance continues, says Sale, even though it is more likely to be articulated by people quite far removed from the front lines where futures and jobs are being lost to technology.

Although Sale is right when he says that pockets of resistance persist, the tradition of direct action initiated by the Luddites is hardly pervasive. Except when they surface as a back-page news item about someone emptying a handgun into his personal computer, reports of people lashing out against technology are rare. Criticism of the politics of technology comes from the lecture circuit, not the shop floor or the staff room. Sale accounts for our complacency by pointing to the complicity of governments and industrialists, who promised all along that so-called labour-saving devices would never become job-killers. Despite the six million jobs worldwide that have been lost to computers, we continue to believe that unemployment and technology are unrelated.

In the *Wired* debate, Kevin Kelly is quick to point out that new jobs have been created in the place of those that have been lost. Sale replies that it is true that some jobs have been created, but that they are created by economic growth, not technology alone. Technology creates jobs only accidentally and indirectly, according to Sale, while the true drivers of economic growth are "warfare, empire, government expansion, resource exploitation, ecological exhaustion, consumption and the manufacture of needs." When economic growth becomes the only imperative and technology makes a job simple enough for a child to do, you can be assured that children will be pressed into the workforce. Whatever the presumed contribution of growth and technology to speed, comfort, wealth, or employment, both exact a price that is becoming steeper every day.

Must we pay this price? Kevin Kelly says no. He believes the techno-mantra that well-intentioned people are more powerful than their machines. If he's right, then we can simply choose to offset the downside of technology, reaping its benefits without paying the price. Kirkpatrick Sale disagrees. He argues that the political qualities of machines are built into them, that whoever or whatever they were originally designed to serve becomes part of their intrinsic nature. Forces are unleashed that cannot be exorcised merely by insisting that this machine or that computer are "tools." If their first master is progress, and their reason for being is profit through enhanced productivity, then they will continue to serve these goals despite our efforts to control them. We cannot avoid being swept along by the political drift inherent in our tools.

Just as it was in the time of the Luddites, this drift is away from the common good. The machine supplants "the customs and habits of the past" with "an ethos of greed and growth," Sale writes.[6] Yet, technology's empire has extended to every nation and every sphere. In return, technology asks only that "its priorities dominate, its markets rule, its values penetrate, and its interests be defended." The principle of reciprocity applies. As the machine's potency rises, ours must decline. In exactly the same way that the tools of the first Industrial Revolution were designed to reduce the craftsman's control over what he was making so, too, today's tools, from robotics on the factory floor to "teaching machines" in the classroom, tend to limit the autonomy and contribution of their operators. Our diminished control over actual production is matched by our diminished role in deciding what should be produced, whether the product is a car, a curriculum, or a country. It is thus entirely consistent that the opinions of technology's "users," either in the workplace or in public debate, are overlooked, marginalized, or silenced. We cannot persist in worshipping machines designed to reduce our power and then wonder at our own powerlessness.

As Sale says to Kelly, "I ask not that we devise some kind of utopia and work toward it, but rather that there be some kind of power of the citizenry, regular and often, to raise questions about, to assess, and to determine whether they want the technologies that are there before them." The lessons to be learned from the Luddites are not just about technology, but are also about citizenship and engagement. What the Luddites will be remembered for is not that they won, but that they resisted.

On Strategy

Kirkpatrick Sale admits that neither Luddites nor neo-Luddites have successfully challenged either technology or the power arrangements that pave its way. But Sale refuses to believe that we are as powerless as we claim to be. After all, when the Luddites marched over the English moors in an attempt to redirect the so-called inevitable march of progress, they too faced great odds. The spoils and spoilage of the first Industrial Revolution – the wealth of capitalists, the seeds of imperialism, the exploitation of child labour, the erosion of communities, and the deskilling of work – retrospectively provided a compelling rationale for their resistance, but the enemy was formidable. While their cause may have failed at the end, for more than a decade the Luddites showed considerable strategic success. In other words, they did something.

To understand the Luddites' tactics, we need to examine their times and their true grievances more closely. The Luddites and their neighbours had just begun to enjoy relatively peaceful and more egalitarian communities. Members of the English working class of 1812 were discovering some prosperity and security. As ordinary citizens learned to read and write, the rigid class distinctions of the past were beginning to fade. These Midland workers had more rights than their predecessors, and with more rights they felt a greater sense of hope and entitlement. In short, they had a lot to lose.

The Luddites were not simplistically opposed to change or to machinery. Despite their detractors' efforts to link them with mindless resistance to technology, the Luddites were actually quite selective in targeting only those machines that made their lives worse. Machines that made work easier, or that produced better or stronger or more beautiful products, they left alone. It was not machinery, but machinery "hurtful to commonality," as one Luddite wrote in a letter, that deserved to be smashed.

This violence had to be put down in the name of law and public order, or so the story goes. Conventional histories put particular emphasis on the Luddites' violent acts, first against machines and later against factory owners. The movement did not begin this way, however, nor was violence ever its dominant strategy. The Luddites did what well-behaved protesters do today. They petitioned Parliament, demanding that fair trade and labour laws be legislated. Their demands were ignored. Later, the Luddites served notice to employers when they planned to target particular factories, giving management fair warning to negotiate new arrangements, but these efforts failed as well. Only when they had exhausted more civil strategies did the Luddites begin their attacks on the machinery itself. Only then did they get the attention of their government, which responded by sending 14,000 troops into three small counties – a force larger than the one then fighting Napoleon.

Others before them had opposed and attacked machines, and their actions had not inspired this kind of counterattack. But the Luddites were a different breed of machine-breakers. They were not just resisting what weaving technology was doing to their jobs and to the quality of their lives. They understood that technology was redistributing power, taking it away from workers and giving it to management and capitalists. They connected technology to the shift of yet more power to the already powerful. It was this insight that made the Luddites far more dangerous than mere machine-breakers could ever be. The elites of British society paid attention to the Luddites because power was at stake.

When the government sent in troops against the workers on behalf of the industrialists, it made clear where its allegiance lay. When the soldiers failed to quell the rebellion, and the Luddites' neighbours refused to give them up to the authorities, the government seized on a radical solution. When Parliament decided to make the destruction of a machine a capital crime, the ruling classes sided irrevocably with machines and their owners, and against the interests of citizens. When eighteen Luddites were hanged, the Luddite rebellion was over and the machine age had truly begun.

Although the Luddites' ultimate failure is indisputable, as a citizens' political movement Luddism was remarkable. Activists like Kirkpatrick Sale are interested in the Luddites not just because they want to re-examine the links between societal disintegration, corporatism, and technology, but because they think the Luddites' history may reveal effective ways to organize resistance.

This re-examination turns up some useful observations. David Noble points out that the Luddites felt entitled to attack the machines because, unlike us, they were not mesmerized by the religions of techno-worship and corporate invincibility. They cut to the chase. As Noble writes, "Forced to choose between technological innovation and their own futures, the Luddites had no problem making that choice and acting on it."[7]

True, the Luddites knew what they wanted, but their strength also arose from different assumptions about how to organize themselves. They were as free from managerialism as they were from technopoly. Kirkpatrick Sale claims Luddism succeeded because, although each cell organized under the same banner, it determined its own priorities and tactics. The movement had no leader and many leaders at the same time. Whenever a unit marched, someone would announce himself to be "General Ned Ludd." Everyone was in charge; everyone was responsible.

So, in addition to making connections between technology and power, the Luddites succeeded because they approached problems directly, were unburdened by techno-worship, and shared responsibility. They had two other elements in their favour. First, they were supported and protected by their communities. Despite strong-arming by government troops and offers of reward money, almost no neighbour betrayed a Luddite. Second, the Luddites simply believed that together they could win – at least until the government decided they were the enemy.

Modern-day Luddites face more formidable obstacles and can claim fewer assets. However, we have one powerful force in our favour: making connections. When the first Luddites began their attacks on machines, only a small insightful group probably realized that technology would undo the conditions that people were beginning to enjoy. But today's Luddites can find sympathizers numbering in the millions – ordinary people who have first-hand knowledge that technology is the clockwork of the global city, the reason and the excuse for the deterioration of lives, families, schools, and communities. Denying technology's role is becoming more difficult, which is why the propaganda machines of globalization and markets are in overdrive. We can see intermittent and encouraging signs that, despite the lies, people are growing conscious that corporate power is being amassed at the expense of democracy and everything else we care about. Millions of people want to believe that alternatives exist for themselves and their children.

The Dominion commissioners believed that we could have something else on our side too. If education can teach the child consciousness beyond self-interest – "to see the whole, of which his life is only but a part," as the commissioners put it – then our schools can still be our best defence against an unthinkable future, and our best hope for a better one.

Ed.com cannot help us reclaim through information or competition what we have lost as individuals, families, and citizens. Our children and our schools will become either what we make them, or what we let others profit from. When we rethink what is worth knowing, we would do well to remember the words of H.G. Wells: "Human history becomes more and more a race between education and catastrophe."

Unless we act soon, with conscience and with consciousness, it will be no contest.

ACKNOWLEDGEMENTS

I am equally indebted to friends I work beside and colleagues I have never met. Many people who feel passionately about protecting public education are ironically committed to documenting its vulnerability. They have shared their work and their insights with great generosity. I have many favours to return.

Jonathan Webb, senior editor at McClelland & Stewart, has been appropriately patient, impatient, encouraging and critical – in other words, he has been the perfect editor. Our partnership has been a pleasure.

My husband, Dwight Renneberg, learned once again that dinner may have to wait, and proved more than once that no file – and no conversation – is gone forever.

Notes

Preface

1. "Ontario Plummets to 46th Place in U.S./Canada School Spending," CCPA *Education Monitor* 1, no. 3 (summer 1997): 23.
2. Virginia Galt, Jennifer Lewington, Brian Laghi, Craig McInnes, Rhéal Séguin, Gay Abbate, "Power Struggle Rocks Canada's Schools," *Globe and Mail*, 11 October 1997, A1.
3. Virginia Galt, Jennifer Lewington, Brian Laghi, Craig McInnes, Rhéal Séguin, Gay Abbate, "Polls Show People Supportive of Teachers," *Globe and Mail*, 11 October 1997, A8.
4. Greg Crone, "Study Ponders Teacherless Society," *Ottawa Citizen*, 9 October 1997.
5. The Ministers [sic] Round Table on Technology in Learning, report of the meeting, 24 March 1997.
6. Patrick Dare, "Minister Wants $4B to Give Each Student a Computer," *Ottawa Citizen*, 12 December 1995.
7. Lehman Brothers, "Selected Growth Stocks," *Investment Opportunities in the Education Industry*, 9 February 1996.
8. Ontario Royal Commission on Learning, *For the Love of Learning*, summary (Toronto: Queen's Printer for Ontario, 1994), 7.
9. Veronica S. Lacey, "The Role of Information Management in Restructuring Education" (paper prepared for the Invitational Conference on Restructuring Education, Haarlem, Netherlands, 16–20 April 1994), 7.
10. Information Technology Association of Canada (ITAC), *Education Statement*, June 1994, 5.

Chapter 1

1. Peter Applebome, "School as America's Cure-all," *New York Times*, 12 January 1997.
2. William J. Clinton, "1997 State of the Union Address," 4 February 1997 (http://www.whitehouse.gov/wh/sou97/).

3. National Film Board of Canada, *Manufacturing Consent: Noam Chomsky and the Media*, Peter Wintoniuk and Mark Achbar, producers, 1994.
4. John Ralston Saul, *The Doubter's Companion: A Dictionary of Aggressive Common Sense* (Toronto: Penguin, 1995), 115.
5. United Nations Conference on Trade and Development (UNCTAD), cited in "Seven Troubling Problems Linked to Globalization," *CCPA Monitor* 4, no. 7 (December 1997/January 1998).
6. H.R. Higham, speech on behalf of Sergio Marchi, federal minister of industry, to the Canadian Education Industry Summit: The First Canadian Conference to Provide Compelling Reasons for Investment in the Education for Profit Industry, Toronto, 24 September 1997.
7. Tony Clarke, "Confronting the Big Business Takeover of Canada," *CCPA Monitor* 4, no. 3 (July/August 1997).
8. Lloyd Axworthy, speaking to the Information Technology Association of Canada (ITAC), 28 February 1995, 9.
9. Anthony Wilson-Smith, "Future Imperfect," *Maclean's*, 30 December 1996, 18.
10. *Ibid.*
11. Andrew Jackson, *The Future of Jobs* (Ottawa: Canadian Centre for Policy Alternatives, January 1997), 7.
12. *Ibid.*
13. Campaign 2000, *Child Poverty in Canada: Report Card 1997*, brochure (Toronto: Family Services Association of Canada, 1997).
14. Jackson, *op. cit.*
15. Jackson, *op. cit.*, 3.
16. Jackson, *op. cit.*, 8.
17. United Nations Conference on Trade and Development (UNCTAD), *op. cit.*
18. Mark Kennedy, "Martin Vows to Help Poor Children," *Ottawa Citizen*, 10 January 1997, A1–A2.
19. Edward Greenspon, "Poverty Issue Requires Kid Gloves," *Globe and Mail*, 17 February 1997, A4.
20. Edward Greenspon, "Child Poverty Leaves Canadians Divided on Blame," *Globe and Mail*, 17 June 1997, A1.
21. John McMurtry, "The MAI Would Make Corporate Rule Absolute," *CCPA Monitor* 4, no. 4 (September 1997).
22. *Ibid.*
23. *Ibid.*
24. *Ibid.*
25. Jeff Sallot, "Human-Rights Protest Noisy but Non-violent," *Globe and Mail*, 26 November 1997, A8.

26. Jane Kelsey, "APEC Created Solely to Serve Business Interests," *CCPA Monitor* 4, no. 3 (July/August 1997).
27. http://www.tgmag.ca, and links.
28. Stewart Goodings, addressing the 1997 Public Education Forum of the People's Summit on APEC, Vancouver, 19 November 1997.
29. Marita Moll, "Canadian Classrooms on the Information Highway: Making the Connections," in *Tech High: Globalization and the Future of Canadian Education* (Ottawa: Canadian Centre for Policy Alternatives, 1997).
30. Quoted by Larry Kuehn, "Schools for Globalized Business: The APEC Agenda for Education" (paper presented to the Public Education Forum of the People's Summit on APEC, Vancouver, 19 November 1997).
31. Larry Kuehn, "Schools for Globalized Business: The APEC Agenda for Education" (paper presented to the Public Education Forum of the People's Summit on APEC, Vancouver, 19 November 1997).
32. Higham, *op. cit.*
33. Thérèse Laferrière, *Towards Well-Balanced Technology-Enhanced Learning Environments: Preparing the Ground Choices Ahead* (Toronto: Council of Ministers of Education, Canada, 1997).
34. Letter from Sergio Marchi, conference program, Canadian Education Industry Summit: The First Canadian Conference to Provide Compelling Reasons for Investment in the Education for Profit Industry, Toronto, 24 September 1997.
35. Council of Ministers of Education, Canada: Third National Forum on Education (TNFE), discussion paper, July 1997.
36. Robert Fulghum, *All I Really Need to Know I Learned in Kindergarten* (New York: Ivy Books/Ballantine Books, 1986).
37. Carolyn Abraham, "Ontario Sets Out Vision for High Schools," *Ottawa Citizen*, 20 September 1996, A3.
38. Meeting of the Partners Committee, "Transitions from School to Work: Career Choices for Youth with Disabilities Project," National Educational Association of Disabled Students (NEADS), Ottawa, 5 February 1996.
39. William Thorsell, "Notes for Keynote Address" (paper presented at the Second National Consultation on Education, Edmonton, 9 May 1996).
40. Nova Scotia Teachers' Union, *Research Report on Outcomes-Based Education: A Project of the NSTU Curriculum Committee*, November 1996.
41. David Berliner, "Educational Psychology Meets the Christian Right: Differing Views of Children, Schooling, Teaching and Learning" (paper presented to the American Psychological Association, Toronto, August 1996).

42. Ontario Ministry of Education and Training, "What Students Are Expected to Know, Be Able to Do and Value When They Graduate from Secondary School in Ontario," draft, undated.

43. Stanley Arnowitz, and Henry A. Giroux, *Education Under Siege: The Conservative, Liberal and Radical Debate Over Schooling* (Massachusetts: Bergin and Garvey, 1985), ix.

44. National Governors' Association, "NGA and ECS Chairman Governor Tommy G. Thompson and IBM CEO Louis V. Gerstner Jr. Announce Education Summit," press release, 28 September 1995.

45. "You Can Forget Goals 2000, Now It's Summit 1996," editorial, *Executive Educator* 18, no. 5 (May 1996): 6.

46. Graham Verbatim Reporting Limited, Transcription of John Snobelen speech, 6 July 1995.

47. "The Mike Harris Round Table on Common Sense in Education," 25 January 1995.

48. Ontario Royal Commission on Learning, *For the Love of Learning*, short version (Toronto: Queen's Printer for Ontario, December 1994), 3.

49. Environics Research Group Ltd., *Focus on Education*, November 1997.

50. *Ibid.*

51. Coalition for Education Reform, *D-: Could Do Better, What's Wrong with Public Education in Ontario and How to Fix It* (Toronto: Author, 1994).

52. Fraser Institute, *Toward the New Millennium: A Five-Year Plan for the Fraser Institute*, 1997.

53. Helen Raham, "Revitalizing Public Education in Canada: The Potential of Choice and Charter Schools," special issue of *Fraser Forum*, Fraser Institute, August 1996.

54. Portions of John Ralston Saul's speech were broadcast on *Sunday Morning*, CBC Radio, 16 February 1997.

55. Carolyn Abraham, "Ontario Worked on Plan to Drop 10,000 Teachers," *Ottawa Citizen*, 12 January 1997, A1.

56. Marc Zwelling, of Vector Research and Development, Inc., memo to David Moss of Ontario Secondary School Teachers' Federation (OSSTF), 11 October 1996.

57. Doug Hart, "Public Expectations and Satisfaction: Attitudes of Graduates, Employers, Parents and the Public Toward Education in Canada" (paper presented to the Canadian Society for the Study of Education, St. John's, Newfoundland, 14 June 1997).

58. Carolyn Abraham, "Snobelen to Lift Construction Ban on Schools Next Year," *Ottawa Citizen*, 20 November 1996, A4.

59. Speaking notes for Education and Training Minister John Snobelen, 13 January 1997, 6.

60. Virginia Galt, "Ontario Under Fire over Education Proposals," *Globe and Mail*, 25 November 1996, A5.

61. Graham Fraser, "Dole Plays Age Card in Acceptance Speech," *Globe and Mail*, 16 August 1996, A1.

62. Gerald Caplan, "Demoralizing Teachers and Confusing Parents a Recipe for Disaster," *Ottawa Citizen*, 8 October 1996, A11.

63. "S Stands for Shame," editorial, *Ottawa Citizen*, 30 September 1996, A12.

64. "Demoralizing Approach," *Ottawa Citizen*, 30 September 1996, A8.

65. Abraham, 20 November 1996, *op. cit.*

66. John Ibbitson, *Promised Land* (Toronto: Prentice Hall Canada, 1997).

67. Arthur Kelly, "Chalk Full of Ideas: The Education Minister Considers More Than Just the Bottom Line," *Biz Magazine*, Spring 1996, 9.

Chapter 2

1. Jim Coyle, "Judge Puts Tory Agenda on Hold," *Toronto Star*, 4 November 1997, B1.

2. Herbert M. Kliebard, "The Cardinal Principles Report as Archeological Deposit," *Curriculum Studies* 3, no. 2 (1995): 197–208.

3. Jennifer Lewington and Graham Orpwood, *Overdue Assignment: Taking Responsibility for Canada's Schools* (Toronto: John Wiley and Sons, 1993).

4. Atlantic Provinces Education Foundation, *The Atlantic Canada Framework for Essential Graduation Learnings*, October 1995.

5. Ontario Ministry of Education and Training, *Putting Students First: Ontario's Plan for Education Reform*, brochure (http://www.edu.gov.on.ca/eng/document/brochure/tabloid/tabloid.html, November 1997).

6. "Education Ideas Lack Credit," editorial, *Ottawa Citizen*, 26 April 1996, A12.

7. Ontario Ministry of Education and Training, *Excellence in Education: High School Reform*, discussion paper (Queen's Printer for Ontario, 1996).

8. "Sir John A. McDonalds®," editorial, *Ottawa Citizen*, 26 February 1997, A14.

9. Virginia Galt, "Ontario Under Fire over Education Proposals," *Globe and Mail*, 26 November 1996, A5.

10. Duff McCay and Company, *1996 Ontario Budget Highlights*, 23 September 1996.

11. The Ministers [*sic*] Round Table on Technology in Learning, report of the meeting, 24 March 1997, confidential document.

12. See, for example, David Livingstone, "Computer Literacy, the 'Knowledge Economy' and Information Control: Micro Myths and Macro Choices" in Marita Moll, ed., *Tech High: Globalization and the Future of Canadian Education* (Ottawa: Canadian Centre for Policy Alternatives, 1997), 99–116.

13. Cited by David G. Stratman, address to the Massachusetts Association of School Superintendents Summer Institute, 1997.

14. Holly Sklar, *Z Magazine*, reprinted in "The United States Index," *CCPA Monitor*, 4, no. 6 (November 1997): 3.

15. *Ibid.*

16. Clinton E. Boutwell, "Profits Without People," *Phi Delta Kappan* 79, no. 2 (October 1997): 107.

17. Dan Gardner, "Silicon Snake Oil in the Classroom," *Ottawa Citizen*, 12 November 1997, A17.

18. Software Human Resources Council, *Software – A World of Opportunity: A Guide to the Canadian Software Industry and Its Careers* (Ottawa: Author, 1997), 2–3.

19. Speech by the Honourable Hedy Frye, Ottawa, 9 October 1997.

20. David Livingstone, "Computer Literacy, the 'Knowledge Economy' and Information Control: Micro Myths and Macro Choices" in Marita Moll, ed., *Tech High: Globalization and the Future of Canadian Education* (Ottawa: Canadian Centre for Policy Alternatives, 1997), 104.

21. *Ibid.*

22. *Ibid.*

23. *Ibid.*

24. *Ibid.*

25. Canadian Labour Force Development Board, *CLFDB Matters* 1, no. 3 (1997): 5.

26. Jean Bourque, letter to the editor, *Ottawa Citizen*, 18 March 1997.

27. "Learning from Ontario's Schools," *Globe and Mail*, 16 June 1997, A20.

28. David C. Berliner and Bruce J. Biddle, *The Manufactured Crisis: Myths, Fraud and the Attack on America's Public Schools* (Toronto: Addison-Wesley, 1995).

29. Jennifer Lewington, "Young Canadians Lack Elite Skills, Science Test Finds," *Globe and Mail*, 30 January 1997, A1.

30. Warren Gerrard, "Science Education Goes Under Microscope: Curriculum, Teachers Blamed for Poor Grades," *Ottawa Citizen*, 24 February 1997, A4.

31. Jeffrey Simpson, "In the End, Everybody Lost When the Teachers Walked Out," *Globe and Mail*, 11 November 1997.

32. Judith Wiener, "If Grade 3 Testing Is Any Indication," *Globe and Mail*, 26 November 1997.
33. Kevin Bushweller, "Teaching to the Test," *American School Board Journal* 184, no. 9 (September, 1997): 24.
34. François Casas, and Diane Meaghan, "Standardized Tests: Why They Cannot Measure Educational Quality," *FWTAO Newsletter*, March/April 1995, 20.
35. "Cheating Case Reveals Testing Mania," *Fairtest Examiner*, Summer 1996, 3.
36. Casas and Meaghan, *op. cit.*
37. Lloyd R. Grann, editor's comments, *Testing African-American Students* (Morristown, NJ: Aaron Press, 1991).
38. See, for example, National Center for Fair Open Testing, *Fairtest Examiner*, spring, summer, fall 1997.
39. Grann, *op. cit.*
40. Stephen H. Smith and Olaf Jorgenson, "Test Prep 101," *American School Board Journal* 184, no. 9 (September 1997).
41. "Is the SAT fair? You decide" (http://www.testprep.com/cbdata.html, 04/12/97).
42. Gerrard, *op. cit.*
43. Gerrard, *op. cit.*
44. Personal communication with the executive director of the teacher organization involved. Source withheld by request.
45. Gerald Bracey, "The fourth Bracey report on the condition of public education," *Phi Delta Kappan*,76, no. 2 (October 1994): 115–127, cited by Philip Nagy, *International Comparisons of Student Achievement in Mathematics and Science* (Toronto: Ontario Institute for Studies in Education, February 1996), 1.
46. David F. Robitaille, Alan R. Taylor and Graham Orpwood, *The Third International Mathematics and Science Study – The TIMSS-Canada Report, Volume 2* (Vancouver: University of British Columbia, 1997), 19.
47. Philip Nagy, *International Comparisons of Student Achievement in Mathematics and Science* (Toronto: Ontario Institute for Studies in Education, February 1996), 6.
48. *Putting Students First: Ontario's Plan for Education Reform, op. cit.*
49. J. Myron Atkin and Paul Black, "Policy Perils of International Comparisons: The TIMSS Case," *Phi Delta Kappan* 79, no. 1 (September 1997): 22–28.
50. David Ireland, "Canadian Students Do Better than Results Indicate," *CCPA Education Monitor* 1, no. 2 (Spring 1997): 13–16.
51. *Ibid.*

52. *Ibid.*
53. Lewington, *op. cit.*
54. David F. Robitaille, Alan R. Taylor and Graham Orpwood, "Demographic Characteristics of the TIMSS Countries, Table 1-2," *The Third International Mathematics and Science Study – The TIMSS-Canada Report: Volume 1* (Vancouver: University of British Columbia, 1996).
55. Virtual Knowledge, a division of Virtual Entertainment, *Children's IQ and Achievement Test,* brochure.
56. Erin St. John Kelly, , "CD-ROM Tests Child's IQ at Home," *Globe and Mail,* 1 February 1997, C8.
57. Virtual Knowledge, a division of Virtual Entertainment, *Children's IQ and Achievement Test,* handbook, 61.
58. John G. Weiss, "It's Time to Examine the Examiner" in Asa G. Hilliard, ed., *Testing African-American Students,* (Morristown, NJ: Aaron Press, 1991), 116.
59. "Is the SAT Fair? You decide," *op. cit.*
60. Smith and Jorgenson, *op. cit.*
61. *Ibid.*
62. "This Is ETS" (gopher://etsis4.ets.org: 70/00/about.ets/, 02/26/97).
63. "Whole Language: What's the Fuss?" an interview with Harvey Daniels in *Rethinking Schools: An Agenda for Change,* ed. David Levine, Robert Low, Bob Peterson and Rita Fenario (New York: New York Press, 1995), 122.
64. "This is ETS," *op. cit.*
65. Peter Cohen, speaking to the Canadian Education Industry Summit: The First Canadian Conference to Provide Compelling Reasons for Investment in the Education for Profit Industry, Toronto, 24 September 1997.
66. Sylvan advertisement, *Globe and Mail,* 13 November 1997, C5.
67. Sylvan Learning Centers (http://www.educate.com/1 . . . enters/partnerships.html, 02/26/97).
68. "This is ETS," *op. cit.*
69. http://www.edweek.org/ht . . . 1%26Testing%26Service%29
70. Listserve communication from mlombardi@bctf.bc.ca, "Response to Ranking Schools in the Media," 27 February 1997.
71. Council of Ministers of Education, Canada, "Education Ministers Discuss Partnerships with Private Sector Leaders," press release, 18 February 1997.
72. Jennifer Lewington, "Work Experience Programs Lag Behind Demand," *Globe and Mail,* 24 February 1997, A7.
73. *Ibid.*

74. Council of Ministers of Education, Canada, "Ministers of Education to Take Steps to Improve Students' Science Performance," press release, 18 February 1997.
75. Canadian Society for the Study of Education, *Common Framework of Science Learning Outcomes (2nd draft): A Response*, undated.
76. *Ibid.*
77. Council of Ministers of Education, Canada, "Pan-Canadian Education Projects on Target," press release, 23 September 1997.
78. Thérèse Laferrière, *Towards Well-balanced Technology-Enhanced Learning Environments: Preparing the Ground Choices Ahead* (Toronto: Council of Ministers of Education, Canada, 1997).
79. Genesis 1.26.
80. "High-tech Hallelujah," *Ottawa Citizen*, 13 November 1995.

Chapter 3

1. Software Human Resources Council, *Software – A World of Opportunity: A Guide to the Canadian Software Industry and Its Careers* (Ottawa: Author, 1997).
2. Marita Moll, "Information Technology in the Classroom: Pits and Pendulums – A Poe-esian Look at Planning" (Presentation to Digital Knowledge Conference, Toronto, 6 February 1996).
3. *Ibid.*
4. *Ibid.*
5. Council of Ministers of Education, Canada, "Developments in Information Technologies in Education" (document prepared for the 13th Conference of the Commonwealth Education Ministers, Botswana, 28 July–1 August 1997).
6. "Gates to Give Book Proceeds to Schools," *Executive Educator* 18, no. 2 (January 1996): 6.
7. John Ralston Saul, *The Unconscious Civilization* (Concord, Ont.: Anansi Press, 1995), 136.
8. Neil Postman, *Technopoly: The Surrender of Culture to Technology* (New York: Alfred A. Knopf, 1992).
9. Information Highway Advisory Council, *Connection, Community, Content: The Challenge of the Information Highway* (Ottawa: Ministry of Supply and Services, September 1995), xv.
10. Ronald E. Anderson, presentation on the results of a survey published by the International Association for the Evaluation of Educational Achievement (IEA), to the Round Table of EI Members in OECD

Countries on Questions of Education in a Changing Society, Saint Petersburg, Florida, 4 December 1996.

11. Mary Gooderham, "Turning Kids into Technotots Has Parents Computing Benefits," *Globe and Mail*, 3 October 1995.

12. Larry Boisvert, "Made in Canada, Serving the World," *Canadian Technology*, winter 1996–97, 3.

13. The Royal Commission on New Reproductive Technologies, *Proceed with Care*, final report, (Ottawa: Canada Communications Groups Publishing, November 1993).

14. World Council of Indigenous People, "Presumed Dead but Still Useful as a Human Byproduct," undated.

15. Marshall McLuhan, *Understanding the Media: The Extension of Man* (Toronto: McGraw-Hill, 1964), vii.

16. Victor Dwyer, "Surfing Back to School: High-Tech Glory or Glorified Play?" *Maclean's*, 26 August 1996.

17. Jerry Mander, "Technologies of Globalization" in *The Case Against the Global Economy*, ed. Jerry Mander and Edward Goldsmith (San Francisco: Sierra Club Books, 1996), 345.

18. Sally Armstrong, "The Way We Were," *Homemaker's*, October 1996, 4.

19. Joe Chidley, "Toxic TV: Is TV Violence Contributing to Aggression in Kids?" *Maclean's*, 17 June 1996, 36.

20. Quoted by John Haslett Cuff, "Turn on, Tune in, Take Charge of Media Literacy," *Globe and Mail*, 23 June 1997.

21. Patricia Herdman, "In Our Own Voice: What Canadians Are Saying About Violent Entertainment," Coalition for Responsible Television (CRTV), 21 April 1997.

22. Brian Burke, "The Moral and Political Significance of the V-Chip," Centre for Educational Priorities (http://www.cep.org, December 5, 1997).

23. Chidley, *op. cit.*

24. Tom Harper, "V-Chip on Cutting Edge of Spicer's Television Crusade," *Toronto Star*, 24 February 1996, L3.

25. *Ibid.*

26. *Ibid.*

27. Carol Goar, "American Networks to Rate TV Shows," *Toronto Star*, 1 March 1996, A2.

28. Dennis Wharton, "Broadcasters Chip in $2M for V-Chip Alternative," *Variety*, 24–30 July 1995, 20.

29. V-Chip Quotable Quotes (http://www.cep.org, December 5, 1997).

30. Harper, *op. cit.*

31. "Cash in the Chip," editorial, *Marketing Magazine*, 11 December 1996.

32. Wharton, *op. cit.*

33. Alison Mitchell, "TV Executives Promise Clinton a Violence Ratings System by '97," *New York Times*, 1 March 1996, A1.
34. *Ibid.*
35. Thomas Ferguson, "Bill's Big Backers," *Mother Jones*, November/December 1996, 63.
36. *Ibid.*
37. Burke, *op. cit.*
38. George Jonas, "Warning, Provocative Thoughts," *Toronto Sun*, 26 May 1997, 11.
39. Patricia Herdman, "Big Wind, Loud Thunder, No Rain," unpublished essay, 9 October 1996.
40. Herdman, "In Our Own Voice . . .", *op. cit.*
41. *Ibid.*
42. Christopher Harris, "Screening What's on the Screen," *Globe and Mail*, 3 September 1997, A1.
43. *Ibid.*
44. *Ibid.*
45. Rick Salutin, "The Spread of Mighty Morphin Anxiety," *Globe and Mail*, 11 November 1994, C1.
46. John Haslett Cuff, "Charade of Justice Follows Thousands of Wartime Rapes," *Globe and Mail*, 12 November 1996, A15.
47. David F. Noble, *Progress Without People: New Technology, Unemployment and the Message of Resistance* (Toronto: Between the Lines, 1995), 9.
48. *Ibid*, 11.
49. *Ibid*, 12.
50. *Ibid*, 145.
51. Saul, *op. cit*, 18.
52. Saul, *op. cit*, 74.
53. Saul, *op. cit*, 105.

Chapter 4

1. "Microsoft Industry to Spend $1 Billion," Windows 95 supplement, *Globe and Mail*, 24 August 1995.
2. "'Smart' Schools Linked to Internet," *Times Educational Supplement*, 21 February 1997, cited in *ATA News* (Alberta Teachers' Association), 25 March 1997, 10.
3. "Heated Underwear for Students a Hot Topic," *Edmonton Journal*, 26 February 1997, cited in *ATA News* (Alberta Teachers' Association), 25 March 1997, 6.
4. Andrew Carver, "Quotes of the Week," *Ottawa Sunday Sun*, 8 April 1997, 6.

5. Seymour Papert, 1984, cited in Larry Cuban, *Teachers and Machines: The Classroom Use of Technology Since 1920* (Toronto: Guidance Centre, 1986), 72.

6. Ontario Royal Commission on Learning, *For the Love of Learning*, vol. 4 (Toronto: Queen's Printer for Ontario, 1994), 4.

7. Gerry Smith, "Education Meets Technology," *Minds in Motion*, fall 1989, 65.

8. International Symposium on Education Revolution with Internet, ERI '96, symposium flyer; Kyushi Institute of Design, Fukuoka, Japan, 4–6 December 1996.

9. Richard Worzel, "Planning the Revolution," TEACH, January/February 1997, 7.

10. Melanie Franner, "ITAC Addresses Technology in Education Issues," *MacBiz Reporter*, 7 September 1994, B8.

11. Information Highway Advisory Council, *Connection, Community, Content: The Challenge of the Information Highway*, final report (Ottawa: Ministry of Supply and Services, 1995), 158.

12. Jeffrey Hecht, *Project Homeroom, Project Schoolroom, and Regular School: Innovations in Team Teaching, Interdisciplinary Learning and the Use of Technology*, a final report on the project at the Maine East High School (Illinois State University: Technological Innovations in Educational Research Lab, 1994).

13. Victor Dwyer, "Surfing Back to School: High-Tech Glory or Glorified Play?" *Maclean's*, 26 August 1996, 45.

14. McLaughlin, John, "Education Limited," *American School Board Journal*, 184, no. 3 (March 1997): 19.

15. "Quotable Quotes," *Apple Education Digest*, winter 1996 (http://204.96. 17.75/educ . . . sources/eddigestw96.html, 03/12/97).

16. Jeffrey Frank, "Preparing for the Information Highway: Information Technology in Canadian Households," *Canadian Social Trends*, Statistics Canada, N38, Catalogue 11-008E, autumn 1995, 5.

17. Karen Southwick, "Are Corporate Technology Initiatives More PR than Philanthropy?" *Electronic School*, March 1997, A13.

18. Neil Gross, "A Notebook for Every Student? How Microsoft and Toshiba Are Scrambling to Stoke the Education Market," May 5, 1997 (http://www.businessweek.com:80/1997/18/6352590.htm).

19. Henry Jay Becker, "A Truly Empowering Technology-Rich Education – How Much Will It Cost?" *Educational IRM Quarterly*, 3, no. 1 (September 1993): 267–271.

20. Andrew Tausz, "How Tech Firms Court the Key Education Market," *Globe and Mail*, 15 October 1996, C6, cited by Marita Moll in "Canadian Classrooms on the Information Highway: Making the Connections,"

Tech High: Globalization and the Future of Canadian Education (Ottawa: Canadian Centre for Policy Alternatives, 1997), 37.

21. Vector Research and Development, Inc., "Results of the Canadian Teachers' Federation (CTF) National Issues in Education Poll," June 1996.
22. John M. Deutch, U.S. deputy secretary of defense, "Opportunity to Change" (http://www.nap.edu/readi . . . techgap/opportunity.html).
23. Douglas D. Noble, "The Overselling of Educational Technology," *Educational Leadership*, 54, no. 3 (November 1996): 19.
24. Ibid.
25. National Commission on Excellence in Education, *A Nation at Risk: The Imperative for Educational Reform* (Washington, D.C.: U.S. Government Printing Office, 1983).
26. Ibid.
27. Noble, *op. cit.*, 21.
28. Ibid.
29. Chris Pipho, "Stateline: The Summit of 1996," *Phi Delta Kappan*, 77, no. 10 (June 1996): 655.
30. Karen Southwick, "Are Corporate Technology Initiatives More PR than Philanthropy?" *Electronic School*, March 1997, A13.
31. Judith Haymore Sandholtz, Cathy Ringstaff and David C. Dwyer, *Teaching with Technology: Creating Student-Centered Classrooms* (New York: Teachers' College Press, 1997).
32. Ena L. Baker, Mary Gearhart, Joan L. Herman, *Apple Classrooms of Tomorrow (ACOT) Evaluation Study, First and Second Year Findings*, 1990, 9.
33. Ibid.
34. Ibid.
35. Sandholtz et al, *op. cit.*
36. David C. Dwyer, "Apple Classrooms of Tomorrow: What We've Learned," *Educational Leadership*, 51, no. 7 (April 1994): 4–10.
37. Council of Ministers of Education, Canada, "Developments in Information Technologies in Education" (document prepared for the 13th Conference of the Commonwealth Education Ministers, Botswana, 28 July–1 August 1997).
38. Neil Postman, "Education and Technology, Virtual Students, Digital Classroom," *Our Schools, Our Selves*, 7, no. 2 (December 1995): 69–79.
39. Ursula M. Franklin, *Every Tool Shapes the Task: Communities and the Information Highway* (Vancouver: Lazard Press, 1996), 11.
40. Postman, 1995, *op. cit.*
41. "Microsoft's Bill Gates Meets with Chicago Students and Teachers" (http://www.microsoft.com/education/k12/resource).

42. Neil Postman, *Of Luddites, Learning and Life*, 1993, 26, cited in David Berliner and Bruce Biddle of *The Manufactured Crisis* (Toronto: Addison-Wesley, 1995), 317.
43. Lowell Monke, "Computers in Education: The Web and the 'Plow' Confronting Technology" (http://www.public.iastate.edu/~lmonke/online°doc.html).
44. Sandholtz et al, *op. cit.*, 92.
45. David C. Dwyer, "The Imperative to Change Our Schools" in Charles Fisher, David C. Dwyer, Keith Yocam, eds. *Education and Technology: Reflections on Computing in Classrooms* (San Francisco: Jossey Bass, 1996), 24.
46. Lynne Ainsworth, "Juggling Act – Balancing the Pros and Cons of New Technology in the Classroom," *Profile* 7, no. 1 (February 1997), York University.
47. Theodore Roszak, "Dumbing Us Down," *New Internationalist*, no. 286 (December 1996).
48. Gerald Bracey, "Research," *Phi Delta Kappan*, 77, no. 2 (October 1995): 150–51.
49. Sandholtz et al, *op. cit.*, 94.
50. *Ibid.*
51. Theodore Roszak, *The Cult of Information* (Berkeley: University of California Press, 1994).
52. Monke, *op. cit.*
53. Sherry Turkle, *Life on the Screen: Identity in the Age of the Internet* (New York: Simon and Schuster, 1995).
54. Speech by Diane Ravitch, former U.S. assistant secretary of education, as quoted in Neil Postman, "Education and Technology, Virtual Students, Digital Classroom," *Our Schools, Our Selves* 7, no. 2 (December 1995): 69–79.
55. Postman, 1995, *op. cit.*
56. Sandholtz et al, *op. cit.*
57. John O'Neill, "A Conversation with Clifford Stoll," *Educational Leadership* 54, no. 3 (November 1996): 14.
58. Roszak, 1996, *op. cit.*
59. "Prime Minister's Remarks at the Ottawa Launch of Cable in the Classroom," 4 October 1995, transcript.
60. Victor Dwyer, *op. cit.*, 44.
61. *Ibid.*
62. Larry Cuban, *Teachers and Machines: The Classroom Use of Technology Since 1920* (Toronto: Guidance Centre, 1986), 89.
63. Sandholtz et al, *op. cit.*

64. R. Chodzinski, "Prerequisite Computer Skills for the Beginning Teacher: A Cyber Leap to the Next Millennium," (paper presented to the International Seminar on Teacher Development, Brock University, May 1997).

65. Council of Ministers of Education, Canada, *op. cit.*, 14.

66. Ivor F. Goodson and J. Marshall Mangan, "The Ideology of Computer Literacy" (unpublished paper, Faculty of Education, University of Western Ontario, 7 January 1994).

67. *Ibid.*

68. Council of Ministers of Education, Canada, *op. cit.*, 15.

69. Microsoft, "Educators See a Dramatic Transformation in Learning When Students Use Technology to Learn Anytime, Anywhere," press release, 23 April 1997.

70. The Ministers [sic] Round Table on Technology in Learning, 24 March 1997, confidential document.

71. "IBM Shares Results from Field-Test of Technology," *Education Week on the Web*, 26 February 1997.

72. David C. Dwyer, 1996, *op. cit.*, 31.

73. William J. Clinton, "1997 State of the Union Address," 4 February 1997 (http://www.whitehouse.gov/wh/sou97).

74. Council of Ministers of Education, Canada, *op. cit.*, 28.

75. Thomas R. Ellinger and Garry M. Beckham, "South Korea: Placing Education on Top of the Family Agenda," *Phi Delta Kappan* 78, no. 8 (April 1997): 624–25.

76. *Ibid.*

Chapter 5

1. *CTV 2000-PLUS*, 1995-96.

2. Marita Moll and Heather-jane Robertson, "Backwash from the Technological Wave: Critical Perspectives on the Impact of Information Technology on Public Education" (paper presented to the Canadian Society for the Studies of Education, Memorial University, St. John's, Newfoundland, 12 June 1997).

3. Peter D. Hart Research Associates, "The Schools of the Future," *The Polling Report*, 28 July 1997, 2.

4. Moll and Robertson, *op. cit*, 6.

5. *Tech High: Globalization and the Future of Canadian Education*, Marita Moll, ed. (Ottawa: Canadian Centre for Policy Alternatives, 1997), 34.

6. Lawrence Surtees, *Wire Wars: The Canadian Fight for Competition in Tele-communications* (Scarborough, ON: Prentice Hall, 1994), xvi.

7. George Emerson, "See Johnny. See Johnny Surf. Surf, Johnny, Surf," *Canadian Business / Technology*, spring 1997, 36.

8. Henry J. Becker, "How Exemplary Computer-Using Teachers Differ from Other Teachers: Implications for Realizing the Potential of Computers in Schools," *Journal of Research on Computing in Education*, 26, no. 3 (1994): 291–321.

9. "Ontario Plummets to 46th Place in U.S./Canada School Spending," *CCPA Education Monitor* 1, no. 3 (Summer 1997): 23.

10. Canadian Teachers' Federation, "Summer 1997 Vector Poll Shows Reducing Class Size as Highest Priority for Public Education Spending," *Canadian Teachers' Federation Economic Service Notes*, September/ October 1997, 1997-8, 1-3.

11. "Futurescape," advertising supplement, *Globe and Mail*, 26 January 1994.

12. Victor Dwyer, "Surfing Back to School: High-tech Glory or Glorified Play?" *Maclean's*, 26 August 1996, 41.

13. "Futurescape," *op. cit.*

14. Emerson, *op. cit.*

15. Asia Connects 1997 (http://www.tgmag.ca).

16. Doug Knox and Wendy Cumming, *Linking Education to Technology*, Continental P.R. Communications, SchoolNet Communications/ Partnerships Plan, 1995/96.

17. Mac Prescott, memo to the SchoolNet Advisory Board regarding international agreement signed with Mexico, 12 June 1996.

18. Doug Hull, letter to Marita Moll, 3 December 1997.

19. Theodore Roszak, "Dumbing Us Down," *New Internationalist*, no. 286 (December 1996).

20. "Information Technology: Boon or Bane?" *The Futurist*, January– February 1997, 12.

21. Howard Rheingold, *The Virtual Community: Homesteading on the Electronic Frontier* (Reading, MA: Addison-Wesley, 1993), 5.

22. Doreen Judica Vigue, "Educators Fighting a Web of Deceit," *Boston Globe*, 27 May 1997, (http//www.computernewsdaily).

23. Willa Walsh. "Notes and News: National Educational Computing Conference," *The Bookmark* 38, no. 3 (March 1997).

24. "Branch Resolutions to Annual General Meeting," New Brunswick Teachers' Association *NBTA News*, 39, no. 8 (29 April 1997).

25. Jean-Claude Couture, "Teachers' Work: Living in the Culture of Insufficiency" in Marita Moll, ed., *Tech High: Globalization and the Future of Canadian Education* (Ottawa: Canadian Centre for Policy Alternatives, 1997).

26. *Technology in Education: Meeting the Challenges of the Information Age*, conference program, Toronto, 1997.

27. Rob Greenwald, Larry V. Hedges and Richard D. Lane, "The Effect of School Resources in Student Achievement," *Review of Education Research*, 66, no. 3 (fall 1997).

28. Apple Macintosh computer advertisement, *Saturday Night Magazine*, December 1993.

29. *Statscan Education Quarterly Review* 3, no. 3 (fall 1996).

30. Jennifer Lewington, "Computer Gap Hurts Poor, Report Says," *Globe and Mail*, 1 November 1996, A5.

31. Statistics Canada, Centre for Education Statistics, *The National Longitudinal Survey of Children and Youth*, 1994–95, initial results, April 1997.

32. Progressive Conservative Party of Canada, "Response to Questionnaire from the Canadian Teachers' Federation," 27 April 1997.

33. Andrew Trotter, "IBM Shares Results from Field-Tests of Technology," *Education Week on the Web* (http://www.edweek.org/ht, February 26, 1997).

34. Alex Molnar, Walter C. Farrell Jr., James H. Johnson Jr. and Marty Sapp, "Research, Politics and the School Choice Agenda," *Phi Delta Kappan*, 78, no. 3 (November 1996): 242.

35. *Ibid.*

36. Marge Scherer, "On Savage Inequalities: A Conversation with Jonathan Kozol," *Educational Leadership* 50, no. 4 (December 1992/January 1993).

37. *Ibid.*

38. "He said . . . she said," *Apple Education Digest*, winter 1996 (http://204.96.17.75/educ).

39. *Ibid.*

40. Andrew Trotter, "IBM Shares Results from Field-Tests of Technology," *Education Week on the Web*, February 26, 1997.

41. Jeannine Aversa, "FCC Approves Plan to Hook Schools, Libraries to Internet," *Detroit Free Press*, 8 May 1997.

42. Roszak, *op. cit.*

43. "The Information Highway," *New Internationalist*, no. 286 (December 1996).

44. Cathy Majteny and Michelle Fleet, "Wiring Africa," *New Internationalist*, no. 286 (December 1996).

45. Ursula Franklin, *The Real World of Technology* (Concord, Ont.: Anansi, 1990) 126.

46. Roszak, *op. cit.*

47. Charles Hoban, *Focus on Learning: Motion Pictures in the School*, (Washington, D.C.: American Council on Education, 1942), 4, cited in

Lawrence Baines, "Future Schlock: Using Fabricated Data and Politically Correct Platitudes in the Name of Education Reform," *Phi Delta Kappan* 78, no.7 (March 1997): 494.

48. Morton Schultz, *The Teacher and the Overhead Projector*, (Englewood Cliffs, NJ: Prentice-Hall, 1965), 31, cited in Lawrence Baines, *op. cit.*

49. Joe Robinson, "Broadcasting to the Schools of a City," in *Radio and Education*, Levering Tyson, ed. (Chicago: University of Chicago Press, 1931), 91–92, cited in Lawrence Baines, *op. cit.*

Chapter 6

1. Marketing Advisory Council, "Kid Power: Creative Kid-Targeted Marketing Strategies," promotional brochure, Toronto, 12–14 June 1995.

2. Ross Crockford, "Kids on the Block," *Adbusters*, fall 1995, 53.

3. Consumers Union, *Captive Kids: Commercial Pressures on Kids at School* (Yonkers, NY: Author, 1995).

4. Michael Grange, "Teachers Fear Schools May Become Medium for Advertising," *Globe and Mail*, 13 June 1995, A8.

5. Ontario Secondary School Teachers' Federation (OSSTF), *Commercialization in Ontario Schools*, September 1995, 15.

6. Michael J. Jacobson, and Laurie Ann Mazur, *Marketing Madness*, (Boulder, CO: Perfect Books Limited, 1995), 33.

7. *Ibid.*

8. Foundation for Biomedical Research, *Research Helping Animals*, promotional publication (Washington, D.C.: Author, 1993).

9. Joby Warrick, "Whose shade of green?" *Washington Post*, 22 April 1997.

10. *Ibid.*

11. Marianne Manilor, and Tamara Schwanz, "What We're Doing to Stop the Attack on Environmental Education," Centre for Commercial-Free Public Education, 6 May 1997.

12. *Ibid.*

13. Laura Jones, "Trash in Schools," *Fraser Forum*, March 1997 (http://192.197.214.41.84folo.pqi/fraser).

14. Jennifer Lewington, "Companies Buy Screen-saver Time," *Globe and Mail*, 21 April 1997.

15. "Exploiting Students," *CCPA Education Monitor* 1, no. 3 (Summer 1997).

16. Joe Salkowski, "We'll Return to History Class After These Messages," *StarNet Dispatches*, 8 April 1997 (http://www.azstarnet.com/public/dispatches/features/ad.htm).

17. Roy F. Fox, "Manipulated Kids: Teens Tell How Ads Influence Them," *Educational Leadership*, 53, no. 1 (September 1995).

18. Jacobson and Mazur, *op. cit.*, 30.

19. Fox, *op. cit.*

20. John Pungente, YNN *1997–98 Bulletin # 16*, 2 December 1997.

21. George R. Kaplan, "KAPPAN Special Report – Profits R Us: Notes on the Commercialization of America's Schools," *Phi Delta Kappan* 78, no. 3 (November 1996).

22. "Branding," *Adbusters*, spring 1997, 39.

23. "Loveable Egg Page" (http://www.virtualpet.com).

24. Jonathan Mathorpe, "Parents, Teachers Unite against New Drug-Swilling Tamagotchi Toy," *Ottawa Citizen*, 15 June 1997, A5.

25. *Ibid.*

26. Kathryn Montgomery and Shelley Pasnik, "Web of Deception: Threats to Children from On-line Marketing," Centre for Media Education, Washington, D.C., 1996.

27. Centre for Media Education, "Alcohol and Tobacco on the Web: New Threats to Youth" (http://www.cme.org, April 23, 1997).

28. *Ibid.*

29. Montgomery and Pasnik, *op. cit.*

30. http://www.msnbc.com:80/news/69777.asp

31. Jane Weaver, "Making It Safe for Junior to Surf," MSNBC (http://www.msnbc.com:80/news/69777.asp).

32. "New Report Documents Threats to Youth from Alcohol and Tobacco Web Sites," Centre for Media Education, news release (http://www.cm.org/cme).

33. Asia Connects, 1997 (http://www.tgmag.ca).

Chapter 7

1. Langdon Winner, "Do Artifacts Have Politics?" *Daedalus: Journal of the American Academy of Arts and Sciences*, winter 1980.

2. Langdon Winner, "The Handwriting on the Wall: Resisting Techno-globalism's Assault on Education," insert, *MSTE News* 6, no. 2 (1996), Queen's University.

3. Gerald Odening and Brandt Sakakeeny, *Educational Services*, Smith Barney Research, 19 April 1996.

4. John M. McLaughlin, speaking to the Canadian Education Industry Summit: The First Canadian Conference to Provide Compelling Reasons for Investment in the Education for Profit Industry, Toronto, 24 September 1997.

5. John M. McLaughlin, "Curing the Common Cold," *Education Industry Report* 5, no. 6 (June 1997).

6. Rinehart and Lee, "Can the Marketplace Save Our Schools?" cited by Erica Shaker in *Education Limited* (Ottawa: Canadian Centre for Policy Alternatives, 1997), 22.
7. Canadian Education Industry Summit: The First Canadian Conference to Provide Compelling Reasons for Investment in the Education for Profit Industry, Toronto, 24 September 1997, conference program.
8. Kevin Bushweller, "Education, Ltd.," *American School Board Journal* 184, no. 3 (March 1997).
9. John Rosica, *Education Industry Report*, November 1997, cited by Erica Shaker in *Education Limited* (Ottawa: Canadian Centre for Policy Alternatives, 1997), 68.
10. Stephen Beatty, KPMG Peat Marwick Canada, speaking at the Canadian Education Industry Summit: The First Canadian Conference to Provide Compelling Reasons for Investment in the Education for Profit Industry, Toronto, 24 September 1997.
11. *Canadian Teachers' Federation Economic Service Notes*, March 1997, 3-5.
12. Ontario Secondary School Teachers' Federation (OSSTF), *Educators Beware! Privatization and Contracting Out in Public Education*, 1994.
13. *Ibid.*
14. Lehman Brothers, "Glossary of Terms," *Investment Opportunities in the Education Industry*, 9 February 1996.
15. Odening and Sakakeeny, *op. cit.*, 23.
16. Quoted by Erica Shaker in *Education Limited* (Ottawa: Canadian Centre for Policy Alternatives, 1997), 12.
17. Paul Starr, "Computing Our Way to Educational Reform," *American Prospect*, July–August 1996, 58.
18. *Ibid.*
19. Educational Management Group (EMG), promotional materials supplied by Lyle MacLennan on behalf of EMG, February 1997.
20. *Ibid.*
21. Educational Management Group (EMG), *Pan-Canadian Group Project Overview*, undated.
22. *Ibid.*
23. Steve Krafft, "Educational Management Group," *Scottsdale Magazine*, winter 1996, 36.
24. Educational Management Group, 1997, *op. cit.*
25. Kit Kreiger, letter to author, 11 July 1997.
26. Meeting of the SchoolNet Advisory Board (SNAB), Industry Canada, Ottawa, 17–18 July 1997.
27. Lehman Brothers, *Investment Opportunities in the Education Industry*, 9 February 1996, 5.

28. Wilfred Brown, "Major Findings of the CTF National Issues in Education Poll," July 1997 (poll conducted by Vector Research and Development, Inc.), 10.

29. Doug Hart, "Public Expectations and Satisfaction: Attitudes of Graduates, Employers, Parents and the Public Toward Education in Canada" (paper presented to the Canadian Society for the Study of Education, St. John's, Newfoundland, 14 June 1997).

30. Canadian Teachers' Federation, "Gallup Poll Shows Canadians Have Growing Confidence in Public Schools," *Economic Service Notes*, 1997-6, June 1997.

31. Brown, *op. cit.*

32. Brown, *op. cit.*

33. John E. Chubb and Terry M. Moe, "Choice is a Panacea," Goldwater Institute, *Arizona Issue Analysis # 112*, October 1990.

34. Cited in Maude Barlow and Heather-jane Robertson, *Class Warfare: The Assault on Canada's Schools* (Toronto: Key Porter Books, 1994), 189.

35. Alex Molnar, *Giving the Kids the Business: The Commercialization of America's Schools* (New York: Harper Collins, 1996).

36. *Ibid.*, 167.

37. Bob Chase, "Which Charters Are Smarter," *Education Week*, 4 December 1996, 1-2.

38. Canadian Teachers' Federation, *Behind the Charter School Myths* (Ottawa: Author, July 1997), 4.

39. Joe Freedman, "Charter Schools in Atlantic Canada: An Idea Whose Time Has Come" (Halifax: Atlantic Institute for Market Studies, 1997), 7.

40. *Ibid.*

41. Molnar, *op. cit.*, 151.

42. Murray Dobbin, "What Did We Earn in School Today?" *Canadian Forum*, June 1997, 17.

43. Brown, *op. cit.*

44. Lisa Keegan, "Opening Education to Market Forces," *Education Industry Report* 5, no. 1 (January 1997): 3.

45. "Let Choice Blossom," editorial, *Ottawa Citizen*, 11 March 1997.

46. *Ibid.*

47. See, for example, Bruce Fuller and Richard Elmore, *Who Chooses? Who Loses? Culture, Institutions and the Unequal Effects of School Choice* (New York: Teachers' College Press, 1996).

48. Sue Urahn and Dan Stewart, *Minnesota Charter Schools: A Research Report*, Minnesota House of Representatives, St. Paul, MN, 1994.

49. Joseph R. McKinney, "Charter Schools: A New Barrier for Children with Disabilities," *Educational Leadership* 54, no. 2 (October 1996): 22–25.

50. Cathy Wylie, "School-Site Management – Some Lessons from New Zealand" (paper presented to the annual meeting of the American Education Research Association, San Francisco, California, April 1995).

51. Canadian Teachers' Federation, July 1997, *op. cit.*

52. Cathy Wylie, "Finessing Site-Based Management with Balancing Acts, *Educational Leadership* 53, no. 4 (December 1995/January 1996): 54–59.

53. Murray Dobbin, *Charter Schools: Charting a Course to Social Division* (Ottawa: Canadian Centre for Policy Alternatives, January 1997).

54. Fraser Institute, *Toward the New Millennium: A Five-Year Plan for the Fraser Institute,* 1997.

55. National Citizens' Coalition, *Who They Are and What They Do,* February 1997.

56. *Ibid.*

57. Atlantic Institute for Market Studies, *Annual Report* 1995–96.

58. Atlantic Institute for Market Studies, *The Beacon* 3, no. 2 (spring 1997).

59. Freedman, *op. cit.*

60. Stephen B. Lawton, Joseph Freedman, Heather-jane Robertson, in Stephen T. Easton, ed., *Busting Bureaucracy to Reclaim Our Schools* (Montreal: Institute for Research on Public Policy, 1995).

61. Helen Raham, "Revitalizing Public Education in Canada: The Potential of Choice and Charter Schools," *Fraser Forum,* August 1996.

62. Amy Pyle and Doug Smith, "Charter School Test Scores Probed," *Los Angeles Times,* 7 October 1997, B1.

63. Doug Thomas and Kim Borwege, "A Choice to Charter," *Phi Delta Kappan* 78, no. 1 (September 1996): 30.

64. Chester E. Finn Jr. and Diane Ravitch, "Education Reform 1995–96," Hudson Institute, 33

65. Wayne Jennings, "Charter Schools and Private Practice Educators," *AEPP Enterprising Educators Newsletter,* April 1997, 5.

66. F. Howard Nelson, American Federation of Teachers, "How Private Managers Make Money in Public Schools," The EAI Experiment in Baltimore (http://www.aft.org . . . EAI).

67. Gerald Odening, speaking to the Canadian Education Industry Summit: The First Canadian Conference to Provide Compelling Reasons for Investment in the Education for Profit Industry, Toronto, 24 September 1997.

68. Janet R. Beales, *Teacher Inc.: A Private-Practice Option for Educators,* Reason Foundation, October 1994.

69. Mary Gifford and Timothy Keller, *Arizona's Charter Schools: A Survey of Teachers* (Phoenix: Goldwater Institute, August 1996), 16–17.
70. Molnar, *op. cit.*, 153.
71. Beatty, *op. cit.*
72. Odening, 1997, *op. cit.*
73. Lehman Brothers, "Definitions of the Market," *Investment Opportunities in the Education Industry*, 9 February 1996, 5.
74. Molnar, *op. cit.*, 96–97.
75. Molnar, *op. cit.*, 96–97.
76. Nelson, *op. cit.*
77. *Ibid.*
78. *Ibid.*
79. *Ibid.*
80. *Ibid.*
81. Molnar, *op. cit.*
82. Philip G. Hill, "Do We Know the Whole Story? The Business-Education Partnership and Corporate Social Responsibility," *The Reporter*, February 1996, 25.
83. Molnar, *op. cit.*, 105.
84. Hill, *op. cit.*
85. "Privatization Experiment in Hartford Comes to an End," *Canadian Principal* 7, no. 6 (March 1996): 1–2.
86. *Education Industry Report* 5, no. 1 (January 1997): 4.
87. *Education Industry Report* 5, no. 2 (February 1997).
88. Nelson Smith, "Standards Mean Business," (paper presented to the 1996 National Education Summit, New York, 26–27 March 1996).
89. Jennifer Lewington, "Grappling with an Ethical Question," *Globe and Mail*, 27 March 1997, C1.
90. Quoted in Philip Hill and Brian McGowan, *Corporate Involvement in Ontario's Catholic Schools*, Ontario English Catholic Teachers' Association (OECTA), 1997, 3.
91. "An Educational Partnership," editorial, *Financial Post*, 10 November, 1994 (Editorial refers to *National Survey on Corporate Support of Education*, study conducted by Spencer Francey Peters Inc. and Cunninghman Gregory and Company, November 1994.
92. Conference Board of Canada, *Ethical Guidelines for Business-Education Partnerships*, draft (Ottawa: Author, 1995).
93. Conference Board of Canada, *Reaching for Success*, conference brochure, Ottawa, June 1993.
94. Godfrey Huybregts, "Business Partnerships: Helping Schools Keep Pace with Technology," *Spectrum*, 1996, 27–29.

95. Norm Lee, "Schools as Learning Organizations," *MSTE News* 5, no. 2 (April 1996), four-page insert, Faculty of Education, Queens University, Kingston.
96. Huybregts, *op. cit.*
97. Huybregts, *op. cit.*
98. Michael Grang. "Publisher Nurtures Growing Relationship," *Globe and Mail*, 27 March 1997.
99. Cited by Robert Kuttner, "Taking Care of Business," *American Prospect*, July/August 1996, 6.
100. Karen Southwick, "Are Corporate Technology Initiatives More PR than Philanthropy?" *Electronic School*, March 1997, A14.
101. Dave Buchanan, "Pepsi High," *CCPA Education Monitor* 1, no. 3 (Summer 1997).
102. George Emerson, "See Johnny. See Johnny Surf. Surf, Johnny, Surf." *Canadian Business/Technology*, spring 1997, 35-42.
103. Ray Beyer, "Scandal for School," letter to the editor, technology section, *Canadian Business*, summer 1997, 9.
104. Ann Kerr, "This School Means Business," *Globe and Mail*, 15 October 1996, C1.

Chapter 8

1. Royal Commission on Industrial Training and Technical Education, *Report of the Commissioners, Parts I and II* (Ottawa: Government of Canada, 1913).
2. William Gibson, quoted by Anne Ward, "Are You Being Served?" *Electronic School*, March 1997, A30.
3. Kirkpatrick Sale, *Rebels Against the Future: The Luddites and Their War on the Industrial Revolution* (Toronto: Addison-Wesley, 1995).
4. "New Accounts of the Luddite Rebellion," *Industrial Worker*, December 1995 (http://www.org/-jw/dec/stories/ludd/html).
5. Kevin Kelly, "Interview with the Luddite," *Wired*, 3.06, June 1995.
6. Kirkpatrick Sale, "Lessons from the Luddites," *The Nation*, June 1995.
7. "Luddites and Friends," *CBC Ideas Transcripts*, CBC Radio, 17 and 24 February 1997.

Index

National Education Association,
U.S., 254
National Geographic Society, 82
National Potato Board, 207
National Science Foundation,
128-29, 131
National Trust, 223
Nesbitt Burns, 18, 287
Netscape Communications Corp., 228
Network for the Evaluation of
Education and Training
Technologies, 137
New America Schools Development
Corporation, 131
New Brunswick Teachers'
Association, 183
New Zealand, charter school in,
262-63
Newfoundland, 2
Nike, 206-8
Nintendo, 203-4, 223, 227
Noble, David, 117, 137, 318
Noble, Douglas, 128
"non-productive" education, 25-26
Nortel, 89
Northern Telecom, 6, 85, 123, 248,
282
Nova Gas, 173
Nova Scotia Teacher's Union, 282

O'Donnell, Rosie, 245, 247
Odening, Gerald, 267-68, 271
Ontario, education reform in, 36-49,
56-58
Ontario Arts Council, 4
Ontario Curriculum Clearing House,
209
Ontario Education Reform Network,
37
Ontario Farm Animal Council, 208
Ontario Federation of Labour, 216
Ontario Institute for Studies in
Education (OISE), 68, 264-65
Ontario Secondary School Teachers'
Federation, 216

open classrooms, 6
Optimedia Canada, 217
Organization for Economic Co-operation and Development (OECD),
20, 28, 75
outcomes-based education (OBE),
25, 33-34, 56, 86; *see also*
"standards"

Papert, Seymour, 123
Paramount, 244
parent councils, 38-40, 46, 212, 272
partnerships between businesses and
schools, 25, 84-85, 278-90
peer teaching, 149
pensions, 14, 15, 17
Pepsi, 212-13
Perelman, Lewis, 122
philanthropy, techno-marketing disguised as, 193-95
Phoneworks, 204
Pizza Hut, 207
Postman, Neil, 93-94, 136, 139,
147-48
postsecondary education, 27
Premont, Roxanne, 253
Princeton Review, 81
print media monopolies, 17
privacy: and the Internet, 228-29; of
student information, 47
privatization of government services,
14, 21, 238-40, 292
privatization of public education, 48,
236-90; *see also* charter schools
Procter and Gamble, 208
proprietary kids magazines (PKMs),
220-22
Provincial Parent Advisory Council,
38-39
Prozac, 214
public broadcasting, 17
public education, defined, 10; public
support for, 37-38, 41-44, 249, 257

"quality assurance," 33

Spiderman comics, 222

"standards," applied to education, 27, 32-35, 131; *see also* outcomes-based education

Starr, Paul, 243

Stentor, 89, 168

Stoll, Clifford, 150

Stratman, David, 189

streaming, 53

student loans, 61

students: advertising aimed at, 199-233; cheating by, 141, 180; effects of computer-based education on, 145-52; effects of standardized tests on, 69; information on, 47; *see also* equity, gender and social

Students' Commission of Canada, 23, 232

Sylvan Learning Systems, 81-83

Syncrude Corp., 255

Tamagotchi, 218-20

Tausz, Andrew, 126

tax credit, for education, 58

teachers: and stress, 184-85; and technology, 152-57, 187-88; education without, 245, 247; non-certified, 47, 267-68; salaries of, 46; working conditions, 48

Teachers for Excellence in Education, 38, 265

teachers' strike (1997), Ontario, 49

teachers' unions, 48-49, 86

teaching assistants, 56

Teaching with Technology, 132

Team Canada trade missions, 23, 26, 173

technological imperative, 97, 157

technology: and values, 100; education, 57, 76, 88; effects on behaviour of, 145-57; political consequences of, 101, 234-36, 244; predictions about, 91-92; resistance to, 96, 117-19, 195,

313-19; worship of, 94-101, 115, 119-20; *see also* computers in the classroom

Technology Incentive Partnership Program, 42

Teenage Mutant Ninja Turtles, 209

Telecommunications Act (1996), U.S., 166

Telelearning Research Network, 171

telephone companies, 168

Telesat Canada, 96, 123

television, 101; in the classroom, 212-14; violence on, 103-16

Tesseract, 273

Test of Grade 3 students (1997), Ontario, 68-71

testing, standardized, 27, 32, 37, 45, 56-57, 64-84, 87; achievement vs. aptitude, 71; computer-based, 81; do-it-yourself packages, 79-80; international comparisons, 75-77; media reports of, 74-75; social bias in, 71-73, 80, 87

Texaco, 211

textbooks, 47, 81, 90-91

TGMagazine, 22-23

Third International Math and Science Study (TIMSS), 75, 77-78, 185

Thompson, Tommy, 131

Thorsell, William, 32

Time Warner, 128

Tiny Toons, 217

Toronto Dominion Securities, 18

trade agreements, international, 20

trade barriers, removal of, 60

trade missions, *see* Team Canada

training for employment, 4, 25-31, 56-57, 61, 74

transfer payments, to provinces, 27

transnational corporations, *see* globalization

tribalism, 231, 292-93

True North Comics, 57

Turk, Jim 216